A Crisis of Beliefs

A Crisis of Beliefs

INVESTOR PSYCHOLOGY AND FINANCIAL FRAGILITY

Nicola Gennaioli and Andrei Shleifer

PRINCETON UNIVERSITY PRESS

Princeton and Oxford

Copyright © 2018 by Princeton University Press

Published by Princeton University Press
41 William Street, Princeton, New Jersey 08540
6 Oxford Street, Woodstock, Oxfordshire OX20 1TR

press.princeton.edu

All Rights Reserved

Library of Congress Control Number: 2018937068
ISBN 978-0-691-18250-6

British Library Cataloging-in-Publication Data is available

Editorial: Joe Jackson and Samantha Nader
Production Editorial: Jenny Wolkowicki
Jacket design: Will Brown
Jacket image courtesy of iStock
Production: Erin Suydam
Publicity: James Schneider
Copyeditor: Karen Brogno

This book has been composed in Bembo Book MT Pro

Printed on acid-free paper. ∞

Printed in the United States of America

10 9 8 7 6 5 4 3 2 1

To Maura with love
To Nancy with love

CONTENTS

ACKNOWLEDGMENTS

We are grateful to a number of people and institutions who helped us, both with the research that has led to this book and with the book itself. Our greatest debt is to our research collaborators, starting with Pedro Bordalo, together with whom we developed the formulation of diagnostic expectations central to this work. We are also indebted to Katherine Coffman, Robin Greenwood, Rafael La Porta, Yueran Ma, and Robert Vishny, all of whom worked with us on the research incorporated into this book.

The book benefited from the intellectual input of many other colleagues. Foremost among them are Sam Hanson and Adi Sunderam from Harvard Business School, who read and extensively commented on the whole manuscript. Sam's comments on the initial chapters were so comprehensive that we concluded the book had been "samitized." Adi, in addition to offering his detailed comments, came up with the book's title.

We also benefited from the detailed comments of several close readers. Former Secretary of the Treasury Tim Geithner read the initial chapters on the financial crisis, offering many suggestions but also recording some disagreements. His views were extremely important to us and influenced our interpretation of many events, even when we ultimately stuck to our guns. Other careful readers included Fausto Panunzi, Stefano Rossi, Matthew Rutherford, Joshua Schwartzstein, Jeremy Stein, René Stulz, Nancy Zimmerman, and two anonymous reviewers from Princeton University Press.

We relied on the help of enormously conscientious and talented research assistants, including Serena De Lorenzi, Paul Fontanier, Giovanni Montanari, and Gianluca Rinaldi. Angela Ma, while still an undergraduate at Harvard, put together the figures for this book but also managed the organization of the whole effort.

Our research for this book benefited from financial support of several donors, including the European Research Council (GA 647782), Pershing Square Venture Fund for Research on the Foundations of Human Behavior, and Howard Zimmerman.

We would like to thank Joe Jackson of Princeton University Press for organizing an extremely professional publishing effort.

Gennaioli would like to thank many people at Bocconi University: administrators for providing excellent logistic support and colleagues from many departments for creating a stimulating, fun, and friendly atmosphere. Special mention goes to Francesco Corielli, Carlo Favero, Fulvio Ortu, and Stefano Rossi.

Finally, Shleifer would like to thank Harvard Business School for its hospitality during the 2017–18 academic year. Both the Finance Unit, with its Initiative on Behavioral Finance and Financial Stability directed by Robin Greenwood, and the Negotiations, Organizations, and Markets (NOM) Unit, headed by Brian Hall, provided a great deal of intellectual help. The NOM Unit also offered a highly sought after office in which to spend a relatively peaceful year.

All these contributions, in their own ways, were indispensable, although we retain full responsibility for the remaining errors.

A Crisis of Beliefs

Introduction

The collapse of the investment bank Lehman Brothers on Sunday, September 14, 2008, caught almost everyone by surprise. It surprised investors, who dumped stocks and brought the market index down by 500 points on Monday. It surprised policymakers, who rushed to rescue other financial institutions after declaring for months that there would be no government bailouts. It also surprised economic forecasters. Only six weeks before the Lehman bankruptcy, in early August 2008, both the Federal Reserve and professional forecasters predicted continued growth of the U.S. economy. Contrary to that prediction, the U.S. financial system nearly melted down after the Lehman bankruptcy, and the economy slid into a deep recession. This happened despite extraordinary—and ultimately successful—government efforts to save the financial system after Lehman.

Why was the Lehman crisis such a surprise? After all, fragility has been building up in the financial system for quite some time. In the mid-2000s, the U.S. economy went through a massive housing bubble. As home prices rose, households levered up to buy homes with mortgages. Banks and other financial institutions levered up to hold mortgages and mortgage-backed securities. As the bubble deflated after 2006, the financial system

1

experienced considerable stress, as reflected in runs on financial institutions, followed by bankruptcies, rescues, and mergers. Yet the system and the economy stayed afloat until the fall of 2008, supported by successful interventions by the Federal Reserve aimed to avoid a financial panic. By mid-2008, investors and regulators expected that, despite the deflating housing bubble, the situation was under control. On May 7, 2008, Treasury Secretary Henry Paulson felt that "the worst is likely to be behind us." On June 9, 2008, Fed Chairman Ben Bernanke stated that "the danger that the economy has fallen into a 'substantial downturn' appears to have waned."

The relative quiet before the storm, expressed in both the official and private-sector forecasts of the economy and the speeches of government officials, gives us important clues as to why Lehman was such a surprise. It surely was not the news of Lehman's financial weakness per se, since the investment bank was in trouble and expected to be sold for several months prior to its September bankruptcy. U.S. banks more generally were making large losses for several months as the housing and mortgage markets deteriorated, and no major economic news surfaced that weekend. Nor can the surprise be attributed to the government reiteration of its "no bailout" policy. For if that were the reason for the collapse, the markets would have bounced back as soon as it became clear on Monday that bailouts were back in. In fact, markets bounced around a bit but continued their slide as the financial system deteriorated over the next several weeks, despite all the bailouts.

The evidence on the beliefs of investors and policymakers instead tells us that the news in the Lehman demise was the extreme fragility of the financial system compared to what was previously thought. Despite consistently bad news over the course of 2008, investors and policymakers came to believe that they had dodged the bullet of a major crisis. The pressures building up from home price declines and mortgage defaults were attenuated by the belief that the banks' exposure was limited and alleviated by effective liquidity support from the Fed. The risks of a major crisis were neglected. The Lehman bankruptcy and the fire sales it ignited showed investors and policymakers that the financial system was more vulnerable, fragile, and interconnected than they previously thought. Their lack of appreciation of extreme downside risks was mistaken. The Lehman bankruptcy had such a huge impact because it triggered a major correction of expectations.

Ten years after Lehman, economists agree that the underestimation of risks building up in the financial system was an important cause of the financial crisis. In October 2017, the University of Chicago surveyed a panel of leading economists in the United States and Europe on the importance of various factors contributing to the 2008 Global Financial Crisis. The number-one contributing factor among the panelists was the "flawed financial sector" in terms of regulation and supervision. But the number-two factor among the twelve considered, ranking just below the first in estimated importance, was "underestimation of risks" from financial engineering. The experts seem to agree that the fragility of a highly leveraged financial system exposed to major housing risk was not fully appreciated in the period leading to the crisis.

These judgments are made with the benefit of hindsight. The world, however, has witnessed an extensive history of financial bubbles, expanding credit, and subsequent crises as the bubbles deflated. Errors in beliefs appear in multiple narratives. Classic studies such as Kindleberger (1978), Minsky (1977), and more recently Reinhart and Rogoff (2009) argue that the failure of investors to accurately assess risks is a common thread of many of these episodes. Rajan (2006) and Taleb (2007) stressed the dangers from low probability risks to financial stability. Even before the Lehman bankruptcy, Gerardi et al. (2008) drew attention to expectation errors in the developing subprime crisis. Since the 2008 crisis, a great deal of new systematic evidence on credit cycles, both for the United States and worldwide, has been developed, starting with the pioneering work of Greenwood and Hanson (2013). Much of this work points to errors in expectations over the course of the cycle. Here we take this point of view further and put inaccurate beliefs at the center of the analysis of financial fragility.

To this end, we seek in this book to accomplish three goals. First, we would like to show that survey expectations data are a valid and extremely useful source of information for economic research. Expectations in financial markets tend to be extrapolative rather than rational, and this basic feature needs to be integrated into economic analysis.

Second, we seek to provide an empirically motivated and psychologically grounded formal model of expectation formation that can be used across a variety of domains, from lab experiments to studies of social beliefs to dynamic analyses of financial and macroeconomic volatility. In economics, nonrational beliefs have been typically formalized using so-called adaptive expectations, which describe mechanical extrapolation of past trends into the future. This approach has been criticized on the grounds that individuals are forward-looking in that they react to information about the future, not only to past trends. We develop a more realistic nonmechanical theory of belief formation, building on evidence from psychology. In this theory, decision makers react to objectively useful information, but in a distorted way.

Third, we use this model of expectation formation to account for the central features—including both market outcomes and beliefs—of the 2008 crisis both before and after Lehman and to explain credit cycles and financial fragility more generally. With the model of expectations we propose, many empirically established features of financial markets emerge in otherwise standard dynamic economic models. Getting the psychology right allows us to shed light on the conditions under which financial markets are vulnerable to booms and busts. It may also help in thinking about the role of economic policy.

Expectations Data

A natural starting point for assessing the significance of financial "instability from beliefs" is to analyze the beliefs themselves. This entails not only directly measuring expectations of market participants and systematically testing whether these beliefs are rational, but also characterizing the type of mistakes (if any) that investors make.

This enterprise is feasible because a wealth of available survey data reports the beliefs of investors, corporate managers, households, and professional forecasters. These data offer important insights on whether, in 2008 and in other historical episodes, investors appreciated the risks building up before the crisis or alternatively failed to see the trouble coming. More generally, survey data help identify regular patterns in beliefs during economic fluctuations, needed to develop better theories of expectation formation and credit cycles.

Our approach is a natural extension of the long-standing research agenda in behavioral finance. Traditional behavioral finance tests the rationality of beliefs *indirectly*, by looking at the predictability of security returns. Because returns should be mostly unpredictable when markets are efficient, the consistent findings of predictability are taken to be evidence that expectations are not rational. Here we take the next step and argue that actual expectations data should become a direct target of investigation. These data can shed additional light on what investors think and how they trade, but also on market behavior. The focus on beliefs is pivotal in high leverage situations, such as the study of credit cycles, because changes in expectations can trigger massive dislocations in the financial system, as we saw after the Lehman bankruptcy.

Although rather obvious, the use of survey expectations as direct targets of economic analysis has been quite controversial in economics, for an important methodological reason. Over the past forty years, macroeconomics has been dominated by the Rational Expectations Hypothesis (REH), and finance by its close relative, the Efficient Markets Hypothesis. These theories, which represent important intellectual achievements of twentieth-century economics, hold that economic agents are rational and, as such, form their expectations about the future in a statistically optimal way, given the structure of the economy. This view has one profound consequence. It implies that expectations are dictated by the structure of the economy itself, so that survey data on expectations are redundant and noisy information. The weakness of this approach is that the REH, like any other hypothesis, cannot be just assumed to hold. Rather, as forcefully argued by Charles Manski (2004), it should be subject to empirical tests. Assessing the statistical optimality of survey data on beliefs is a natural place to start.

For the period leading to the 2008 crisis, we have a good deal of data on the expectations of homebuyers about future home price growth, on investor beliefs about the risk of home price declines and mortgage defaults, and on forecasts of economic activity made by both private forecasters and the Federal Reserve. We also have a variety of contemporaneous documents and speeches of policymakers, as well as discussions at the Federal Open Market Committee (FOMC) meetings, which shed light on the beliefs of policymakers. We can then ask directly: What were homebuyers, banks, investors, and policymakers thinking as the events leading up to the crisis unfolded?

The answers to this question cast doubt on the "too big to fail" theory of the crisis, which holds that the banks knew the risks but gambled on bailouts. The expectations of bank executives and employees seem to be very similar to those of other investors. Bankers were optimistic about housing markets and made loans as well as personal home purchases accordingly. There is no evidence that bankers understood the risks better than anybody else.

Beliefs are more in line with the classical analyses of Kindleberger (1978) and Minsky (1977) that emphasize excessive optimism before crises. Homebuyers were unrealistically optimistic about future home price growth. Investors in mortgages and in securities backed by these mortgages, including financial institutions, considered the possibility that home prices might fall but did not fully appreciate how much and what havoc these declines would wreak. And macroeconomic forecasters from both the private sector and the Federal Reserve did not, in forming their expectations, recognize the risks facing the U.S. financial sector and the economy as late as the summer of 2008. The evidence does not suggest that investors or policymakers were totally naïve or oblivious to the risks in the financial system. Rather, they did not fully appreciate tail risks until the Lehman collapse laid them bare.

The data on beliefs prior to the Lehman crisis point to two key patterns: the extrapolation of past home price growth into the future, and the neglect of unlikely downside risks. Extrapolation of past home price growth sheds light on the housing bubble. Neglected downside risk explains how the financial system became so leveraged. This levering up of both households and financial institutions was most plausibly supported by the widely shared beliefs that the prices of homes were unlikely to collapse and that financial institutions were protected from bad shocks by diversification and hedging.

Neglect of downside risk explains how it took a year between initial bad news and the Lehman bankruptcy to ignite a financial panic. As home prices started falling, beliefs began deflating as well, leading to an unwinding of unwanted risk exposures. Starting in the summer of 2007, this unwinding led to mortgage defaults, foreclosures, fire sales of assets, liquidations, runs on some financial institutions, and other correlates of distress. But markets did not collapse, despite the deflating housing bubble, and the financial system held together for over a year. In part, this was due to successful liquidity interventions from the Fed. But it was also due to the continued belief that banks were not vulnerable to extreme tail risks, even if home prices fell. The Lehman bankruptcy was a massive surprise precisely because it laid bare these extreme downside risks. Investors learned that they were wrong in thinking that the situation was under control. This was the making of the financial crisis and of the Great Recession that followed, driven by erroneous beliefs.

Beliefs tie together the transmission mechanisms of the crisis, which are well understood by economists (Brunnermeier 2009). Prior to Lehman, the financial system already faced significant instability, such as asset fire sales, bank runs, and rescues of failing institutions, but there was no major disruption because investors did not anticipate a full meltdown. After Lehman, the very same amplification mechanisms could no longer be controlled without capital injections, and the financial system nearly collapsed before the government injected capital to prevent massive insolvencies. Lehman was an eye opener. It proved that financial institutions were much more exposed to risk than previously thought. To understand the pivotal role of the Lehman bankruptcy in the crisis, one needs to understand the evolution of beliefs.

Looking at beliefs data also sheds light on financial fragility more broadly, beyond the 2008 crisis. A great deal of survey data on investor and professional forecaster expectations about not only stock markets, individual stocks, and credit markets, but also the real economy, are available and can be examined. The evidence presented in this book—both new and summarized from earlier studies—suggests that extrapolation of past trends is in fact a common feature of expectations held by investors, corporate managers, and professional forecasters. This is in line with studies of other bubble episodes (Kindleberger 1978; Glaeser 2013; Greenwood, Shleifer, and You 2018). Neglect of risk, as pointed out by Rajan (2006) and Taleb (2007), is pervasive as well. The neglect of downside risk is present in several documented instances of financial innovation, such as portfolio insurance and index options (Coval, Pan, and Stafford 2014) and other episodes of credit expansion (Baron and Xiong 2017). The kinds of patterns we see in 2008 appear in other financial and economic episodes.

The expectations data actually tell us something deeper. Across many economic domains, forecast errors are predictable, even among professional forecasters. Expectations are too optimistic in good times and too pessimistic in bad times. This stands in contrast to the Rational Expectations Hypothesis, which holds that statistically optimal forecasts should use all available information, thereby avoiding predictable errors. The failure of standard economic models to account for expectations is a major gap in the analysis because it assumes away a potentially critical source of instability. There is enough evidence to take the "instability from beliefs" hypothesis seriously.

The Psychology of Expectations

The empirical challenges that expectations data present to the REH are only the beginning of the story. It takes a theory of expectations to replace the existing theory. Naïve theories of irrational beliefs cannot explain how extrapolation and neglected downside risk are connected and how they come and go, around 2008 or in general. Adaptive expectations, a theory of mechanical extrapolation of past trends, can explain the growth of the housing bubble but not why the system stayed afloat after the bubble started deflating in 2006 or why a single event such as the failure of Lehman induced such a drastic revision of expectations.

9

This brings us to the second goal of this book: to move from the analysis of expectations data to a new theory of expectation formation that can account for the facts. We present one psychologically founded theory of expectation formation, which we call Diagnostic Expectations. We have developed this theory over the past several years together with Pedro Bordalo and have taken it both theoretically and empirically to a number of different domains with Katherine Coffman, Yueran Ma, and Rafael La Porta. The theory is surely not the last word in modeling expectations, but it suggests that one can make some progress in understanding the reality of financial markets by moving away from the REH in a psychologically realistic direction.

In developing this model of expectations, we are guided by four principal considerations. First, we would like a theory of beliefs to be biologically and psychologically plausible, and in particular based on the evidence on human judgment obtained in experimental data. Psychologists have for decades studied judgment under uncertainty and the biases it entails, and a theory of beliefs might as well start with this evidence.

Second, we would like a theory of beliefs to be portable in the sense proposed by Matthew Rabin (2013). That is, we would like the same theory to explain evidence in psychological experiments, social judgments individuals make, financial markets, and perhaps other domains. There is no compelling reason to think that belief formation in financial markets is different from that anywhere else. One can argue, of course, that in financial markets, unlike in other domains, rational arbitrageurs profitably trade to eliminate the effects of belief distortions of irrational "noise traders" on security prices. Yet this objection has long been rejected in finance: Arbitrage is limited by capital constraints and risk aversion of arbitrageurs, and it typically does not eliminate inefficiencies in market prices (DeLong et al. 1990; Shleifer and Vishny 1997).

Third, we would like a theory in which beliefs are forward-looking. Before the rational expectations revolution, economists relied on models of adaptive expectations, in which decision makers mechanically extrapolate the past rather than react to news. These models were effectively criticized by Robert Lucas (1976), who argued, using both logic and evidence, that economic agents react to news about the future in forming their beliefs. The evidence from psychology also shows that humans do not update mechanically. They revise their beliefs about the probabilities of different events on the basis of information. The question the Lucas critique leaves open is not whether economic agents are forward-looking and react to information but rather whether they do so by the right amount. In our approach they do not.

Finally, we would like a theory of belief formation to be testable using survey evidence on beliefs. The available evidence shows that survey expectations are not noise and that both investors and managers make decisions in line with their stated beliefs. To us, these beliefs are as significant a component of empirical data that economic models need to explain as any other. A successful model of belief formation must as a start account for measured beliefs.

The model of expectations we describe builds on the famous representativeness heuristic of human judgment under uncertainty initially proposed by psychologists Daniel Kahneman and Amos Tversky in 1972. According to Kahneman and Tversky (1983), "an attribute is representative of a class if it is very diagnostic, that is, if the relative frequency of this attribute is much higher in that class than in a relevant reference class." Representativeness entails a judgment error of overestimating the likelihood of representative attributes in a class.

To illustrate, suppose someone is asked to predict the most likely hair color of an Irish person. In several informal surveys we conducted, many people said red. It is absolutely the case that red hair is objectively more common among the Irish than among other humans: 10 percent of the Irish have red hair, compared to 1 percent elsewhere. But because red hair is a representative attribute of the Irish, people tend to believe that the Irish are even more likely to have red hair than they actually do. Judgments by representativeness contain a kernel of truth in that they respond to information in the objectively correct direction. However, they do so excessively. For this reason, people overestimate the percentage of Florida residents older than age 65 or the share of African Americans who live in poverty, and underestimate the likelihood of unrepresentative types, such as Republicans supporting abortion.

Judgment by representativeness is a universal decision heuristic, which accounts for many striking experimental findings. It is also tied to the biology of memory, which accounts for mechanisms of selective recall. Representativeness is the foundation of our theory of expectations. It creates a belief distortion that social psychologists call "the kernel of truth": Beliefs exaggerate true patterns in the data, or, in dynamic contexts, they overreact to information. This implies that both beliefs and their errors are predictable from the underlying reality. To see this, go back to the example of the red-haired Irish. Here, people overreact to the information that a person is Irish in estimating the person's hair color. Without the knowledge of a person's nationality, they might have estimated that the hair color of a random person is dark, which is the most common hair color in humans. But once they learn a person is Irish, the recall of red hair is immediate because in the data, red-haired types are *relatively* much more prevalent in the Irish population than elsewhere. As a consequence, when thinking about the Irish, the probability mass shifts too far toward red hair.

Applied to expectations in macroeconomics and finance, representativeness has some distinctive implications. The kernel of truth principle implies that people tend to overweight future outcomes that become more likely in light of incoming data. Just as they overreact to the news that a person is Irish in estimating the color of their hair, they react to macroeconomic news in the correct direction but excessively. Good macroeconomic news makes good future outcomes more representative, and therefore overweighted, in judgments about future states of the world. The converse is true for bad macroeconomic news. The same principles of belief formation that apply to lab experiments and social judgments translate one-for-one into our model of diagnostic expectations.

Under some conditions, diagnostic expectations tie together extrapolation and neglect of tail risk. News pointing to higher likelihood of economic growth causes high-growth scenarios to be representative and recessions to be unrepresentative, leading investors to both neglect downside risk and to display excess optimism about average conditions. News pointing to reduced volatility renders extreme shocks unrepresentative, leading investors to neglect risk. Diagnostic expectations also generate systematic reversals of optimism and pessimism in the absence of news. When trends in news cool off, no particular outcome is representative and expectations revert toward rationality. If the corrective news is bad enough, the left tail becomes representative and investors display excess pessimism. These movements in beliefs are entirely due to investors' overreaction to objectively useful information, not to their mechanical extrapolation of the past.

A formal model of diagnostic expectations satisfies our four criteria for a theory of expectations. It is based on extensive psychological evidence. It is portable in that the same model is applicable to lab experiments, to human social judgments such as stereotypes, and to financial markets. It offers testable predictions about the evolution of expectations in economic and financial contexts. And it is forward-looking in that it is first and foremost a theory of how people react to information. But unlike in the case of rational expectations, the reaction to news is not statistically optimal. Rather, it is distorted by a basic principle of human judgment.

Diagnostic Expectations and Financial Fragility

Diagnostic expectations provide a useful unifying account of the 2008 crisis. They can serve as a foundation of extrapolative beliefs that characterized the housing bubble, which can be seen as updating and overreacting to repeated good news about home prices and general economic conditions. But they can also account for the neglect of downside risk, due to good news both about economic conditions (which rendered the left tail unrepresentative) and about the safety of financial institutions. More subtly, diagnostic expectations can account for the quiet period between the first tremors in housing and financial markets in the summer of 2007, which the Fed contained so successfully, and the eventual Lehman crisis. Even though the housing bubble was deflating and expectations about economic conditions were revised downward, the perception of tail risks remained dampened due to Fed policies and to the "diversification myth," an exaggerated faith in the new insurance mechanisms. Diagnostic expectations may thus explain why both Federal Reserve and private-sector forecasts of future economic activity made as late as August 2008 point to a widely shared—and exaggerated—belief that, despite the early tremors, the situation was under control.

The theory also accounts for the extreme reaction to the Lehman bankruptcy, as the tail risks to the financial system came out into the open and market participants reacted. The Lehman bankruptcy revealed that the situation was far from being under control, that financial institutions were highly interconnected, so that systemic risk was much higher than previously expected. As a consequence, the previously neglected left tail became representative, causing beliefs to overweight the black swan of a financial meltdown. The market panic, asset fire sales, runs on financial institutions, mergers to avoid bankruptcy, and of course government rescues can be viewed as reflecting—at least in part—the massive revision of diagnostic expectations about financial fragility. The Lehman crisis was a crisis of beliefs.

To be sure, this is just a narrative of one important episode. To evaluate the theory more thoroughly, one needs to bring it to more systematic data. Fortunately, since the 2008 crisis, economists have assembled a good number of credit cycle facts that describe the relationship between credit growth, credit valuations, and economic activity. In brief, this research finds that private credit expansion, and especially the expansion of household credit, predicts increased likelihood of future economic crises, as well as low stock returns for banks that extended that credit. This predictable fragility is reflected in debt markets as well. A high share of risky debt issuance in total debt issuance, as well as low yield spreads between risky and safe debt, are indicators of substantial market appetite for taking risk. In the data, these bullish indicators anticipate a reversion in credit conditions, meaning that high risk appetite predicts low returns and subsequent declines in issuance of risky debt. But they also predict slowdown in economic growth. This evidence points with some reliability to predictable credit cycles: Frothy credit market conditions predict both financial and economic trouble ahead. The Lehman crisis and the Great Recession were extremely dramatic, but far from unique.

The predictability of economic outcomes and security returns from credit market conditions suggests that rational expectations models might not be the most natural way to explain the data. Rather, the evidence suggests that instability comes from expectations themselves. Diagnostic expectations formalize this hypothesis, offering a unified account of credit cycles. Good economic news, such as growth in home prices or improvement in economic conditions more generally, makes right-tail outcomes representative. This leads investors to both overestimate average future conditions and to neglect the unrepresentative downside risk, causing overexpansion of both leverage and real investment. When good news stops coming, investors revise their expectations down, even without adverse shocks. These revisions cause credit spreads to revert, the lenders to perform poorly, and economic and financial conditions to deteriorate, leading to deleveraging and cuts in real investment. A severe crisis occurs if arriving news is sufficiently bad as to render left-tail outcomes representative and hence overstated.

The fragility of the financial system here comes entirely from beliefs. Without diagnostic expectations, there surely will be market volatility in response to shocks but no major market stresses without major shocks. Diagnostic expectations change this calculus both because they point to predictable reversion in economic conditions coming from predictable reversion in expectations and because they lead to extreme financial fragility when left-tail outcomes become representative. In an intuitive way, diagnostic expectations supply a theory of a panic driven by shifting representativeness.

Roadmap

In the rest of this book, we develop these ideas more systematically and formally. Chapter 1 summarizes the basic facts about the financial crisis of 2008 and draws attention to several key facts that need to be explained, such as the year-long delay between the onset of bad news about housing and the Lehman bankruptcy. Chapter 2 then presents a variety of evidence, both from surveys and from policymaker speeches and narrative accounts, which summarizes the beliefs during this period. The main message of this chapter is that extrapolation and the neglect of left-tail risk were empirically measurable features of beliefs during the housing bubble and that downside risk was neglected in 2007–2008, even as the bubble was deflating. Rational expectations models, such as "too big to fail" or "bank runs," are not consistent with these facts as long as one takes expectations data seriously.

Chapter 3 introduces a model of a financial system that is standard except that downside risks are neglected. The goal of the model is to assess whether this belief distortion can account for the key features of the crisis. In chapter 3, we simply postulate neglected risk rather than derive it from a micro-founded model of belief formation. We show how the neglect of downside risk can lead not only to excessive expansion of debt that investors perceive to be safe, but also to the levering up of banks that issue such debt to investors and the need to find assets to issue profitable liabilities. When neglected risks resurface, investors realize that credit expansion is excessive and risks are misallocated between them and the banks. The unwinding of original positions causes debt prices to fall severely, triggering major financial instability. The model delivers some stylized facts about a financial crisis without any nonstandard assumptions other than an error in beliefs.

The first three chapters leave us with two questions. First, are extrapolation and neglect of risk general features of beliefs in other episodes of market volatility? The single episode of 2007–2008 allows limited inference, so assessing errors in beliefs more broadly is critical to evaluate their importance for financial fragility. Second, the model of belief distortions in chapter 3 makes several assumptions about the conditions under which beliefs display extrapolation and neglect of risk. Are these assumptions realistic and applicable in other contexts? Here we see the importance of starting with more systematic psychological foundations. These two questions motivate the rest of the book.

In chapter 4, we summarize some of the rapidly growing empirical evidence on expectations. This evidence comes from many sources, including expectations of aggregate stock market returns, expectations of earnings growth of companies, and expectations of credit market conditions. Chapter 4 establishes three major facts that are central to our analysis. First, in cases when multiple data sources about the same expectations are available, survey expectations are extremely consistent across these sources. The traditional dismissal of survey expectations data as noise is rejected by this evidence. Second, investors and managers make decisions that are in line with their stated expectations. When investors expect stock market returns to be high, they put money into equity mutual funds. When corporate managers expect high earnings growth, they plan more investment. On every count we consider, survey expectations appear to be a credible measure of the beliefs of market participants. Third, in several domains, survey expectations are extrapolative. Investors expect high returns on the stock market when past returns have been high. Corporate managers and analysts expect high earnings growth when past earnings growth has been high. Fourth, expectations are not mechanically extrapolative. They depend on the features of the underlying economic process. Beliefs exaggerate the frequency of outcomes that have become objectively more likely. Updating is also more aggressive when the underlying series is more persistent, which is again inconsistent with mechanical extrapolation. Such "sophisticated" extrapolation is a central feature of beliefs demanding explanation.

We also use chapter 4 to summarize the evidence on credit cycles. This evidence most importantly points to predictability of economic conditions and security returns from indicators of credit market frothiness, such as the growth of credit, credit spreads, and risky debt share in total issuance. Such predictability points directly to the need for a theory of expectations.

Chapter 5 presents perhaps the central innovation of this book, which is the model of expectation formation that we developed with Pedro Bordalo. This model builds expectations from the psychological foundations up. We begin by summarizing Kahneman and Tversky's research on representativeness and then describe a formal model of judgment by representativeness and the way it transforms true probability distributions of future outcomes into diagnostically expected ones. We show how this model can account for the findings of famous experiments but more generally explains distorted beliefs such as stereotypes in social domains. We then use the model to account for the stages of the 2008 crisis: the exuberance around the growth of housing prices, the quiet period after the first bad news started to come in, and the collapse of markets after Lehman. Unlike other theories, a model with diagnostic expectations accounts not just for market outcomes during this period but also for the beliefs of the participants.

In chapter 6, we put the various pieces together by presenting a full-blown dynamic economic model of credit cycles with diagnostic expectations. In the model, good news leads to excessively optimistic expectations and overexpansion of credit and economic activity. Critically, such overexpansion is self-correcting even without adverse news, as exaggerated beliefs revert to fundamentals. The model accounts for the credit cycle facts described in chapter 4 but also suggests how representativeness can lead to sharp movements in expectations and activity when tail outcomes become representative.

Chapter 7 summarizes the book. We hope to accomplish three goals. The first is to provide a new narrative of the 2008 financial crisis that assigns a central role to beliefs in accounting both for periods of relative quiet and those of extreme volatility. Second, we hope to demonstrate that survey expectations are a valid and extremely useful source of data for economic analysis. They can be used to test conventional null hypotheses, such as rational expectations. Perhaps more important, expectations data can be used to test and distinguish alternative models of economic fluctuations. Third, we propose to show that beliefs can be modeled in economic analysis starting with first principles of psychology, such as representativeness. Our proposed model of such beliefs—diagnostic expectations—can then be incorporated into standard dynamic economic models, such as that of credit cycles. This model is both rigorous and testable. It disciplines the analysis, as do rational expectations, but fits the evidence on beliefs considerably better.

Perhaps, however, there is a more holistic message to all of this. What we hope to show is that behavioral economics has grown up. It no longer needs to be merely a critique of neoclassical economics. A researcher can start with fundamental psychology, build formal models of beliefs, incorporate those models into standard models of markets, and bring predictions to the data. Tractable and psychologically founded models of beliefs can be integrated into the standard analysis in finance and macroeconomics. This approach may address the concerns about the discipline of the analysis while bringing to it a healthy dose of realism.

CHAPTER 1

The Financial Crisis of 2008

The financial crisis of 2008 is one of the most dramatic economic events in modern U.S. history. It featured an effective meltdown of the U.S. financial system, massive government rescues of financial institutions, and a deep and long-lasting recession. Although a decade later the U.S. economy has recovered almost completely, the crisis has left behind fundamental questions about the fragility of the financial system and its impact on the real economy. In this chapter, we present the basic narrative of the origins of the financial crisis, the crisis itself, and its immediate aftermath.

We begin with the 2008 crisis for two reasons. First, despite being dramatic, this crisis is actually fairly typical, sharing the essential features of many others. It grew out of a bubble in the housing market, which was to a large extent financed with mortgage debt. The growth of mortgages led to a huge expansion of household leverage, but also leverage of banks and other financial institutions that were exposed to housing. The crisis was most directly caused by the deflation of the housing bubble beginning in 2006, leading to mortgage defaults, collapses in values of bank assets, losses of financial institutions, and ultimately fire-sale liquidations and massive distress.

The second reason to look closely is that, because the crisis is so recent, and so heavily investigated and discussed by academics, journalists, and policymakers, we know a great deal about what various participants were thinking in real time as the events unfolded. What were the beliefs of households buying homes and taking out mortgages in markets with rapidly rising prices? What was the reasoning of the commercial banks, investment banks, and insurance companies that took on massive and highly leveraged exposures to mortgage debt as home prices rose? What were the beliefs of investors and policymakers *starting* in the summer of 2007, as it became clear that the housing bubble was deflating? Why was the bankruptcy of Lehman Brothers such a pivotal event that radically changed beliefs about the markets and the economy? We have enough data on the crisis of 2008 to begin asking questions about beliefs and expectations underlying the observed behavior.

In this chapter, we summarize the basic facts about the crisis, while in chapter 2 we focus on the beliefs of the participants in this episode. The rest of the book then presents our conceptual take on these issues. Our goal in this book is to interpret historical events, and to this end we need to start with agreed-on facts.

The Housing Bubble and Housing Finance

Every narrative of the 2008 crisis begins with the housing boom. As argued by Robert Shiller, U.S. housing prices rose only moderately, in inflation-adjusted terms, for a century prior to the mid-1990s. Yet, as figure 1.1 shows, during the decade beginning in 1996, housing prices doubled in real terms. Prices rose even more dramatically in parts of the United States with inelastic housing supply, such as major cities (Saiz 2010). Figure 1.1 shows also how this dramatic decade-long increase was

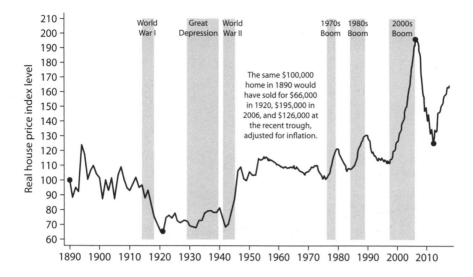

FIGURE 1.1. U.S. Home Values over Time. Robert Shiller's inflation-adjusted index of sale prices of standard existing homes in the United States. The index is set to 100 in 1890. *Source*: Shiller, Robert J. 2016. *Irrational Exuberance: Revised and Expanded Third Edition*. Princeton, NJ: Princeton University Press. Reprinted by permission of Princeton University Press.

followed by price declines that started in 2006 and accelerated in 2007. Within five years, home prices gave up much of their earlier gains.

Owner-occupied housing in the United States is largely financed with mortgages, with 80 to 90 percent of purchase prices typically paid with such debt. The rise of home prices was accompanied by equally dramatic growth in household debt, as figure 1.2 shows. Some of that growth came from home purchases by people who had never owned homes before: The rate of home ownership in the United States rose from 64 percent in 1994 to 69 percent at the end of 2006 (Federal Reserve Bank of St. Louis 2017a). Some of the rise in debt came from existing homeowners moving to more expensive residences. Some of it took the form of second mortgages, as homeowners took on additional debt to finance home improvements. Some of the debt reflected mortgage refinancing,

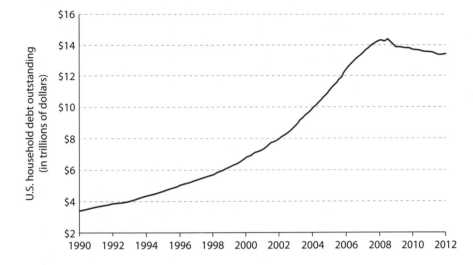

FIGURE 1.2. U.S. Household Debt. Total debt outstanding for U.S. households in trillions of dollars. *Source*: Board of Governors of the Federal Reserve System. 2017. "Debt Outstanding, Domestic Nonfinancial Sectors, Households—LA154104005.Q: 1945–2017." December. https://www.federalreserve.gov/releases/z1/default.htm.

as households took out larger mortgages against homes whose prices had recently appreciated, so as to "cash out" and perhaps spend some of the housing equity. Last but not least, a key feature of the housing boom was investors buying multiple homes for speculative purposes, hoping to re-sell as home prices went up (DeFusco, Nathanson, and Zwick 2017). For all these reasons, household debt in the United States rose from $5.7 trillion in 1998 to $14.0 trillion at the end of 2008, and the ratio of debt to household income rose from about 0.9 to 1.3 over the same period, a truly enormous increase (Board of Governors of the Federal Reserve System 2017; Federal Reserve Bank of St. Louis 2017b).

Two additional features of U.S. housing finance during this decade deserve special mention. First, many households previously unable to get a mortgage because of poor credit scores were now able to do so. In previous times, the share of such subprime mortgages was under 10 percent.

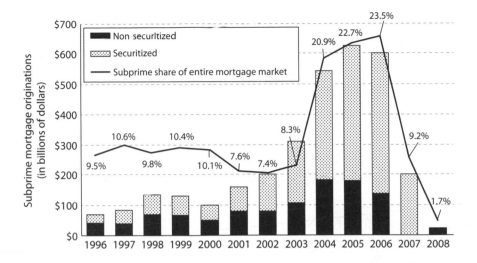

FIGURE 1.3. U.S. Subprime Mortgage Originations. Total U.S. subprime mortgage originations are broken down into those securitized and those non-securitized. U.S. subprime mortgage originations are also given as a percentage of total U.S. mortgage originations. *Source*: Financial Crisis Inquiry Commission, 2011. *The Financial Crisis Inquiry Report: Final Report of the National Commission on the Causes of the Financial and Economic Crisis in the United States.* Washington, DC: U.S. Government Printing Office.

As figure 1.3 illustrates, at the peak of the housing boom from 2004 to 2006, between a fifth and a quarter of new mortgage originations by dollar value were subprime. In 2006, households took out $600 billion of subprime mortgages, and the total over the decade added up to over $2 trillion. Because they ended up defaulting at high rates, subprime mortgages play a crucial role in the narrative of the crisis.

Figures 1.1–1.3 already describe the basic elements of extreme financial fragility. When home prices fall 30 percent or more, and homeowners have borrowed 80 or 90 percent of the price, many households end up with negative equity on their homes and default on their mortgages, especially if they are experiencing financial hardship such as unemployment. Even if they do not lose their homes, their spending capacity falls sharply. Investors who hold these mortgages also lose money when homeowners delay payments or default. The question is what happens to the financial system and to the economy when so much wealth is destroyed and this wealth is held by heavily leveraged entities.

To address this question for the 2008 crisis, we need to describe securitization, a crucial feature of mortgage finance during the housing boom. With securitization, mortgages were packaged and financially reengineered into tradable securities, which could be sold off rather than kept on the banks' balance sheets. Through impressive financial innovation, a large share of these securities were believed to be extremely safe. For this reason, securitization enabled massive increases in leverage and the fragility of the financial system.

Securitization

In the United States during this period, a bank or another financial intermediary that issued a mortgage could do one of three things with it. First, it could keep the mortgage on its own books as an asset. Second, the bank could sell mortgages to the government-sponsored housing finance enterprises (GSEs), Fannie Mae and Freddie Mac, whose liabilities were implicitly guaranteed by the U.S. government. Mortgage-originating banks did this to a substantial extent, but Fannie and Freddie typically only bought conforming mortgages (meaning not too large, not too risky, and sufficiently well documented). Fannie and Freddie sometimes retained these mortgages on their own balance sheets as assets, but more often securitized them, as we describe below. Third, the bank could sell mortgages to private investment banks, which would then securitize and sell them to investors, who thereby took on the risk of mortgage defaults.

Although all kinds of loans can be securitized, including auto loans and student loans, the most rapid growth of securitization occurred in the mortgage market. Such securitization is a financial operation that creates mortgage-backed securities (MBS) in two steps: pooling and tranching. Pooling refers to building a portfolio or pool of mortgages out of individual ones. It creates safety by diversifying away the uncorrelated risks of individual mortgages. Tranching refers to the creation of claims of different seniority out of the pool of mortgages. This means that, to the extent that mortgages in the portfolio default or delay payments, the losses are allocated to the junior tranches first and to the senior ones only after the junior tranches are worthless. Tranching builds in additional safety for the most senior securities. The combination of pooling and tranching is so powerfully risk-reducing that senior tranches were seen as nearly completely safe. Although securitization was not invented during the housing boom, it achieved unprecedented magnitude in the creation of new MBS products, including both agency MBS issued by GSEs and private-label MBS issued by private originators.

The exact reasons for the enormous demand for securitization during this period continue to be debated, but it certainly originated in a huge demand for assets that investors perceived to be safe. Some of that demand came from foreign investors, especially from high-saving Asian countries, who poured trillions of dollars into U.S. markets over this period (Bernanke et al. 2011). Some of the demand came from the increasingly wealthy U.S. households and corporations wishing to keep a share of their wealth in safe assets. By manufacturing AAA-rated senior tranches of MBS, securitization met this demand. Depending on the estimates, 60 percent or more of MBS by dollar value created through the process ended up being rated AAA (Fitch Ratings 2007). By comparison, only about 1 percent of corporate bonds by dollar value receive such ratings (Fitch Ratings 2007).

One might ask what happened to the junior tranches of MBS created in securitizations—the tranches designed to absorb the initial losses when some mortgages in the pool default. Some of these tranches were retained

27

by the financial intermediaries, exposing them to concentrated mortgage risks. But even more were themselves securitized, creating so-called collateralized debt obligations (CDOs). For this, an intermediary would assemble the junior tranches of MBS into another pool and then tranche that pool to create a variety of claims. The senior tranches of CDOs, impressively, were also rated AAA. In the mid-2000s, nearly 70 percent of CDOs by dollar value—not just MBS engineered from original mortgages but CDOs engineered from risky tranches of MBS—were rated AAA. CDOs ended up being held disproportionately by financial institutions and became a major source of their losses in the crisis.

The demand for securitization products was met with supply from both quasi-public and private sources. GSEs securitized conforming mortgages into agency MBS, and then sold them off into the market, keeping some on their own books. Because of implicit government guarantees, agency MBS were perceived as a close substitute for U.S. Treasuries. More consequentially, securitization of mortgages was pursued privately by investment banks using the riskier subprime mortgages as collateral, converting them to a large extent into AAA-rated private-label MBS. These AAA ratings were based not on government guarantees, but on models of default used by the rating agencies.

Securitizations in the mid-2000s reached staggering volumes. By 2007, over $4 trillion of agency MBS was outstanding, in addition to over $2.5 trillion of private-label residential MBS. At its peak in 2006, private-label residential MBS issuance exceeded $1.2 trillion, substantially higher than the issuance of corporate debt. Perhaps even more remarkably, a substantial fraction of these securitizations were backed by subprime mortgages, those too risky to sell to the GSEs. As we saw in figure 1.3, about 75 percent of subprime mortgage originations in the United States were securitized in 2006. In that year, close to half a trillion dollars of subprime mortgages were pooled and tranched into AAA-rated MBS.

Aside from its enormous magnitude, securitization plays an outsized role in the narrative of the financial crisis for three distinct reasons. First, there is the chicken-and-egg problem of whether the growth of credit to subprime borrowers drove the housing bubble or whether alternatively home price growth drove the credit expansion by increasing the value of available collateral. There is growing evidence that loose credit had an influence on home prices—see Mian and Sufi (2017) for a summary of extensive research supporting this view. On the other hand, home prices started growing before the huge expansion of subprime lending in the early 2000s period of very low interest rates, and this growth likely contributed to the expansion of collateral and credit, so there are causal factors running from home prices to credit as well. Our best assessment is that home price growth and credit growth were mutually reinforcing.

Second, the demand for securitized products encouraged fraud and other questionable practices in the subprime mortgage market, including the misrepresentation of borrower income, borrower credit rating, borrower downpayment, and perhaps other information (Keys et al. 2010; Bubb and Kaufman 2014; Piskorski, Seru, and Witkin 2015; Mian and Sufi 2017). There is an ongoing debate whether demand for MBS drove these misrepresentations. How much of the financial crisis can be attributed to such fraud, and how much to home price declines, remains an open question.

Third, and critical from our viewpoint, securitization created a massive misallocation of risk. Investors including financial institutions, hedge funds, sovereign funds, and money market funds that bought AAA-rated MBS or CDOs did so because they demanded safe securities, for reasons of preferences or regulations. When home prices began falling and AAA-rated MBS and especially CDOs lost their value and ratings, these investors not only lost money but ended up holding securities they did not want or even were not allowed to hold for regulatory reasons.

This caused them to sell, leading to major price declines. Risk misallocation is a central feature of our model in chapter 3.

This discussion sums up what securities were issued as a consequence of the housing boom and how they were valued. But who bought this stuff and how did they pay for it?

Buyers of MBS

Figures on the holders of private-label MBS are difficult to come by, but it appears that banks, hedge funds, investment banks, and other leveraged financial intermediaries were significant buyers. They held some of the MBS on their own books. In addition, banks and other intermediaries set up separate legal entities, so-called structured investment vehicles (SIVs), to buy private-label MBS. An SIV would buy a portfolio of predominantly but not completely AAA-rated MBS or CDOs, which would become its assets. The SIV would then finance its assets by issuing short-term liabilities, typically in the form of asset-backed commercial paper (ABCP), which needed to be rolled over every few weeks. As long as money market funds or other buyers of ABCP were willing to roll it over, the bank that owned the SIV would collect the spread between the yield on its assets and the cost of short-term finance. In addition, the banks typically provided SIVs with guarantees of funding in case ABCP funding evaporated. However, banks were required to hold far less regulatory capital against these guarantees and off-balance sheet exposures than would be required if they directly held these assets on their balance sheets. During the crisis, SIVs turned into a major problem for banks, which ended up absorbing SIV losses as MBS and CDO prices plummeted (Acharya, Schnabl, and Suarez 2013).

The International Monetary Fund (IMF) estimates that, prior to the crisis, U.S. banks bought $1.5 trillion of residential MBS, and another

$196 billion of commercial MBS, roughly 20 percent of what was outstanding at the time. An even higher fraction, perhaps 25 percent, of CDOs was bought by banks, particularly in less senior tranches. Erel, Nadauld, and Stulz (2014) estimate that at the peak of the crisis, up to $250 billion of private-label MBS was in SIVs, while Krishnamurthy, Nagel, and Orlov (2014) suggest that 40 percent of AAA-rated private-label MBS went into SIVs. This came on top of other real estate exposures in the form of non-securitized household mortgages and commercial real estate.

The growth of assets on the balance sheets of major commercial and investment banks was reflected in the growth of their leverage. Greenlaw et al. (2008) report that by 2007 the three major investment banks (Goldman Sachs, Morgan Stanley, and Lehman Brothers) saw their equity drop to 3 to 4 percent of their assets. For commercial and investment banks, growth in leverage parallels the growth in assets more generally and not just in this period (Adrian and Shin 2010).

In sum, securitization of potentially risky mortgages, and the large exposure of highly leveraged financial institutions to these securities, had the effect of concentrating the risk of the bubble deflating on the financial intermediaries.

The System under Pressure

Home prices peaked in mid-2006 and started declining afterward, as we saw in figure 1.1. This decline infected the financial system. Not surprisingly, changes in home prices showed up first in the rapid increase in default rates on subprime mortgages, illustrated in figure 1.4. In 2006, annual default rates on these mortgages were just 2 percent, justifying the perceptions of safety implicit in the AAA ratings and the pricing of subprime MBS and CDOs. In 2007, these rates doubled to about

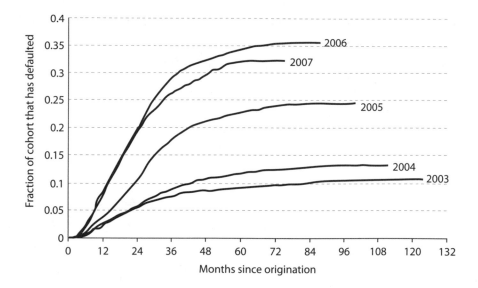

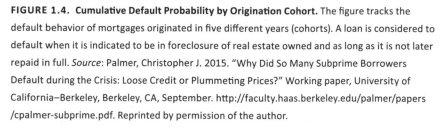

FIGURE 1.4. Cumulative Default Probability by Origination Cohort. The figure tracks the default behavior of mortgages originated in five different years (cohorts). A loan is considered to default when it is indicated to be in foreclosure of real estate owned and as long as it is not later repaid in full. *Source*: Palmer, Christopher J. 2015. "Why Did So Many Subprime Borrowers Default during the Crisis: Loose Credit or Plummeting Prices?" Working paper, University of California–Berkeley, Berkeley, CA, September. http://faculty.haas.berkeley.edu/palmer/papers /cpalmer-subprime.pdf. Reprinted by permission of the author.

4 percent, and eventually rose to 16 percent in 2008 and 2009. These defaults were the highest for the most recent vintages of mortgages, those issued in 2006 and 2007. Within five years, close to a third of subprime mortgages issued in these years had defaulted.

Initially, mortgage defaults led to sharp reductions in the prices of junior tranches of MBS. As the critical figure 1.5 shows, these prices had already fallen sharply by mid-2007. But by the summer of 2007, and increasingly toward the end of 2007, the high rates of default brought about declines in the prices of AAA-rated senior tranches as well. Eventually, junior tranches of subprime residential MBS became essentially

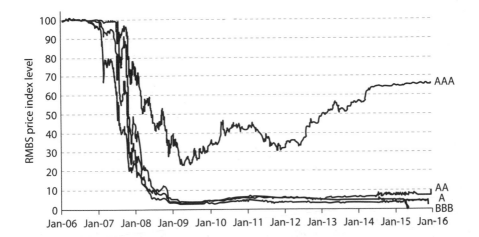

FIGURE 1.5. Prices of Residential Mortgage-Backed Securities. The figure shows the Markit ABX Home Equity Index (ABX.HE), which tracks the performance of residential mortgage-backed securities (RMBS) of different issuer ratings. *Source*: Markit. 2017. "ABX Home Equity Index (ABX. HE): 2006–2017." Accessed August 15, 2017. https://ihsmarkit.com/products/markit-abx.html.

worthless, while the senior ones fell to as low as a third of their initial value before recovering starting in 2009.

The financial system came under stress almost immediately once the prices of AAA-rated MBS began to decline, and strains began to be felt by late spring and especially by August 2007. Subprime mortgage lending, and the creation of subprime MBS from these mortgages, came to a halt. In April 2007, a leading subprime mortgage lender, New Century, filed for bankruptcy protection. In June 2007, the investment bank Bear Stearns suspended redemptions from its funds holding MBS. In July, Countrywide Financial, a major underwriter of subprime mortgages, warned of "difficult conditions"; it was eventually acquired in January 2008. Interbank lending rates rose sharply. More worrisome, the declines in MBS values put huge stress on the short-term financing of MBS holdings, especially in SIVs. As figure 1.6 shows, in the summer

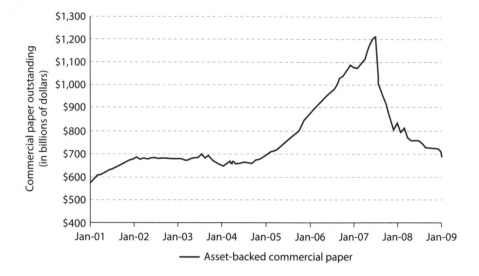

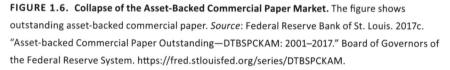

FIGURE 1.6. **Collapse of the Asset-Backed Commercial Paper Market.** The figure shows outstanding asset-backed commercial paper. *Source*: Federal Reserve Bank of St. Louis. 2017c. "Asset-backed Commercial Paper Outstanding—DTBSPCKAM: 2001–2017." Board of Governors of the Federal Reserve System. https://fred.stlouisfed.org/series/DTBSPCKAM.

of 2007, the asset-backed commercial paper market froze, so SIVs could no longer maintain their MBS holdings without injections of cash from their sponsors. They had to get this liquidity or, alternatively, liquidate their holdings.

The Federal Reserve responded to the problems in financial markets. Starting in late 2007, it intervened energetically by cutting interest rates, supplying liquidity, and arranging acquisitions of troubled institutions. Critically for what was to happen later, the Fed described the problem as one of liquidity, meaning that banks and SIVs had trouble rolling over their short-term liabilities that financed their MBS holdings. These short-term liabilities needed to be guaranteed or replaced. The cocktail of lower interest rates, collateralized loans to institutions seeking liquidity, and rescues of troubled financial institutions through acquisitions by healthier ones appeared to stabilize the financial system by early 2008.

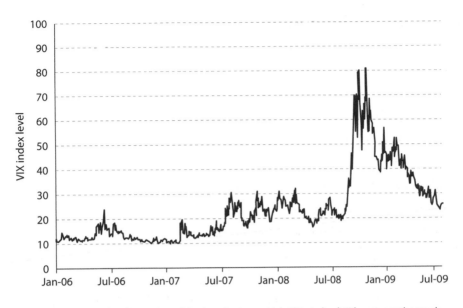

FIGURE 1.7. VIX. The Chicago Board Options Exchange Volatility Index (VIX) captures the stock market's expectation of volatility. It is computed using S&P 500 index options. *Source*: Federal Reserve Bank of St. Louis. 2017d. "CBOE Volatility Index: VIX—VIXCLS: 1990–2017." Chicago Board Options Exchange. https://fred.stlouisfed.org/series/VIXCLS.

Figure 1.7 presents the VIX index describing expectations of stock market volatility implied by S&P 500 options. It shows the index rising substantially in the summer of 2007, but then stabilizing for a year and actually declining in the spring and summer of 2008, prior to the Lehman crisis. The behavior of VIX demonstrates two points. First, the market expected higher volatility after the housing bubble started deflating and the turbulence in the summer of 2007, but it did not expect anything like the extraordinary volatility after the Lehman bankruptcy. Second, while investors did not feel that the financial system was all the way back to normal, the Fed interventions effectively reduced risk perceptions until Lehman.

A prescient paper by Greenlaw et al. (2008) was presented at a University of Chicago–sponsored conference well attended by Fed officials in late February 2008. The paper pointed to severe stress in markets for short-term financing, but also centrally focused on mortgage losses facing banks. The paper's authors noted that some estimates indicated mortgage losses of $250 billion by the end of 2007, and some doomsday scenarios forecast total mortgage losses of up to $500 billion. The authors also quite accurately predicted that such severe losses would lead to the withdrawal of short-term finance, necessitating the liquidation of MBS portfolios in fire sales, leading to further price declines and deterioration of balance sheets of intermediaries. They warned that the U.S. financial system might be facing insolvency and not just illiquidity if capital was not rebuilt. In their view, this posed a serious threat to bank lending and the economy.

During the next six months, home prices fell further, defaults on subprime MBS continued to mount, and MBS prices continued to fall, including now those of senior tranches (figure 1.5). Short-term financing and interbank markets continued to experience severe stress. The Fed massively expanded its liquidity operations. One important event during this period was the rescue of one of the largest investment banks, Bear Stearns, through acquisition by JPMorgan Chase, which required substantial assistance from the Federal Reserve. Remarkably, despite all the stress, the financial system held together through the summer of 2008.

Lehman

The calm lasted until early September. On September 7, the GSEs Fannie and Freddie were placed into government conservatorship, essentially nationalized. This was perhaps the single most significant step in fixing the financial system, but it came too late. Over the weekend of September 13–14, the Fed and the Treasury failed to successfully organize a rescue of one of the largest investment banks, Lehman Brothers, which declared bankruptcy on September 14. Rumors that Lehman, with its huge exposure to MBS and real estate, was illiquid and perhaps insolvent circulated for several months, arguably since the rescue of Bear Stearns (Sorkin 2009). But it was widely assumed that Lehman was too big to fail, and as such would be rescued by the government through a sale to a larger and healthier bank, dismemberment, and at least liquidity guarantees. After all, it was a bigger and more financially interconnected bank than Bear Stearns.

Except that in the Lehman case, the government did not save it. The reasons for the decision not to rescue Lehman remain controversial. U.S. Treasury Secretary Henry "Hank" Paulson blamed British officials for a failure to approve the takeover of Lehman by Barclays, a British bank, over the critical September 13–14 weekend. Many believed at the time that the senior management of Lehman was so arrogant and divorced from reality in its failure to sell the bank earlier that a furious Paulson wanted to teach them a lesson (Sorkin 2009). Paulson was adamant, both before and during that weekend, that moral hazard was rampant and that, unlike in the Bear Stearns case, the U.S. government would not be putting up any money to facilitate a takeover of Lehman, possibly discouraging some suitors. He and other government officials faced intense political pressure from Congress not to rescue Lehman.

It is an open question which of these arguments prevailed over that fateful weekend, but a few weeks later, as it became clear that the failure of Lehman precipitated a financial meltdown, the principal policymakers offered an explanation. According to this account, the Fed had no legal authority to rescue Lehman either by buying some of its assets in a takeover by a third party or by guaranteeing its liquidity because it could only do so if confident that Lehman was solvent. Because the officials did not have such confidence, they were in no position to save Lehman. As Ben Bernanke, then the Federal Reserve chairman, later said with respect to Lehman, "We did everything we could" (Bernanke 2015).

Laurence Ball (2018) questions this account. He argues that the law is ambiguous, and that the Fed and Treasury officials did not try very hard to find out whether Lehman could be legally saved. In fact, the government was adamant for months that it would put no money into a Lehman rescue. Ball suggests that the story that the government had no legal authority to rescue Lehman was made up after the fact, once the catastrophe became apparent. Ball's story is bolstered in part by the fact that the largest insurance company, AIG, was rescued right after the Lehman bankruptcy, and the fears about its solvency were perhaps as real. Given the incompleteness of the record, it is hard to learn exactly what is true, and we might never know. But the effects of Lehman's bankruptcy were extreme.

Lehman's bankruptcy shocked financial markets, and its effects obviously surprised both investors and regulators. Lehman's failure caused the stock market to drop 500 points on Monday, September 15, and triggered a series of major rescues of financial institutions. As figure 1.7 illustrates, the perception of volatility as measured by VIX exploded. At the same time as it chose not to save Lehman, the government arranged the rescues of an even larger investment bank, Merrill Lynch, through its acquisition by Bank of America, as well as of the large insurance company, AIG, which was selling insurance against the default of mortgage-backed securities. In both instances, the immediate problem was the demand by creditors of the institutions for more collateral, prompted in part by concerns about their solvency.

The failure of Lehman precipitated the second largest financial crisis in U.S. history after the Great Depression. Financial markets were chaotic and disrupted, and short-term financing came to a halt except for that using government securities as collateral. Figure 1.8 shows the mas-

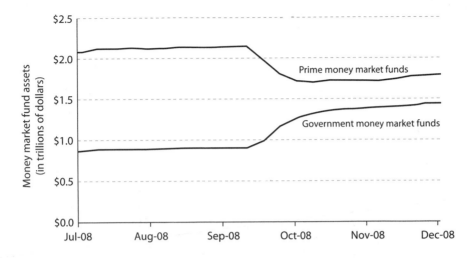

FIGURE 1.8. Money Market Fund Assets. The figure shows how investors ran from prime money market funds that lent to holders of MBS toward government money market funds. *Source*: Investment Company Institute. 2008–2012. "Weekly Money Market Fund Assets." www .ici.org/research/stats.

sive reallocation of investment in money market funds from so-called prime funds, which provided short-term financing to investment banks like Lehman for their MBS holdings, toward funds that invested in U.S. Treasuries. In the course of a few weeks, about half a trillion dollars of liquid savings left these types of funds as investors flew to the safety of government debt and away from securities they previously but no longer thought to be safe.

Figure 1.9 presents the evidence on haircuts for repo, the overnight loans collateralized by securities. A haircut of near zero means that a lender is willing to lend almost a dollar overnight backed by a dollar of securities as collateral. A haircut of 40 percent means that the lender is only willing to extend an overnight loan of 60 cents against the same collateral. Clearly the markets saw a severe deterioration of the terms of short-term financing of MBS holdings, which meant that, without large capital commitments, these holdings could not be maintained.

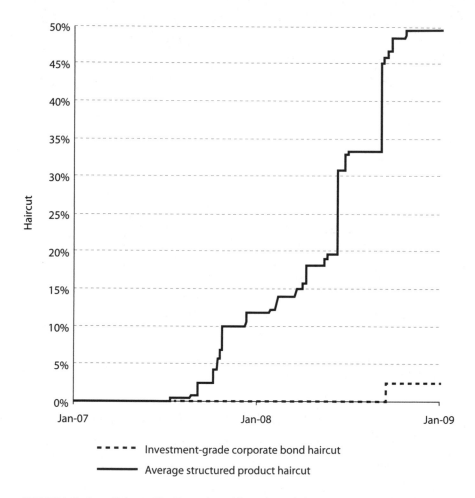

FIGURE 1.9. Repo Haircuts. The figure shows bilateral repo haircuts on structured products and investment-grade corporate bonds. *Source*: Gorton, Gary, and Andrew Metrick. 2010a. "Haircuts." *Federal Reserve Bank of St. Louis Review* 92 (6): 507–19. Reprinted by permission of the authors.

Why was Lehman so pivotal? Surely there is nothing special about Lehman per se. We would have seen the same market distress if it were AIG or Merrill Lynch. So, what was the real news in the Lehman bankruptcy that caused such a sharp market reaction that surprised both investors and policymakers? What did the markets and policymakers learn that they did not know before? Certainly the news was *not* that

Lehman was in deep trouble, since this was known for months. The policymakers in fact were publicly trying to convince Lehman to merge with another company for close to half a year. Nor was it news that the housing bubble was deflating, since by September this was very old news as well. Nor was it news that financial institutions were losing hundreds of billions of dollars, since that too was widely understood at the time.

Markets appear to have learned two things from the Lehman filing. The first is that the government was willing to let a systemically relevant financial institution go bankrupt. Although Secretary Paulson repeatedly and extremely publicly insisted that there would be no more bailouts, markets did not quite believe him. Most investors thought that the government would blink. Ironically, the government made a U-turn on this policy immediately after the Lehman bankruptcy.

The failure of Lehman was probably news in another way. What became clear over that fateful week is that the financial system was in a meltdown that was very hard to control. Investors, and possibly regulators as well, learned that financial institutions facing hundreds of billions of dollars in losses were highly interdependent, both because of their complex derivatives and other contracts with each other and because they were holding similar assets. The bankruptcy of Lehman accelerated the unwinding of derivatives contracts and sales of assets by investors who sought to rebuild their own capital and liquidity. This process rekindled fire sales and made the meltdown even harder to stop. There is little evidence in the pre-Lehman record that policymakers fully appreciated the system-wide liquidation forces that would be unleashed.

In response to rapidly falling asset prices and the evaporation of short-term financing, banks and investment banks had to sell assets to repay their creditors. Such fire sales led to further declines in MBS prices, the further need to liquidate, and precisely the vicious circle accurately described by Greenlaw et al. (2008) in February 2008. Figure 1.10, which

FIGURE 1.10. Residential Mortgage-Backed Securities (RMBS) Fire Sale. AAA-rated RMBS prices (as captured by the ABX.HE RMBS index) exhibit a classic fire sale. *Source*: Markit. 2017. "ABX Home Equity Index (ABX.HE): 2006–2017." Accessed August 15, 2017. https://ihsmarkit.com /products/markit-abx.html.

will be critical to our analysis in chapter 3, shows the price patterns of AAA-rated MBS between January 2008 and January 2013, when prices recovered. From the start of 2008 to the spring of 2009, prices of the safe tranches of MBS collapsed by nearly 70 percent, only to recover by 120 percent in the following few years. This picture looks like a classic fire sale, with the typical V-shaped price pattern.[1]

The Fed and the Treasury responded aggressively to the Lehman fallout, recapitalizing financial institutions, making equity injections, arranging mergers, providing loans against risky collateral, and eventually buying up hundreds of billions of dollars of agency MBS and putting

---

1. Merrill et al. (2014) analyze a data set of MBS transactions by insurance companies, whose risk exposures are heavily regulated, and find direct evidence of fire sales of stressed securities.

them on the Fed's balance sheet. This ended up being sufficient to stabilize the financial system by the spring of 2009, a truly extraordinary accomplishment for which both the Fed and the Treasury officials justly received considerable praise. These accomplishments should not be underestimated; it is easy to imagine the U.S. financial system and economy going into a decades-long decline if the problems were not fixed.

But massive damage was done. The U.S. economy slid into a major recession, which came to be known as the Great Recession, and did not recover for several years. Over a decade after the crisis, the loss of output relative to trend was estimated at $2 trillion. Housing prices continued to decline; construction virtually stopped and then remained moribund even longer than the rest of the economy. Unemployment peaked at 10 percent in October 2009 (U.S. Bureau of Labor Statistics 2012).

Several studies have explored the causal links from the financial crisis to the Great Recession. Two mechanisms have received substantial support. The first is the standard bank lending channel: As banks' balance sheets deteriorated due to their exposure to housing and MBS, they curtailed lending to firms and households, which in turn cut investment in physical capital and consumption of durables. Studies such as Chodorow-Reich (2014) and Benmelech, Meisenzahl, and Ramcharan (2017) provide supportive evidence for this channel. The second is the household debt channel: As families lost their equity in housing, and even defaulted, they cut their spending, thus deepening the recession. This channel was investigated in a number of compelling studies by Atif Mian and Amir Sufi (2009, 2011, 2014a), culminating in a 2014 book. They suggest that the United States would have had a major recession even without the financial crisis, since the households lost so much wealth after the housing price collapse. There is some evidence that corporate losses also contributed to the recession (Giroud and Mueller 2017), but the evidence here is less extreme than that for financial institutions and households.

Financial System Losses

It is useful to estimate the magnitude and timing of the financial system losses. The answer informs the crucial question of whether the market collapse could have been anticipated before the failure of Lehman. The answer also helps quantify the magnitude of the amplification mechanisms, such as runs and fire sales, which brought the financial institutions close to insolvency.

We rely on the estimates of financial system losses from the International Monetary Fund, which also enables us to see how the magnitudes evolved over time. Already in October 2007, the IMF projected mark-to-market losses for all holders of asset-backed securities (including mostly MBS) and CDOs of about $200 billion. In March 2008, the IMF provided more detailed estimates. It estimated about $720 billion of global losses on all securities (including corporate debt), of which about half, or $340 billion to $380 billion, would accrue to banks. Most of that, according to the IMF estimates, would come from subprime MBS and CDOs. It also appears that the IMF expected half of those total bank losses to accrue to U.S. banks—roughly $200 billion. These estimates are similar to the baseline scenario of Greenlaw et al. (2008). Losses on this scale arguably did not constitute an existential threat to banks, but would have created a major hole in bank capital and a major obstacle to future bank lending.

By October 2008, these loss estimates had risen sharply—and these are the numbers before the asset liquidations went into full swing. The total expected loss estimate rose to $980 billion; the bank share stayed at half of that or roughly $500 billion. Interestingly, the IMF forecast substantial losses on AAA-rated MBS as well. At that point, the IMF also estimated bank loan write-downs (separately from securities) of up to $300 billion. If one attributes half of the losses to the U.S. banks, projected U.S. bank losses would add up to $400 billion. This gets closer to an existential threat—even before the full effects of Lehman worked through the system.

In April 2009, the IMF estimated total write-downs of $1.07 trillion on loans, and $1.64 trillion on securities. The IMF also revised sharply upward the share of these losses accruing to banks, in part because of the massive declines in the prices of CDOs that the banks held disproportionately. Specifically, the IMF projected loan losses of $600 billion and security losses of $1 trillion for banks. If we take half of this share to be U.S. banks, the projected losses rise from $400 billion to $800 billion. In fact, in October 2009, the IMF estimated the losses of U.S. banks as $654 billion for loans and $371 billion for securities, roughly $1 trillion total.

Several points about these numbers should be mentioned. First, one can say that even losses of $1 trillion are not huge in the context of the entire U.S. financial system, where the stock market value can move by that amount in the course of a few weeks or even days without major disruptions. But this calculation misses the essential and obvious point that banks are heavily leveraged, and losses of even a few percent of their capital can threaten both their solvency and their ability to do business. Even absent the existential threat, banks heavily exposed to subprime severely curtailed their lending, as Chodorow-Reich (2014) and others show persuasively.

Second, we focused on the risks to U.S. banks rather than the losses of other financial institutions and foreign banks. Since security markets are integrated, to the extent that various leveraged investors sell together, price declines and losses affect them all. While we focused on banks, fire sales bankrupted several hedge funds, mutual funds, and even insurance companies.

Third, while Lehman precipitated a crisis that would have probably destroyed the U.S. financial system without major government interventions, the projected losses were both huge and hugely threatening to both the financial institutions and the economy even before Lehman. These losses represented risks to solvency and survival that were rising over several months, a point which will become central to our interpretation of the evidence.

Fourth, both before but especially after the Lehman bankruptcy, the losses became much more extreme because of fire sales and liquidations, as short-term financing of security holdings evaporated. These fire sales, together with deteriorating fundamentals, explain how losses mounted from $400 billion to as much as $1 trillion for U.S. banks alone. In retrospect, the Greenlaw et al. (2008) worst-case scenario in February 2008 turned out to be rosier than reality.

To summarize, what the U.S. economy experienced during this period is an almost classic credit crisis. The housing bubble, and its subsequent deflation, are the obvious cause. This bubble was financed with mortgages, substantially converted into MBS, which led to the tremendous growth in leverage of both households and financial institutions. As home prices started falling, the leverage cycle unwound, leading to massive losses in the financial system, liquidations, and declines in asset prices. As the financial system collapsed, only massive government interventions succeeded in reviving it.

In the period leading to the collapse of the bubble, the economy (including both households and financial institutions) was bearing a great deal of home price risk. Yet market participants appear not to have fully appreciated the extent of this risk, judging by the vast demand for and manufacture of AAA-rated MBS and especially CDOs that assigned a very low price for that risk, as well as the willingness of the financial sector to retain massive exposure to home price risk. Nor does the evidence suggest that either market participants or policymakers appreciated the magnitude of the exposure of financial institutions to housing risk, and the interdependencies between them that posed major systemic risk once home prices started falling. But these are just impressions based on behavior rather than direct evidence on beliefs.

In chapter 2, we take a closer look at the evidence of what various parties said, modeled, and predicted. This evidence on beliefs clarifies the choices of investors and policymakers, as well as the critical market outcomes. What were the expectations sustaining the housing bubble? What was the thinking behind the massive production of AAA-rated assets from risky mortgages? What were the beliefs in 2007–2008 when it became clear that the housing bubble was deflating, and why did the markets remain calm? Why was Lehman so pivotal in triggering the crisis? Our goal is to understand the financial crisis based on much more direct evidence of what the participants were thinking.

CHAPTER 2

What Were They Thinking?

C hapter 1 described a sequence of choices made by households, financial institutions, investors, and policymakers that led to the financial crisis as the housing bubble deflated. Critically, the events of 2008 including Lehman surprised both investors and policymakers. This suggests that they may have neglected some key risks in the system, such as the probability of major mortgage defaults, or the extent to which the financial sector was vulnerable to them, or both. We now assess this possibility by asking: What were market participants thinking when they made their choices? Answering this question is possible because the recency of the 2008 crisis, and the abundance of accounts, allows a closer look at what happened. And it matters because it helps us compare and evaluate several theories of the crisis.

Of course, documenting that ex ante beliefs did not anticipate the 2008 crisis is not enough to prove judgment errors. Foresight errors of this sort may in fact be due to bad luck, not necessarily to suboptimal inference. Notwithstanding these difficulties, this chapter shows that there are good reasons to think that distorted beliefs played an important role in the making of the crisis. At the end of the chapter, we use this evidence on beliefs to assess several theories proposed to describe the 2008 crisis. In chapter 4, we present systematic evidence of forecast errors in financial markets. Bad luck cannot explain these predictable errors, which only reinforces the possibility that it cannot explain the Lehman surprise either.

To analyze beliefs, it is useful to distinguish two sub-periods that also correspond to distinct sets of facts we outlined in chapter 1. The first is the period of the home price increases and securitization, from the early 2000s until the summer of 2007. This period witnesses rapid growth in home prices and a boom in the issuance of private-label mortgage-backed securities (MBS), and it ends as investors become aware that home prices are falling and intermediaries suffer their first runs on short-term financing. What were the beliefs that sustained the growth of home prices, mortgage finance, and securitization? The second period runs from the summer of 2007 to the Lehman collapse in September 2008. Why did the deflation of the bubble take so long to lead to a full-blown crisis? What were market participants and policymakers thinking, especially after March 2008, as they watched the financial system disintegrate first slowly and then all at once?

Beliefs from the Early 2000s to the Summer of 2007

We start from beliefs about home price growth, which are the critical determinants of banks' investment in mortgages and securitization. There is only limited data on the expectations of long-term home price growth during this period. One fascinating source is the surveys conducted by Case, Shiller, and Thompson (2012) in four U.S. counties—Alameda, California; Middlesex, Massachusetts; Milwaukee, Wisconsin; and Orange, California. The first and the last counties are in California, which experienced very rapid home price growth. Among other questions, Case, Shiller, and Thompson elicited expectations of long-term price growth by asking: "On average, over the next ten years, how much do you expect the value of your property to change each year?" During the five-year period before 2008, those numbers averaged about 11.6 percent in Alameda County, 8.1 percent in Middlesex County, 9.5 percent in Milwaukee County, and 13.2 percent in Orange County—all annual expected growth rates. These forecasts were roughly in line with the extremely rapid home price growth witnessed prior to the surveys, but they were way off the future realized long-term home price growth in these counties. Historically, home price growth has been strongly mean reverting, so expectations of continued price growth of this sort are unrealistic.[1] In a more recent study, Kuchler and Zafar (2017) find related evidence of households using local home price growth to forecast future national growth of home prices.

Expectations of this kind are fairly standard in behavioral—though not in neoclassical—economics. They are called "extrapolative" in the sense that they extend high price growth into the future and become highly inflated after several years of rapid price growth. Such expectations play a key role in just about every empirically plausible narrative of housing bubbles, and the bubble of the 2000s is no exception (see Case, Shiller, and Thompson 2012; Glaeser 2013; Glaeser and Nathanson 2017; DeFusco, Nathanson, and Zwick 2017). As we show in chapter 4, extrapolation describes market beliefs quite generally.

But how does one go from the optimism about home prices to rapid leveraging up by households and especially by financial intermediaries? How does this optimism about average price growth lead to securitization and vast issuance of AAA-rated mortgage-backed securities? After

---

1. Other studies documenting extrapolative expectations toward housing by U.S. households include Niu and van Soest (2014); Armona, Fuster, and Zafar (2016); and DeFusco, Nathanson, and Zwick (2017).

#	Name	Scenario	Cumulative loss	Probability
(1)	Aggressive	11% HPA over the life of the pool	1.4%	15%
(2)		8% HPA for life	3.2%	15%
(3)	Base	HPA slows to 5% by end-2005	5.6%	50%
(4)	Pessimistic	0% HPA for the next 3 years, 5% thereafter	11.1%	15%
(5)	Meltdown	−5% for the next 3 years, 5% thereafter	17.1%	5%

FIGURE 2.1. Conditional Forecasts of Mortgage Default and Losses. Analysts at Lehman Brothers understood the consequences of home price declines. However, they severely underestimated the probability and the magnitude of these declines. *Source*: Mago, Akhil, and Sihan Shu. 2005. "HEL Bond Profile across HPA Scenarios." *U.S. ABS Weekly Outlook*, Lehman Brothers Fixed-Income Research, August 15.

all, for 60 to 70 percent of collateralized debt obligations (CDOs) to be rated AAA, even with all the safety benefits of pooling and tranching, investors must expect home prices to be extremely unlikely to decline substantially, so mortgages default very rarely. The belief in the safety of mortgages and of AAA-rated MBS and especially CDOs is central both to securitization and to massive levering up by the intermediaries.

The first piece of evidence comes from a table, reproduced here as figure 2.1, from the Lehman Brothers' *U.S. ABS Weekly Outlook* on August 15, 2005, close to the peak of the housing bubble. This table, unearthed by Foote, Gerardi, and Willen (2012), describes five scenarios for home price appreciation (HPA) for a pool of subprime mortgages: "aggressive," with HPA of 11 percent over the life of the pool (very similar to expectations documented by Case, Shiller, and Thompson); "less aggressive" with 8 percent HPA; "base" with HPA slowing down to 5 percent per year by the end of 2005; "pessimistic" with HPA of 0 percent for three years and 5 percent thereafter; and "meltdown" with −5 percent HPA for the next three years and 5 percent thereafter.

Several points are noteworthy. First, the table attaches a 50 percent probability to the "base" scenario in which home prices continue to grow at a brisk pace, though perhaps not as brisk as in the previous decade. In fact, the table attaches the probability of 95 percent to the four scenarios other than the meltdown. These scenarios do not contemplate any home price declines, with merely a brief period of no price growth at worst. As a consequence, they entail at worst minor losses on junior tranches of subprime MBS and none on the AAA-rated tranches. In the view of Lehman analysts in 2005, home prices are almost certain to keep rising even if they take a brief and unlikely pause.

Second, the table considers its meltdown scenario, in which home prices depreciate by 5 percent a year for three years and then revert to steady growth. Even in this meltdown scenario, junior tranches of MBS are at risk, but AAA tranches are completely safe.

Of course, what happened to housing prices, and to subprime MBS including AAA-rated tranches, is much worse than the meltdown scenario described by the Lehman forecasters. As figure 1.1 showed, home prices fell much more, junior tranches of subprime MBS were largely wiped out, and critically, AAA tranches lost hundreds of billions of dollars in value as well. Forecast errors of this magnitude are probably due to the analysts attaching too low a probability to a large home price decline, a draw they did not even fathom. Nor is there a reason to think that Lehman analysts were exceptional or just marketing MBS and CDOs: Optimistic beliefs about both average home price appreciation and downside risk were common among other market participants examined by Foote, Gerardi, and Willen (2012). Consistent with such beliefs, banks retained large amounts of CDOs and lower-rated MBS on their own books, guaranteed structured investment vehicle (SIV) holdings, and levered up. They literally put their money where their mouth was.

Cheng, Raina, and Xiong (2014) present evidence that, at least with respect to home price expectations, securitization specialists working at investment banks were just like everybody else. The authors put together

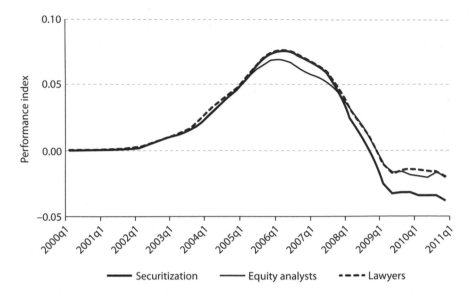

FIGURE 2.2. Investment Performance of Homebuyers. The figure above shows the performance of three groups of homebuyers. Securitization specialists do not appear to have a better understanding of the risk of home prices falling, as they are no more successful at timing the housing bubble. *Source*: Cheng, Ing-Haw, Sahil Raina, and Wei Xiong. 2014. "Wall Street and the Housing Bubble." *American Economic Review* 104 (9): 2797–829. Reprinted by permission of the authors.

data on home purchases by these specialists during the 2000s and on price performance of these homes. As figure 2.2 reproduced from that study shows, the investment bankers working on securitization did just what everybody else did: They bought homes in the mid-2000s and experienced initial price increases and then sharp declines. There is no evidence that they had a superior understanding of the risk that home prices fall.

Another crucial piece of the puzzle is how one goes from beliefs about the distribution of scenarios for home prices to the conversion of mortgages into AAA-rated MBS. How does 60 percent of the value of CDOs become rated AAA? Of course, the principal reason is that securitization involved pooling and tranching, which to a very substantial extent did protect AAA-rated MBS holders. But not enough, so there is at least a possibility that something went wrong. Two types of explanations have been offered. The first is that AAA ratings on MBS and CDOs were issued by rating agencies, which compromised their ratings to compete for business from investment banks. There is surely some truth here, but this cannot be the whole story. After all, a lot of MBS and CDOs were retained by banks or acquired by sophisticated investors such as hedge funds, so the notion that they were all duped by the rating agencies seems farfetched.

A deeper problem has been identified by Jarrow et al. (2008) and developed in a series of papers by Coval, Jurek, and Stafford (2009a, 2009b). The authors argue that both investment banks and rating agencies relied on incorrect models to value MBS and especially CDOs. Some of the mistakes came from excessively optimistic assumptions about home prices, as we already saw in figure 2.1. But another key error came from underestimating the correlation in the defaults of individual mortgages, i.e., the neglect of the systematic component in these risks. The central assumption behind the rating of AAA tranches is a low correlation in default rates between mortgages, making a pool much safer than individual mortgages. Once this correlation becomes even a bit higher than assumed, as Coval, Jurek, and Stafford show, defaults eat through the junior tranches fast and get to the senior tranches faster than anticipated. The authors present persuasive evidence that such errors had a material impact on the rating and pricing of CDOs.

Systematic errors from incorrect models used for CDO ratings reinforce the errors in forecasts of scenarios of future home prices. A higher than anticipated incidence of defaults, especially of correlated defaults, substantially raises the risks of AAA tranches, as figure 1.5 showed. Mortgage defaults were much higher, and more highly correlated, than the models of CDO risks predicted, leading to market losses on AAA-rated tranches. The modeling failures led to a neglect of downside risk of MBS and CDO portfolios.

The available data on beliefs thus suggest that before 2007, many market participants were overly optimistic about home price growth and downside risks to home prices, to AAA-rated MBS and CDOs, and therefore to balance sheets of banks. Such optimism is the main pillar of the "neglected risk" model of the financial crisis we describe in chapter 3. From this perspective, by some time in 2007 the financial system was extremely vulnerable. Financial institutions maintained on their balance sheets, and through various guarantees, substantial and highly leveraged exposures to overpriced assets. The assets were overpriced both because of the housing bubble and because the risk of MBS, especially AAA-rated CDOs, was not accurately priced in. The tail risk was underestimated by financial institutions as well as by investors.

Beliefs after 2007

In the summer of 2007, when it became apparent that home prices were falling, at least the junior tranches of private-label MBS were losing substantial value and even senior tranches were seen as much riskier than previously thought (see figures 1.1, 1.4, 1.5, and 1.10). The declines in private-label MBS prices led to a major liquidity crisis in which several SIVs and some investment banks could not roll over their short-term funding. The asset-backed commercial paper market came to a halt in August 2007. Yet markets got around this problem with short-term borrowing, largely with the help of lower interest rates and collateralized lending facilities from the Fed, such as the Term Auction Facility and later the Primary Dealer Credit Facility. The financial system did not collapse; it continued to limp along for over a year. The question is why. How is it possible that even when markets learned that home prices were falling, and that even AAA-rated MBS was at substantial risk, calm prevailed for another year? Why did it take the Lehman bankruptcy for the system to go into a freefall?

Our best judgment is that for a year after the summer of 2007, neither investors nor policymakers fully appreciated the tail risks that had built up in the financial system. The liquidity interventions starting in the summer of 2007 calmed markets down and perhaps assured investors and policymakers that they would stay calm, despite the fact that the losses of financial institutions kept growing at a brisk pace. Securitization also contributed to the belief that banks' exposure to home price declines was limited, creating a perception of safety. In this sense, the relative calm between the summer of 2007 and September 2008 points again to neglected tail risk. If risks were properly understood, markets should have strongly reacted already in the summer of 2007, when it was clear that the home price bubble was deflating. Instead, markets remained relatively calm, as we saw in figure 1.7. As we argue in chapter 5, insufficient reaction to incoming bad news was due to an exaggerated perception of financial system safety, which lasted until Lehman failed.

The warnings from the International Monetary Fund (IMF) and well-informed observers such as Greenlaw et al. (2008) in the spring of 2008 were not effective. Neither market participants nor policymakers appear to have fully appreciated the full extent of bank exposure and losses and the systemic solvency risks. As long as financial intermediaries were able to maintain and refinance their holdings of MBS, even with the help from the Fed, the system was seen as stable. The authorities had several effective mechanisms of addressing the shortages of liquidity, from lending money to intermediaries while taking risky collateral to arranging takeovers of weak institutions. As we saw in the introduction, both Bernanke and Paulson believed in late spring that the worst was over. Even as late as July–August 2008, a collapse did not seem likely or imminent.

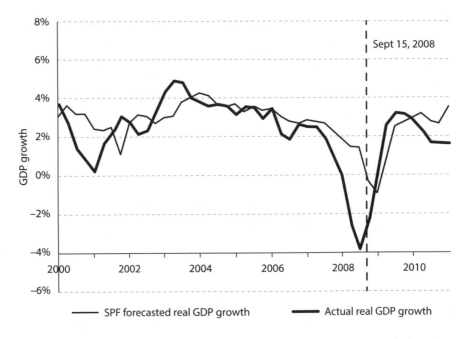

FIGURE 2.3. Forecasted and Actual Real Economic Growth over the Next 12 Months from the Survey of Professional Forecasters (SPF). *Source*: Federal Reserve Bank of Philadelphia. 2017a. "Survey of Professional Forecasters: 1968–2017." https://www.philadelphiafed.org/research-and-data/real-time-center/survey-of-professional-forecasters.

Since neglect of risk even after 2007 is important to our analysis, we document it in some detail. We first consider forecasts of economic growth, both from the Survey of Professional Forecasters (SPF) and from the Federal Reserve Greenbook, a document prepared for the Federal Open Market Committee (FOMC) meetings. Figure 2.3 presents SPF forecasts for real GDP for the following year, as well as actual growth rates during this period. Figure 2.4 presents the corresponding Greenbook data. These figures are organized so that, at every point in time, they report a forecast for the next twelve months of real GDP growth as well as the actual realization of that growth for those same twelve months.

Figure 2.3 shows that SPF forecasts for real GDP growth for the next twelve months averaged 1.36 percent as late as the third quarter of 2008,

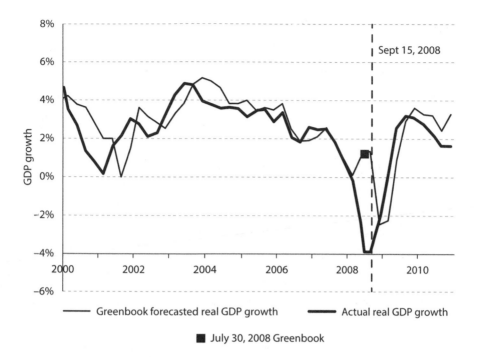

FIGURE 2.4. Forecasted and Actual Real Economic Growth over the Next 12 Months from the Federal Reserve Board Greenbook. *Source*: Federal Reserve Bank of Philadelphia. 2017b. "Greenbook Data Set: 1966–2012." Board of Governors of the Federal Reserve System. https://www.philadelphiafed.org/research-and-data/real-time-center/greenbook-data.

when in reality that growth turned out to be *negative* 3.90 percent. In the fourth quarter, even after Lehman, the consensus forecast falls but only to −0.40 percent, which sharply overstates the future reality. Figure 2.4 shows that the Fed Greenbook, with all the Fed's access to information, did not do much better. The June 2008 Greenbook forecast next year real GDP growth at 1.13 percent, which was actually revised slightly upward on July 30. Both SPF and Fed forecasters were in for a major surprise.

Perhaps most remarkable in this regard is a document prepared by the Fed forecasting staff on July 30, 2008, for the August 5, 2008 FOMC meeting. As the governors were aware of the stresses in the financial system, the staff was asked to prepare the forecasts for the scenario of "severe financial stress," which was the worst case they considered. As the forecasters described it, "in this scenario credit losses and solvency concerns intensify for many financial institutions, restricting their ability to supply credit and causing them to tighten lending standards more than in the baseline." In this scenario, the Fed forecasters expected −0.4 percent real GDP growth in the second half of 2008, with real growth rising to 0.5 percent in 2009 and 2.6 percent in 2010. The unemployment rate in this scenario was expected to peak at 6.7 percent in 2009. It actually peaked at 10 percent. Six weeks before Lehman, the Fed forecasters had no idea what was coming.

Equally informative is the discussion of these forecasts by the FOMC members. Most of them are concerned about the stresses in the financial system, and there is a clear agreement that financial institutions stand to lose hundreds of billions of dollars in real estate loans and securities. But even some of those concerned say they are not as pessimistic as the "severe financial stress" scenario. Other FOMC members, particularly some regional bank presidents, appear utterly oblivious. One stated, "I say that the level of systemic risk has dropped dramatically and possibly to zero."[2] It is hard to conclude from this evidence that six weeks before the Lehman bankruptcy people in that room comprehended the fragility of the financial system, unless they chose not to mention it.

This forecasting record is echoed by both the conduct and the speeches of the regulators. In 2013, Fed governor Jeremy Stein retrospectively summarized the feelings during that period as follows:

> The first serious tremors associated with the crisis were felt in August 2007, with BNP Paribas suspending redemptions on its money

---

2. See page 51 of the transcript of the August 5, 2008 FOMC meeting.

market funds and investor runs on multiple asset-backed commercial paper programs. At this point, there was no longer any real doubt about the nature of the shock confronting us—even if its precise magnitude was yet to be determined. And yet it was more than a full year until the failure of Lehman Brothers in September 2008, which ignited the most intense part of the crisis. Moreover, during the interval from the start of 2007 through the third quarter of 2008, the largest U.S. financial firms—which, collectively, would go on to charge off $375 billion of loans over the next 12 quarters—paid out almost $125 billion in cash to their shareholders via common dividend and share repurchases, while raising only $41 billion in common equity. This all happened while there was a clear and growing market awareness of the solvency challenges they were facing. Indeed, the collective market cap of these firms fell by approximately 50 percent from the start of 2007 through the end of June 2008. (Stein 2013)

Nor was the private sector, as evidenced by both forecasts and dividend payouts, alone in underestimating system risks. On August 22, 2008, three weeks before Lehman, Federal Reserve Chairman Ben Bernanke gave a speech at the flagship gathering of central bankers in Jackson Hole, Wyoming. Bernanke is deeply concerned about the stresses facing the financial system, which he refers to as a "financial storm," and explains several government interventions during the previous year, including the rescue of Bear Stearns. Bernanke is uncomfortable about such rescues and mentions the problem of "too big to fail" multiple times. He characterizes the stresses in the financial markets as problems of liquidity and short-term funding, which the Fed seeks to address. He does not mention systemic risks of major insolvencies or of a crisis. It is difficult to read this speech as one by a captain whose ship is about to go down.

But the point here is not just the understandable lack of perfect foresight by private forecasters, the Greenbook, financial institutions, or even high-level officials. Rather, it appears that both the Fed and the private sector saw the decline in home prices, in MBS prices including AAA-rated tranches, in bank balance sheets, and in market liquidity as serious but manageable problems, rather than as the precursors of a meltdown. Until September, a broad financial crisis and a deep recession were either seen as unlikely or not mentioned in a polite conversation.

In light of this evidence, it is understandable why the meltdown after the Lehman bankruptcy came as such a surprise. It made it clear to both investors and regulators that systemic risk was much higher than they thought. Heavily exposed to housing and highly interdependent, the entire financial system became extremely fragile and unstable. Lehman's bankruptcy brought this reality to mind and triggered a meltdown. It also made clear that without public assistance—which the officials were adamant they were not providing until after the Lehman bankruptcy—the financial system was bankrupt. Only the extremely aggressive government actions to boost the capital of financial institutions, and not just their liquidity, immediately after Lehman convinced markets that the system would survive. It is hard to imagine, in retrospect, that the Treasury and the Fed would have let Lehman go if they understood what would happen afterward.

This brings us back to the fundamental question about public policies in the year before the Lehman bankruptcy: How much were the policies shaped by the neglect of risk, how much by a lack of legal authority to intervene in the financial sector, and how much by the fear of spooking markets and precipitating an earlier crash? Some policymakers were surely worried about financial fragility for some time. As early as April 2008, the Treasury prepared and shared with the Fed a proposal, called the "Break the Glass" Bank Recapitalization Plan, to massively shore up bank capital. This proposal went nowhere. There were also expressions of substantial concern from several officials at the New York Fed. But these concerns did not prevail; policymakers supported the liquidity of the financial system but did little to shore up capital of financial institutions until after Lehman. Why this relative passivity?

The "lack of legal authority" view has many merits. After all, banks until the summer were in compliance with formal regulatory requirements, and bank regulators had no legal power to force them to stop dividends or raise equity unless they really looked weak, like Citibank. The investment banks in most trouble, such as Lehman, were not even regulated by the Fed, making it difficult to force them into a merger on terms they did not like. The crisis actually started on the periphery of the financial system not regulated by the Fed, such as investment banks, foreign banks, and insurers.

Policymakers also had fairly limited political capital to intervene — or to expand their authority—until after Lehman. Secretary Paulson used his persuasive powers to convince Congress to let the government take over the government-sponsored housing finance enterprises (GSEs), which were surely insolvent and whose bankruptcy would have caused even more damage than that of Lehman. Belief in intentionally risky behavior by banks was widely shared by Congress, central bankers, and presidential candidates, making intervention extremely unpopular. The policymakers could have been fully aware of the problems, aggressive as they could be to fix the financial system, but still severely handicapped to do much until after Lehman.

The policymakers probably did not want to start a meltdown, either. Excessive talk about the solvency of the system would have only spooked market participants and perhaps triggered an earlier crisis at a time when neither the Fed nor the Treasury had the tools to address it. Perhaps the emphasis on liquidity rather than solvency problems was part of this plan.

But to embrace the "we did everything we could" argument in its entirety, one needs to believe many things. Even without legal authority, policymakers had a lot of what political scientists call "soft power." After all, the Fed controlled access to liquidity through the Term Auction Facility and the Primary Dealer Credit Facility, which gave it tremendous influence over Lehman and other borrowers. Few of the financial institutions would have lasted until September without this aggressive liquidity support, which was not used to persuade banks to raise capital.

Policymakers could have also sounded the alarm about the health of the financial system right after the rescue of Bear Stearns and requested forcefully, even if they could not mandate, that banks stop paying dividends and raise more equity. Officials could have spoken early on about solvency problems of financial firms, rather than insisting that the problem was only access to short-term finance. Had they appreciated the risks, participants in the FOMC meeting on August 5, 2008, could have questioned the extraordinary optimism of the staff's "severe financial stress" forecast, rather than go along with it or with the ultra-bullish central forecasts.

It is hard to believe that both the reluctance to wield regulatory powers and the silence about solvency were intended only to preserve the public face of stability. An alternative view is that policymakers genuinely believed that they had things under control, until they didn't. Even the best policymakers did not fully appreciate tail risks building up in the financial system.

The focus on beliefs, then, as reflected in both quantitative forecasts and official speeches, tells us something fundamental about the impending crisis. It tells us that both the private and the official sectors, while aware that the financial system was under stress, did not fully appreciate the systemic risk it faced. As we show in chapter 3, this neglect of systemic tail risk ties the whole story together.

Theories of the Crisis

Perhaps not surprisingly, the financial crisis of 2008 has inspired a number of plausible explanations. A detailed picture of how the events unfolded, combined with an understanding of the beliefs of market participants, helps tease some of them apart. In the remainder of this chapter, we examine these leading theories of the crisis. We begin with the moral hazard theory, which holds that financial institutions were fully aware of the risks in the system, but their incentives were distorted—for instance, by "too big to fail" implicit guarantees. We then consider perhaps the leading theory of the crisis, widely embraced by prominent economists and policymakers, which sees it as principally a liquidity crisis similar to a bank run. We argue that both of these theories miss essential facts of the crisis and conclude that better theories must put expectations first.

Moral Hazard and Distorted Incentives

The moral hazard problem with banks is the favorite of populist politicians and economic theorists. It is also an obligatory and heartfelt concern gravely and earnestly expressed by bank regulators, including senior Fed officials, at every opportunity. At the broadest level, there are two versions of this theory. The first is the "too big to fail" theory, which says that banks take excessive risks, counting on getting the upside if these bets pay off and on a government bailout if they do not. The second version can be called the "fraudulent practices" theory, whereby banks knowingly took excessive risks but then distributed them to unsophisticated investors.

Applied to the financial crisis, the "too big to fail" theory holds that banks wanted to take leveraged bets on housing. They understood that their mortgage and MBS holdings and SIV liquidity guarantees were riskier than the risk ratings indicated, but nonetheless went for it because they counted on bailouts. Because the Fed's regulatory framework accepted AAA ratings of MBS and CDOs at face value, it failed to impose proper risk controls on the banks, which took enormous risks and left the taxpayer on the hook for their losses. The Bear Stearns rescue only deepened the conviction that the Fed stood ready to bail out large institutions.

The "fraudulent practices" theory holds that banks tricked their naïve clients to take out risky mortgages or to purchase seemingly safe securities such as MBS. They originated bad things to distribute them. Bank staff knew of the risks entailed, but hefty bonuses gave them a strong incentive to engineer these transactions. Consistent with this theory, in chapter 1 we mentioned the evidence of fraud in subprime markets.

At the heart of moral hazard theory is the assumption that the banks knew something about housing in general and MBS (and CDOs) in particular that others did not know—namely, that they were riskier than rated. That is, the banks had special information about the risks of their holdings that they concealed from both investors and regulators. The trouble with this assumption is that we have little evidence that the banks had any superior knowledge about the risk of the assets in which they invested, or least in 2005 and 2006. As we have stressed in chapter 1, banks retained massive direct and indirect exposure to housing and were not especially keen to cut it as the "fraudulent practices" theory would predict. To the contrary, as figure 2.1 illustrated, banks showed substantial optimism and disregard for downside risks. Likewise, the study by Cheng, Raina, and Xiong (2014) summarized in figure 2.2 showed that securitization specialists were just as optimistic about real estate as others. This evidence points against the view that bankers knew something about the housing bubble that others did not. When the bubble collapsed, they lost money on their homes, they lost money on equity holdings in their firms, and many lost their jobs. This does not look like superior knowledge.

In fact, the information we have from bank internal statements and other data (such as figure 2.1) suggests that they held beliefs similar to those held by the rating agencies and investors. They were very optimistic until 2007 and tried to sell their holdings and reduce leverage after that, though obviously not fast enough. Fahlenbrach, Prilmeier, and Stulz (2017) present broader evidence that banks usually take their signals from markets and expand their loan portfolios when markets reward them with high equity returns. In this episode, this would have meant deeper involvement with lending and securitization. Stock market valuations of banks reached their highest levels ever in the second quarter of 2007, prior to the summer crisis, suggesting that markets and banks agreed that MBS was a good investment. This is not to say that banks did not try to cheat with asset valuations or delay recognizing losses. Rather, banks went into MBS and CDOs because markets treated this as a good strategy.

In sum, the moral hazard view, appealing as it is politically and theoretically, has trouble fitting the evidence. Perhaps the central feature of the period leading up to the financial crisis is that beliefs and expectations were widely shared: by households, by banks and their employees, by investors, and by the policymakers. Of course, a few contrarian investors turned out to be brilliant ex post, and perhaps were brilliant ex ante, by betting against the CDOs and earning a fortune when the market collapsed. But they were in the minority, often sold short too early and went bankrupt, and do not appear to have played a role in precipitating the crisis. There is no evidence that we know of that the banks themselves were among these brilliant or lucky investors. Rather they went with the flow—not a picture of moral hazard.

Bank Run Models

Perhaps the dominant explanation of the financial crisis is that it was a liquidity crisis, or a bank run. In such a crisis, suppliers of short-term debt to hedge funds, SIVs, or investment banks refuse to roll over their loans or sharply raise haircuts, forcing these shadow banks to liquidate their holdings of securities, perhaps in a fire sale or at a large loss, potentially leading to insolvency. Former Fed Chairman Ben Bernanke is an important adherent of this view, which he offered in his 2010 congressional testimony and repeated frequently in his speeches.

The bank runs narrative begins with the classic Diamond and Dybvig (1983) model. The model is a bit unrealistic in treating random "sunspots" as triggers for a run and was modified to focus on solvency concerns by Goldstein and Pauzner (2005). It was later adapted to the facts of the financial crisis in influential work of Gorton and Metrick (2010a, 2010b, 2012). We briefly discuss all this work. In a 2015 speech at the National Bureau of Economic Research, Bernanke stated that "the Diamond-Dybvig model describes what happened in the financial crisis extremely well."

In the Diamond-Dybvig model, banks have some long-term assets such as loans or projects financed by short-term liabilities, such as demand deposits. There is no deposit insurance. If bank assets are liquidated in the short run, their recovery value is much lower than if they are held to maturity. A key feature of bank liabilities is the first come, first served rule of withdrawing demand deposits: Depositors who try to withdraw their funds are paid in full as long as there is money to pay them; those who ask late are paid nothing if there is no money left.

Diamond and Dybvig describe a self-fulfilling bank run. One day, with no news, some depositors get nervous that they may not get their deposits back and line up to withdraw their money. A small depositor hearing about this line worries that if enough people take their money out, he may be left behind and get nothing. He then lines up to get his money out as well. But as more depositors get in line, other depositors rush to do the same, so as not to be left empty-handed. In this way, every depositor gets in line. This is a run on the bank. To pay the depositors, the bank has to raise cash right away, and to do so it needs to terminate loans or sell assets. But doing so rapidly is inefficient and leads to losses that prevent the bank from paying off the depositors who got in line last, who then end up empty-handed. For no reason at all, this bank is bankrupt, and many of its depositors lose their savings.

Other than terrible distributional consequences of a run, whereby those who got there first are paid in full and the others lose everything, this run is extremely wasteful because productive bank assets are liquidated at a discount early to pay the depositors who got in line first. The bank in the end is insolvent because its liabilities exceed its vastly diminished assets. A totally arbitrary run on a healthy bank doing exactly what it is supposed to do—no moral hazard here—ruins both the bank and its depositors. Deposit insurance in this model is extremely effective and costless; it guarantees liquidity to depositors no matter when they ask, so they do not need to rush to withdraw even if nervous. With deposit insurance, assets are not liquidated and are kept to maturity, and as a consequence all depositors are paid in full, with interest.

The original Diamond-Dybvig model has a stark and unrealistic feature that bank runs are triggered by nonfundamental factors. Goldstein and Pauzner (2005) modify this formulation by assuming more realistically that the probability of an inefficient bank run rises with the level of solvency concerns about the bank. When depositors are worried about a bank's solvency, they line up to withdraw their money, which of course only amplifies the likelihood of insolvency as banks liquidate assets to meet depositor demands. The Goldstein-Pauzner model also has the advantage of having only one equilibrium; there are no runs when banks are far enough from insolvency.

The original Diamond-Dybvig model, as well as the Goldstein-Pauzner reformulation, applies to banks whose liabilities are uninsured deposits and whose assets are projects or loans that are a common pool. The model does not directly apply to a run on a shadow bank, where each short-term loan such as asset-backed commercial paper (ABCP) or repo has its own collateral. In such a situation, there is no obvious externality from one repo holder to the next.

To consider bank runs in this setting, Gorton and Metrick (2010a, 2010b, 2012) focus on collateralized lending and specifically on the financing of long-term AAA-rated MBS holdings by shadow banks such as investment banks and SIVs using repo. Their starting point is that this type of financing relies on low haircuts, so shadow banks are able to borrow close to $1 to finance $1 of holdings. In this case, the shadow bank needs little capital and no major guarantees from a sponsoring bank. The secret of this type of financing is the complete certainty that the collateral is absolutely safe. As long as the providers of short-term finance have such certainty, they do not need to expend resources to find out what the collateral is or whether its value might fall. Put differently, prime money market funds or other repo lenders rely on essentially mechanical transactions. They do not have the know-how to investigate the quality of the collateral and must assume it to be entirely safe. As soon as any suspicion about collateral quality arises, these financiers must sharply raise haircuts or get out.

So, suppose we start with money market funds providing repo financing on total certainty about the sufficiency of collateral, and a small adverse shock raises concerns about its value, perhaps such as that in the summer of 2007. In Gorton and Metrick's view, the financiers either refuse to roll over the debt or sharply raise haircuts to preserve the complete certainty of getting their money back, even overnight. The bank now needs more capital to maintain its holdings. As uncertainty rises a bit more, these concerns (and haircuts) rise sharply, and any shadow or other bank unable to get capital or trigger liquidity guarantees needs to liquidate its assets. Liquidations by one bank further reduce the value of assets, deepening problems for other banks. We are back to widespread inefficient liquidation, just as in the Diamond-Dybvig model.

In the model of Gorton and Metrick, without external support in the form of capital or liquidity guarantees, shadow banks unravel as soon as doubts that collateral is completely safe arise. This model describes elegantly how small shocks can lead to a disaster when long-term assets are financed by short-term safe liabilities. And as in Diamond-Dybvig, either ex ante guarantees of such liabilities by a solvent institution or ex post liquidity rescues by the government effectively solve the problem because they stop asset liquidations.

An Evaluation

Bank run models have several critical advantages. First, they describe something that has clearly happened, both in the summer of 2007 during the ABCP run, and in late summer and September 2008, as investment banks and other shadow banks lost financing in the repo market. Both of these episodes featured dramatic withdrawals of short-term finance. Bank run models also account for the impressive efficacy of liquidity interventions by the Fed during the summer 2007 ABCP collapse, which successfully stabilized the financial system. They also explain why such liquidity interventions work so well—they stop asset fire sales and liquidations and thereby calm down short-term creditors.

This theory also has the advantage of being very convenient to policy-makers. For in its pure Diamond-Dybvig form or even the Gorton-Metrick version, it says that crises are unpredictable, and thus the failure to predict them is not the policymaker's responsibility. The policymaker must be vigilant like a firefighter, but should not even try to be a police-man, since he could not predict when and how a sunspot or a small bad shock would hit. Ex post provision of liquidity by lending against risky collateral or guaranteeing liabilities is the best one can do.

So what is wrong with seeing the financial crisis as a (shadow) bank run? The main problem we see with the liquidity story is that it puts the cart before the horse. The pure Diamond-Dybvig (or Gorton-Metrick) bank run begins with an unexpected withdrawal of short-term finance from a healthy institution, which then precipitates a vicious cycle of asset liquidations and further withdrawals of short-term finance. This is not what happened in 2008. Rather, as we saw from the IMF data, major losses on MBS and other real estate assets built up over time and raised concerns about the solvency of major institutions—including Lehman—from early 2008 when Bear Stearns was saved through acquisition. The losses in hundreds of billions of dollars, and the fear of deepening losses, sparked the short-term finance withdrawals, which then led to the unrav-eling of the system. The Goldstein-Pauzner model is a better description of such bank runs because it connects them to prior losses and solvency concerns. The horse here is major losses and threats to solvency; the bank runs are the cart.

The pure Diamond-Dybvig or Gorton-Metrick view builds on the premise that a crisis begins with a small unanticipated shock. In reality, the shock in 2007–2008 was massive, and more important, it was a long time coming. Even without the fire sales that started in 2007 and accel-erated after Lehman, the financial sector was on track to lose several hundred billion dollars from its direct exposure to real estate, MBS holdings, and guarantees to SIVs. There was a large, observable, and growing insolvency threat to the financial system, which investors and policymakers could see coming. Once insolvency is considered, bank runs are best seen as a final blow to the financial system already severely threatened by large losses, rather than the cause of the crisis. Fire sales, liquidations, and further losses followed these runs, driving financial institutions ever closer to bankruptcy.

This matter is not a minor academic dispute. As we showed in chapter 1, massive losses of financial institutions were clearly predicted by the IMF and others starting in early 2008. This means, if one accepts the Goldstein-Pauzner view of bank runs precipitated by solvency concerns, that the likelihood of such massive runs was at least partly foreseeable as well. And with genuine solvency concerns, liquidity interventions are no longer sufficient to fully stabilize the system. Capital is needed. The policy however turned to capital injections only after Lehman; it saved the financial system but came too late to prevent the Great Recession. Policymakers were way behind the curve.

At the heart of this delayed recognition of vulnerability is neglect of risk. Judging by the quantitative evidence on expectations by both professional forecasters and Fed staff, by the policies pursued by the regulators, as well as by their speeches, the solvency risks and their systemic consequences were not fully appreciated by either markets or policymakers until September 2008, when it was too late to avoid a catastrophe. It is not that the policymakers did not recognize market stresses; they obviously did. Perhaps they saw them as a series of manageable challenges that could be contained. Rather, the ties between individual institutions through fire sales, derivatives clearing, or other mechanisms of contagion were not fully appreciated. The "no bailout" rhetoric and the decision not to rescue Lehman in all likelihood reflected this lack of appreciation.

Fire Sales

A common feature of every serious narrative of the crisis is the importance of costly asset liquidations, or fire sales, as financial institutions lose access to financing. These liquidations lead to losses, to further withdrawal of finance, and eventually to the insolvency of financial institutions and perhaps the whole system. Given their importance, we describe these mechanisms in some detail.

Fire sales are forced sales of assets at below fundamental values occurring because high valuation buyers—in this case, other financial institutions—are themselves in trouble and have no resources to buy assets. In this case, prices drop even lower than the already low fundamental values. We saw the evidence of fire sales with respect to the prices of AAA-rated MBS in figure 1.10.

The significance of fire sales of financial assets was recognized both during the crisis events and in the analyses immediately after. For example, a 2009 report from the U.S. Treasury held that "an initial fundamental shock associated with the bursting of the housing bubble and deteriorating economic conditions generated losses for leveraged investors including banks. . . . The resulting need to reduce risk triggered a wide-scale deleveraging in these markets and led to fire sales." Similarly, a discussion of the crisis by leading American financial economists (French et al. 2010, 67) stated: "A bank that simply suffers large losses may be forced to reduce its risk by selling assets at distressed or fire-sale prices. If other banks must revalue their assets at these temporary low market values, the first sale can set off a cascade of fire sales that inflicts losses on many institutions. Thus, whether through official defaults or fire sales, one troubled bank can damage many others, reducing the financial system's capacity to bear risk and make loans." The Fed justified its guarantees of money market funds as a policy of preventing liquidations of assets at distressed prices.

The foundation of research on fire sales is the idea of debt overhang originally presented by Stewart Myers (1977). According to Myers, high debt reduces the returns to shareholders from making investments because returns accrue to creditors waiting to be paid off. This idea was explored by Hart and Moore (1995), who showed that in some circumstances creating debt overhang could be an efficient mechanism to control free-spending managers, even if it occasionally leads to asset sales or forgone investment. The work on fire sales, beginning with Shleifer and Vishny (1992), builds on these ideas. Shleifer and Vishny pointed to a general equilibrium aspect to debt overhang. If several firms in an industry, which could be the finance industry, face debt overhang at the same time, then prices of assets these firms sell might fall below fundamental values because the natural buyers of these assets are themselves facing debt overhang and cannot invest.

Shleifer and Vishny's 1992 paper dealt with the case of real assets, such as ships or factories. It argued that when highest valuation owners of assets have to liquidate, and high valuation buyers are themselves financially constrained, the valuations would fall as assets are transferred to less efficient but financially less constrained owners. Shleifer and Vishny (1997) applied this concept to the case of financial assets liquidated by hedge funds facing redemptions. The idea in both of these papers is the inability of high valuation buyers to come to the market and pay the full price when the seller is forced to sell because these buyers are themselves financially constrained. This theory was tested, with some supporting evidence, shortly after the paper was written, in the collapse of the well-known hedge fund Long-Term Capital Management (LTCM). As then Fed Chairman Alan Greenspan described that episode in testimony before Congress, "Quickly unwinding a complicated portfolio that contains exposure to all manners of risks, such as that of LTCM, in such market conditions amounts to conducting a fire sale. The prices received in a time of stress do not reflect longer-run potential, adding to the losses incurred" (Greenspan 1998).

These ideas were further developed by Brunnermeier and Pedersen (2009), who presented an elegant model of liquidation cycles in financial markets. In their model, as investors become worried about collateral values of assets they finance, they raise haircuts on the loans, which forces asset sales, which reduce the market value of the collateral but also further raise haircuts, which lead to further liquidations and so on. Brunnermeier and Pedersen's paper motivated the analysis of Greenlaw et al. (2008) that warned about the dangers of mounting bank losses for financial stability. The Gorton-Metrick view of runs is also related to that model.

More generally, fire sales of MBS and other assets became the critical amplification mechanism whereby troubles of some financial institutions spread literally like fire through the financial system in the crisis (see Stein 2013). This mechanism works in reality, in bank run models, but also in our model in chapter 3. Our innovation is to show that the recognition of expectation errors is the shock that fire sales amplified.

Summary

The two standard interpretations of the financial crisis—moral hazard and bank runs—fail to account for some basic features of the data, especially data on beliefs. The moral hazard view does not come to grips with the basic fact that households, financial institutions, and policymakers all shared the optimism about the housing market and securitization. To the extent that there was trickery by banks, it seems minor compared to the tidal wave of the growth of home prices and MBS markets that swept them along. The evidence suggests that the banks shared the optimism and sought to exploit it and, like everyone else, got into trouble when home prices collapsed.

Nor is the evidence consistent with the view that the crisis was an unanticipated run on reasonably healthy banks and shadow banks. Like almost everyone else, the banks predicted the future of housing and MBS incorrectly, and paid the consequences. By 2008, both investment and commercial banks were staring into the abyss of massive losses, which caused fire sales as banks tried to rebuild capital, as well as ignited a series of runs. Traditional liquidity interventions by the Fed could delay but not stop a major crisis and a deep recession. The crisis looked exactly like what one would expect when banks' balance sheets are severely compromised, and they need to cut loans and sell assets to raise capital. Here as well, both investors and policymakers failed to see the tail risks to the financial system from massive losses in housing related assets. The calm before Lehman underscores the importance of beliefs in shaping market outcomes.

In the rest of the book, we develop our view that errors in beliefs and expectations are central to understanding the 2008 financial crisis and credit cycles more generally. In chapter 3, we present a model of the financial system tailored explicitly to understanding the crisis. The model seeks to capture the essential features of shadow banking and its fragility in the world of neglected risk and expectation errors. We suggest that the main elements of the crisis we discussed in chapters 1 and 2 are captured by this model.

In subsequent chapters, we consider more general models of expectations and belief formation, seeking in part to micro-found the analysis in chapter 3. In chapter 4, we present the evidence on survey expectations in financial markets and the economy. We show that these beliefs deviate systematically from rational expectations—the assumption that economic agents optimally use the true model of the economy to form their beliefs. In chapter 5, we then present our alternative to rational expectations, which we call diagnostic expectations. This model is explicitly derived from psychology of how people process information. Finally, in chapter 6, we present a more general approach to modeling credit cycles seeking to understand both the basic features of the crisis we have outlined until now and the more systematic features of the data on credit, beliefs, and the real economy.

CHAPTER 3

A Neglected Risk Model
of the Financial Crisis

This chapter presents a basic model of financial fragility with neglected downside risk.[1] The model describes a financial system in which financial intermediaries such as banks engage in a risk transformation, but is explicitly motivated by the 2008 crisis, capturing the narrative of chapters 1 and 2. The model has two ingredients: strong demand for safe assets and neglect of downside risk. Demand for safe assets comes from investors who are more patient than intermediaries but unwilling to hold risky claims. To satisfy this demand, intermediaries hold risky assets and use them as collateral to back the liabilities they issue. Intermediaries also pool risky assets in order to render their cash flow safer, which allows them to issue even more debt. These transactions lead to growth in leverage, which reflects debt issuance by intermediaries, and to the expansion of the financial sector making risky investments and retaining risk on its books. Under rational expectations, this arrangement is efficient and the financial system is robust, since debt issuance is limited by a recognition of downside risks.

---

1. The analysis in this chapter is based on two papers by Gennaioli, Shleifer, and Vishny (hereafter GSV 2012, 2013), although here we use a different formulation.

Here our second assumption becomes critical. When both intermediaries and investors neglect downside risk in the performance of the assets, debt is perceived to be safer than it is. In this case, the financial sector expands too much, risk sharing is no longer efficient, and the system is fragile. If bad news brings neglected risks to mind, risk-averse investors dump safe debt on the market. Under some conditions, this leads to fire sales and ex post misallocation of risk.

In the context of 2008, we view intermediaries as traditional banks or investment banks, the assets as mortgages, the safe debt as AAA-rated mortgage-backed securities (MBS), the transformation of mortgages into such debt as securitization, and the investors as hedge funds, pension funds, or sovereign funds demanding safe assets. The neglected risk is that of very low returns on housing, and therefore on AAA-rated MBS, which we discussed extensively in chapters 1 and 2, or of other bad shocks that may hurt banks. We do not model the additional maturity transformation whereby AAA-rated MBS is financed by short-term liabilities such as asset-backed commercial paper (ABCP) or repo. In fact, our central message is the fragility of the system resulting from overexpansion and risk misallocation rather than from the maturity transformation. Short-term liabilities would add another source of fragility, as in models of bank runs. But we show that a simple model of neglected risk, even if it abstracts from bank runs, can describe both the basic features of the crisis and the beliefs of the participants.

Following our discussion in chapter 2, we make the simplifying assumption that everyone in the economy—both the intermediaries and investors—holds the same beliefs. While this assumption is too strong, it captures the evidence from chapter 2 that markets were driven by widely shared but incorrect expectations. In this chapter we take the beliefs of market participants as given. In the second half of the book, we derive beliefs from a more fundamental psychological model.

We proceed in three steps. First, we consider an initial model in which payoffs on all risky assets are perfectly correlated with each other, so there is no scope for diversification from pooling and, moreover, the total volume of assets is fixed. The only question in that model is how much AAA-rated debt can be manufactured using these risky assets as collateral. We examine the consequences of neglected risk in that model. Second, we allow for the endogenous determination of the volume of loans being issued, so the intermediary decides how many loans to issue based on what it can finance with AAA-rated debt. This modification allows us to study the impact of neglected risk not only on bank leverage, but also on the total size of the financial sector and its liquidity. Third, we consider intermediary-specific idiosyncratic risk and the benefits of trading and pooling assets before the portfolio is tranched and safe debt is manufactured. We describe how these successive extensions all increase the level of fragility. Along the way, we discuss which aspects of the financial crisis the model can explain.

Neglected Risk, Leverage, and the Crisis

There are two periods $t = 0, 1$ and two types of agents: intermediaries and investors. The representative intermediary maximizes expected discounted profits over the two dates:

$$\Pi_0 + \beta_I \Pi_1, \qquad (3.1)$$

where Π_t is the expected profit of the intermediary at date $t = 0, 1$ and $\beta_I < 1$ is the intermediary's discount factor.

The intermediary maximizes profits by issuing safe debt, such as AAA-rated MBS, against a portfolio of mortgages. These mortgages yield a stochastic repayment $\tilde{X} \in [0, +\infty)$ at $t = 1$, distributed with a probability density function $f(\tilde{X})$ that is increasing from the left tail and decreasing toward the right tail (extreme outcomes are unlikely).[2]

At $t = 0$ the intermediary issues N debt claims collateralized by cash flow $\tilde{X}$. Each debt claim promises a face-value payoff of 1. Debt is sold to investors, and the intermediary keeps the residual equity. For our purposes, this tranching of mortgages into a safe and risky portion can happen inside a separate legal entity such as a trust or a structured investment vehicle (SIV), and we refer to this financial arrangement as securitization.

Investors are patient and wealthy agents interested in safe debt, such as pension funds, sovereign funds, or hedge funds. At $t = 0$, a representative investor receives a large endowment W and uses it to buy debt. This investor is more patient than intermediaries: Its discount factor is $\beta_h > \beta_l$. Critically, investors have a strong preference for debt that defaults with probability less than δ^*. They are risk neutral with respect to debt with default probability below δ^*. To hold debt with default probability above δ^*, however, investors demand a high risk premium: They discount payments of such debt by an extra factor $\epsilon \ll 1$ such that $\epsilon\beta_h < \beta_l$. The parameter δ^* captures the investors' "preferred habitat": It pins down the risk investors can comfortably tolerate. We think of it as very small (e.g., $\delta^* < 0.0001$), which generates demand for AAA-rated debt.

There are gains from trade between intermediaries and investors: Patient investors are willing to pay more for the debt than it is worth to the intermediaries, but only if the debt is safe enough. The leading example again is the tranching of mortgage portfolios in securitization to create AAA-rated MBS. The kink in investors' risk preferences captured by δ^* renders our analysis highly tractable and intuitive, but as shown

---

2. Formally, $\lim_{\tilde{X}\to 0} f(\tilde{X}) = \lim_{\tilde{X}\to +\infty} f(\tilde{X}) = 0$ and there exist thresholds X_L and X_H, with $0 < X_L \leq X_H$ such that $f(\tilde{X})$ is increasing for $X < X_L$ and decreasing for $X \geq X_H$.

by Gennaioli, Shleifer, and Vishny (GSV 2012) our qualitative results extend to smoother preferences.[3]

Equilibrium under Rational Expectations

Before introducing neglected risk, we solve this model when the beliefs of both intermediaries and investors are formed using the true density $f(X)$. To sell debt to patient investors, intermediaries must respect their risk tolerance δ^*. This constraint restricts the quantity of safe debt that can be issued. Suppose that the representative intermediary issues N units of debt using its portfolio of loans as collateral. Since each debt claim promises one unit, debt is repaid in full if the realized cash flow is high enough, i.e., if $\tilde{X} > N$, but defaults otherwise. To satisfy investors' risk tolerance, the probability of default must be lower than δ^*:

$$\int_0^N f(\tilde{X})d\tilde{X} \leq \delta^*. \tag{3.2}$$

We call equation (3.2) the "AAA constraint." If this constraint is violated, debt is too risky and investors attach a low value to it. Because the AAA constraint is easier to satisfy when less debt is sold (N is lower), it determines the volume of securitization.

---

3. In GSV (2012), the preferred habitat assumption was captured by infinite risk aversion, which can be viewed as a special case of our preferences for $\delta^* = 0$ and ϵ set at the level such that the valuation is at the lowest possible cash flow realization. Under such extreme risk intolerance, however, investors would never be willing to hold debt if the lowest possible cash flow is zero. The case of infinite risk aversion only yields meaningful results when the support of $\tilde{X}$ is bounded away from zero (the case considered in GSV 2012).

If the AAA constraint is satisfied, investors' reservation price for a unit of debt is given by:

$$p(N) = \beta_h \left[1 - \int_0^N \left(1 - \frac{\tilde{X}}{N} \right) f(\tilde{X}) d\tilde{X} \right].$$ (3.3)

By risk neutrality, this is the discounted face value of debt minus its expected shortfall in default. In default, each unit receives a pro rata share $\tilde{X}/N$ of the available cash flow.

Consider how the price and quantity of safe debt issuance are set. Because investors' wealth W is assumed to be high, they bid up the market price of debt until it converges to their reservation value. Equation (3.3) then pins down the equilibrium price of safe debt at $t = 0$.

To find the equilibrium quantity of debt, consider intermediary profits as a function of debt issuance N. The intermediary earns issuance revenues $Np(N)$ from investors and retains the risky tranche payoff $max(0, \tilde{X} - N)$. Using equations (3.1) to (3.3), the representative intermediary chooses optimal issuance N to maximize profits:

$$max_N (\beta_h - \beta_l) \left[N - \int_0^N (N - \tilde{X}) f(\tilde{X}) d\tilde{X} \right] + \beta_l \int_0^{+\infty} \tilde{X} f(\tilde{X}) d\tilde{X}$$

$$s.t. \qquad \int_0^N f(\tilde{X}) d\tilde{X} \leq \delta*.$$ (3.4)

The objective function in equation (3.4) says that profits increase in the amount of debt issued N: By tranching more safe debt out of $\tilde{X}$, the intermediary earns the valuation gap $(\beta_h - \beta_l)$. Other things equal, intermediaries want to issue as much safe debt as possible. At the same time, they need to satisfy the AAA constraint, which limits how much they can sell.

At the rational expectations optimum, the intermediary issues just enough debt $N*$ that the AAA constraint is binding:

$$\int_0^{N^*} f(\tilde{X})d\tilde{X} = \delta^*. \tag{3.5}$$

At this point, gains from trade are maximized. Investors' desire to delay consumption is satisfied to the highest extent possible given their risk tolerance. Intermediaries profit from selling debt at investors' reservation price of equation (3.3). In addition, because intermediaries are better risk bearers, they retain the junior tranche of the cash flow. Under rational expectations, the issuance of safe debt and the allocation of the risk of the junior tranche are both efficient. Neither crises nor fire sales happen.

Neglected Downside Risk and Market Equilibrium

We model neglected risk by assuming that at $t = 0$, when debt is issued, intermediaries and investors hold the same beliefs that satisfy the following definition.

Definition 3.1. *Agents neglect downside risk below $\underline{X}$ when their perceived cash flow distribution $f^\theta(\tilde{X})$ underestimates the tail to the left of threshold $\underline{X}$. Specifically, $f^\theta(\tilde{X})$ satisfies:*

$$\int_0^X f^\theta(\tilde{X})d\tilde{X} < \int_0^X f(\tilde{X})d\tilde{X} \qquad \text{for all } X \leq \underline{X}.$$

The superscript θ parameterizes the nonrational beliefs of market participants. In chapter 5, we provide a psychological foundation for this parameter θ, but we do not use it in this chapter. The above definition formalizes in reduced form the key features of the market participants' beliefs discussed in chapter 2: neglect of left-tail risk, which occurs when the probability $Pr(\tilde{X} \leq X)$ of any left-tail realization below $\underline{X}$ is underestimated. As the mortgage repayment $\tilde{X}$ is naturally linked to home prices growth, this formalization captures the beliefs in figure 2.1 that market participants underestimated the likelihood of a housing crash.

Definition 3.1 only entails underestimation of left-tail events, while being silent on the perception of cash flows above the threshold $\underline{X}$. Several belief structures are consistent with this definition of neglected risk. If definition 3.1 applies over the entire support of $\tilde{X}$, so $\underline{X} \to +\infty$, then the believed distribution $f^\theta(\tilde{X})$ first order stochastically dominates the truth $f(\tilde{X})$. In this case, not only probabilities of low cash flows are underestimated but probabilities of high cash flows are overestimated. This special case yields both neglected downside risk and the inflated assessments of average home price growth as described by Case, Shiller, and Thompson (2012).

But definition 3.1 also allows for neglected downside risk to coexist with neglected upside risk while leaving the average assessment unchanged. Formally, the perceived distribution $f^\theta(\tilde{X})$ could be a mean-preserving concentration of the truth $f(\tilde{X})$. This is the case originally considered in GSV (2012), which assumes that all unlikely events are underestimated, including those in the right tail.

Due to the convenient "kinky" investor preferences, our results on debt issuance are insensitive to the nature of beliefs above $\underline{X}$. Other results such as those on the overexpansion of mortgage financing also rely on inflated mean beliefs of the Case-Shiller-Thompson type. For this and other reasons, characterizing the full shape of beliefs $f^\theta(\tilde{X})$ is useful. The psychologically founded model of beliefs in chapter 5 offers testable conditions under which beliefs jointly exhibit neglect of downside risk and overestimation of the mean.

To compute equilibrium debt issuance with neglected risk, note that the only difference between this case and rational expectations is that both investors and intermediaries now use the distorted density $f^\theta(\tilde{X})$ rather than the true one $f(\tilde{X})$. As a consequence, the equilibrium face value of debt N^θ under neglected risk is determined by the distorted AAA constraint:

$$\int_0^{N^\theta} f^\theta(\tilde{X})d\tilde{X} = \delta^*. \tag{3.6}$$

By comparing equation (3.6) to equation (3.5), proposition 3.1 follows (proofs in the appendix):

Proposition 3.1. *Provided $\underline{X} > N^*$ in definition 3.1, neglected downside risk boosts the issuance of safe debt relative to rational expectations, $N^\theta > N^*$.*

When $\underline{X} > N^*$, neglect of downside risk is severe enough to dampen the perception of default risk at the rational expectations issuance level N^*. This relaxes the AAA constraint, allowing the intermediary to expand the issuance of safe debt.

In this way, neglect of risk can account for excessive securitization. For a fixed amount of assets such as mortgages, intermediaries create and sell excessive amounts of AAA-rated debt such as MBS. They have an incentive to do so because of the strong demand for safe debt by investors. Importantly, there is no trickery by intermediaries in this model. Rather, neglect of risk creates an opportunity for financial innovation, and competitive intermediaries exploit this opportunity to the hilt, in this case by manufacturing vast quantities of AAA-rated debt. Market forces capitalize on incorrect beliefs. More generally, we expect new financial products to load up precisely on the risks investors do not fully appreciate. Under rational expectations, financial innovation would improve risk-sharing and welfare. With neglected risk, in contrast, it creates inefficient risk-sharing and the possibility of crises. We next consider this claim in detail.

Financial Fragility and Risk Misallocation

In this most basic example, the quantity of mortgages is held constant, so neglected risk causes financial fragility through a misallocation of risk

87

between intermediaries and investors. To see this, note that with neglected risk the *true* probability of default, computed using the true density $f(\tilde{X})$, is given by

$$Pr(\tilde{X} < N^\theta) = \int_0^{N^*} f(\tilde{X})d\tilde{X} + \int_{N^*}^{N^\theta} f(\tilde{X})d\tilde{X} = \delta^* + \int_{N^*}^{N^\theta} f(\tilde{X})d\tilde{X}, \quad (3.7)$$

which exceeds investors' risk tolerance δ^*. By encouraging issuance of debt perceived to be safe, neglected risk raises default risk under the true cash flow distribution. As a consequence, investors hold debt that is too risky for their taste. They are willing to bear default risk of at most δ^*, but end up bearing more. This is the cause of risk misallocation and financial fragility.[4]

The financial crisis unfolds when the hidden risks of "safe debt" resurface and investors realize that they are outside of their preferred habitat. Suppose that this occurs at $t = 0$, right after debt is issued. This may be due to the arrival of bad news about mortgage default rates or house price dynamics, as in the summer of 2007, which brings to mind the possibility that debt defaults are more likely than previously thought. To simplify, suppose that after receiving bad news intermediaries and investors wake up and become fully rational: They replace their beliefs $f^\theta(\tilde{X})$ with the true density $f(\tilde{X})$. This is a shortcut: Our model of beliefs in chapter 5 tightly characterizes the evolution of market participants' beliefs.

When at $t = 0$ neglected risks resurface, investors realize that the debt they bought is just not safe enough and violates their preferred habitat δ^*, as per equation (3.7). Bad news need not be terrible. It just needs to be bad enough that the investor is reminded of the possibility of bad states.

---

4. Ideally, intermediaries should bear cash flow risk when $\tilde{X} \in (N^*, N^\theta]$. With neglected risk, however, this cash flow risk is inefficiently borne by investors. This is due to neglected downside risk, which implies $N^\theta > N^*$.

When this happens, the perceived default risk jumps above δ^*. In light of investors' preferences, their reservation value for the debt claims drops to

$$p_{inv}^{crisis} = \epsilon \beta_h \left[1 - \int_0^{N^\theta} \left(1 - \frac{\tilde{X}}{N^\theta} \right) f(\tilde{X}) d\tilde{X} \right], \qquad (3.8)$$

which is well below the original valuation due to the fact that $\epsilon \ll 1$.

In contrast, intermediaries' reservation value for safe debt is given by:

$$p_{int}^{crisis} = \beta_l \left[1 - \int_0^{N^\theta} \left(1 - \frac{\tilde{X}}{N^\theta} \right) f(\tilde{X}) d\tilde{X} \right]. \qquad (3.9)$$

Because $\epsilon \beta_h < \beta_l$, the resurfacing of neglected risk causes intermediaries to value safe debt more than investors do. Formally (3.9) is higher than (3.8). Patient investors value saving vehicles, but are very unwilling to bear the previously neglected risk.

The misallocation of risk is now evident and triggers a market response. To get rid of previously neglected risks, investors dump debt claims on the market, putting a strong downward pressure on prices. Intermediaries are the liquidity providers, willing to buy the safe debt shed by investors.

How much trading occurs and how much do debt prices drop? The answer depends on the liquid wealth of the intermediaries, which summarizes their ability to buy back the originally issued AAA-rated debt. At the time of debt issuance, the liquid wealth of intermediaries is equal to the issuance revenues $N^\theta p(N^\theta)$ raised from investors.[5] Suppose that

---

5. With abuse of notation, $p(N^\theta)$ denotes the equilibrium price computed in equation (3.3) using distorted beliefs:

$$p(N^\theta) = \beta_h \left[1 - \int_0^{N^\theta} \left(1 - \frac{\tilde{X}}{N^\theta} \right) f^\theta(\tilde{X}) d\tilde{X} \right].$$

intermediaries distribute a fraction $1 - \sigma > 0$ of these resources while retaining a fraction $\sigma < 1$. For now, we take the savings rate σ as exogenous, but later endogenize it. When neglected risks resurface, the liquid wealth of intermediaries is then given by $\sigma N^{\theta} p(N^{\theta})$.

Using expressions (3.8) and (3.9), we can establish:

Proposition 3.2. *When neglected risk resurfaces, the secondary market outcomes are as follows:*

a) *If* $\sigma \geq p_{inv}^{crisis} / p(N^{\theta})$, *all debt is bought back by intermediaries and the market price of debt is given by* $\min(\sigma p(N^{\theta}), p_{int}^{crisis})$.

b) *If* $\sigma < p_{inv}^{crisis} / p(N^{\theta})$, *intermediaries can buy only some debt* $(\sigma N^{\theta} p(N^{\theta}) / p_{inv}^{crisis})$, *investors retain the rest of it, and the secondary market price of debt is given by* p_{inv}^{crisis}.

When intermediaries hold enough liquid wealth, in case (a), they are able to buy back from investors all debt issued at $t = 0$. The market price of debt is below the issuance price, so investors lose money and intermediaries profit. But there are two upsides. First, risks are reallocated efficiently: Risk-averse investors no longer need to bear excessive default risk. Second, debt prices are high and might even be equal to intermediaries' reservation price for debt (equation (3.9)). As a consequence, despite neglected risks, investor losses are limited.[6] When intermediaries hold enough liquid wealth, they provide backstop insurance to investors. Neglected risk creates some volatility in asset prices, but no major risk misallocations.[7]

---

6. Once again, intermediaries' reservation price in equation (3.9) may be quite close to the issuance price, provided intermediaries are patient enough, i.e., $\beta_l \approx \beta_h$, and neglected risks are not too high, i.e., $N^{\theta} \approx N^*$.

7. One may argue that even in this case neglected risk may be socially costly, for it destroys the supply of safe assets. This reasoning abstracts from the possibility

When in contrast the liquid wealth of intermediaries is low, as in case (*b*) above, their ability to buy back debt from investors is limited. In this case, the resurfacing of neglected risks triggers a financial crisis with two features. First, prices are well below their "fundamental value" given by intermediaries' willingness to pay, as in a classic fire sale. Second, investors are stuck with excess default risk, so that risk is misallocated, which is socially costly.

This crisis captures the key features of our narrative in chapter 1. First, starting with the summer of 2007 and accelerating after the Lehman bankruptcy, many investors interested in safety dumped AAA-rated MBS on the market. The supply of assets was enormous, given the initial neglect of risk. Second, commercial and investment banks, which held the risky tranches from securitization, either through direct holdings of risky loans or through liquidity guarantees to SIVs, also ended up bearing losses. These losses, along with high leverage and illiquidity, reduced intermediaries' ability to support the price of MBS in secondary markets. The end outcome was a fire sale in which the prices of MBS fell dramatically and investors remained burdened with assets they perceived to be too risky. In 2007, liquidity provision by the Fed sufficed to generate enough demand to prevent a meltdown. After Lehman's collapse in 2008, liquidity concerns were dwarfed by solvency concerns that required capital to restore confidence.

The chain of causality described in figure 3.1 relies on two assumptions. The first is the kink in investors' preferences around their limit of

---

that when intermediaries buy back all debt they can transform the $N^\theta - N^*$ excess units into junior (equity) claims. This would restore the preferred habitat default risk δ^* for the remaining debt, allowing intermediaries to sell it back to investors. Allowing for this possibility changes intermediaries' willingness to pay, increasing the equilibrium price in case (*a*) of proposition 3.2.

FIGURE 3.1. Transmission from Neglected Risk to Financial Crisis.

risk tolerance. This feature makes the economy vulnerable to crises even in the presence of small neglected risk, because investor valuation is extremely sensitive to minor changes in perceived risk. Such kinky preferences are not necessary for our analysis; they just micro-found an amplification mechanism. The second ingredient is limited liquid wealth of intermediaries. This is a key factor necessary for the occurrence of fire sales and crises. With substantial liquid wealth (or borrowing capacity), the consequences of neglected risk are minor, as in case (*a*) of proposition 3.2.

Although we have so far taken limited liquid wealth as given, this is an important choice variable for intermediaries. We next endogenize this choice and show that doing so amplifies financial fragility. This exercise also allows us to account for another key feature of the pre-crisis period described in chapter 1: the expansion of the supply of loans such as mortgages.

Neglected Risk, the Supply of Loans, and Market Illiquidity

We endogenize the liquid wealth of intermediaries (i.e., the retention rate σ of the previous section) by introducing bank lending. Suppose that intermediaries have access to a technology transforming I dollars lent at $t = 0$ into a repayment $\tilde{A}q(I)$ at $t = 1$. Repayment is stochastic due to the uncertain state of the economy $\tilde{A}$, which is distributed according to density function $h(\tilde{A})$. The state $\tilde{A}$ could be shaped by home prices or macroeconomic conditions. Neglected risk is, once again, captured by a believed density $h^\theta(\tilde{A})$ that satisfies definition 3.1. Using the previous notation, we can define the total cash flow available to outside investors as $\tilde{X} = \tilde{A}q(I)$. The cash flow distribution $f(\tilde{X})$ from the last section is thus induced by the productivity distribution $h(\tilde{A})$ and depends on the level of lending I.

The lending technology $q(I)$ is increasing and concave, due to diminishing borrower credit quality, with $q(0)=0$. This of course was another central feature of the mid-2000s, the expansion of subprime lending. Resources that the bank chooses not to lend are kept as liquid capital and are eventually distributed at the end of $t=0$, after secondary markets clear.

The intermediary chooses how much safe debt N to issue and how many loans I to make so as to maximize its profits. Safe debt continues to have a unit face value so that N units of debt default when $N > \tilde{A}q(I)$. This condition pins down a threshold $\tilde{A} = N/q(I)$ above which full repayment takes place. The objective function of the intermediary is the same as equation (3.4), except that now it exploits the connection between loans made and available cash flows:

$$max_{N,I}(\beta_h - \beta_l)\left[N - \int_0^{\frac{N}{q(I)}}(N - \tilde{A}q(I))h^\theta(\tilde{A})d\tilde{A}\right]$$
$$+ \beta_l q(I)\int_0^{+\infty}\tilde{A}h^\theta(\tilde{A})d\tilde{A} - I. \qquad (3.10)$$

The profit in equation (3.10) consists of three terms. The first term is the rents extracted from investors buying debt. These rents depend on the amount N of debt issued, which in turn depends on lending I through the available cash flow. They are evaluated at a price of debt equal to investors' reservation value when the AAA constraint is binding. The second term is the perceived cash flow from loans. And the last one is the amount lent, I. The liquid wealth of the intermediary is implicitly determined by the difference between debt issuance revenues and lending $pN - I$. This liquid wealth cannot be negative, and it depends on the investors' reservation price $p(N)$ evaluated at the equilibrium issuance N.

Once again, the intermediary must satisfy the AAA constraint:

$$\int_0^{\frac{N}{q(I)}} h^\theta(\tilde{A})d\tilde{A} \leq \delta^*. \tag{3.11}$$

By making more loans I, the intermediary increases its cash flow and can issue more debt N.

At the optimum, the intermediary issues debt until the AAA constraint becomes binding. This identifies a threshold level A^θ of economic conditions satisfying

$$\int_0^{A^\theta} h^\theta(\tilde{A})d\tilde{A} = \delta^*.$$

Neglect of risk raises the threshold economic conditions A^θ. When market participants are more optimistic, more debt is issued, which repays fully only under better conditions. With lending I, safe debt issuance is given by $N^\theta(I) = A^\theta q(I)$, which increases in lending I and is above its counterpart under rational expectations.

Proposition 3.3. *With neglected risk:*

i) *The level of lending is higher than under rationality: $I^\theta > I^*$.*

ii) *If the perception of average economic conditions $\int_0^\infty \tilde{A}h^\theta(\tilde{A})d\tilde{A}$ is sufficiently above the truth $\int_0^\infty \tilde{A}h(\tilde{A})d\tilde{A}$, the intermediary does not carry any liquid wealth:*

$$I^\theta = p(N^\theta(I^\theta))\, N^\theta(I^\theta).$$

When market participants neglect downside risk and inflate average expected outcomes, our model yields overinvestment in mortgages, as in (*i*), but also low liquidity of intermediaries, as in (*ii*). To gain intuition for these results, note that at the optimum the marginal benefit of lending is given by:

$$q'(I^\theta)\left[(\beta_h - \beta_l)\left(\int_0^{A^\theta} \tilde{A}h^\theta(\tilde{A})d\tilde{A} + A^\theta(1-\delta^*)\right) + \beta_l\int_0^{+\infty} \tilde{A}h^\theta(\tilde{A})d\tilde{A}\right].$$

The first term in square brackets captures the intermediary's profit from debt issuance. By lending more, the intermediary obtains more collateral, relaxes the AAA constraint, and expands the supply of safe debt, which is profitable. In the presence of neglected risk this mechanism is more powerful and strengthens the intermediary's incentive to lend.

The second term in brackets captures the intermediary's profits from holding the risky tranche of mortgages. When intermediaries are optimistic about the average expected state of the economy, i.e., $\int_0^{+\infty} \tilde{A}h^\theta(\tilde{A})d\tilde{A}$ is large, an additional loan looks very profitable. This effect also enhances the incentive to lend.

Proposition 3.2 says that when the second effect is strong enough, the intermediary's incentive to make loans is much stronger than the debt issuance revenues these loans generate. As a result, an intermediary optimistic about the payoff from the risky tranche that it retains has an incentive to max out its lending, potentially beyond the issuance revenues received. Such an intermediary puts all its resources into loans and leaves no spare liquid wealth, $I^\theta = p\,(N^\theta\,(I^\theta))\,N^\theta\,(I^\theta).$[8]

Crucially, neglected risk itself causes illiquidity and fire sales. The updated chain of events leading to financial crises is described in figure 3.2.

---

8. Because the return on the marginal loan is diminishing, each additional loan sustains a progressively smaller expansion of safe debt. If the intermediary is optimistic about the loan's average return, however, it still finds it optimal to finance it. By doing so, the intermediary expects to earn more profits from the risky tranche.

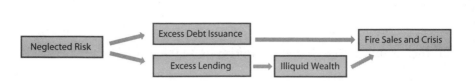

FIGURE 3.2. Neglected Risk, Excess Lending, and Illiquidity.

The key mechanism connecting neglected risk to financial crises is the overexpansion of the financial sector. With neglected risk, intermediaries expand lending to marginal borrowers and create debt from securitizing these loans at the same time. It is not just that debt creation expands to enable more lending. Lending itself expands to provide fodder for debt creation, which boosts issuance revenues. The large pool of wealth available to investors induces intermediaries to expand their collateralizable cash flow from increasingly marginal mortgages in order to boost debt supply. In addition, intermediaries' optimism about average future conditions raises the expected return from retaining the risky tranche of cash flows, further boosting the incentive to lend. This combination of excess lending and debt issuance creates illiquidity in intermediaries' balance sheets and fragility in the system.

This analysis offers an even closer parallel to the narrative in chapter 1, where we discussed evidence that the demand for securitization actually influenced subprime mortgage lending because these mortgages were needed as fodder for the creation of AAA-rated MBS. The model delivers this mechanism: The demand for AAA-rated debt encourages intermediaries to expand their supply of loans. With neglected risk, such expansion poses systemic threats. In this model, not only the risk allocation but also production is inefficient: There is overlending and thus overinvestment. This mechanism can therefore also account for the evidence on the huge expansion of home construction and mortgage finance described in chapter 1.

Finally, this model naturally yields fire sales of MBS as a by-product of the illiquidity that intermediaries choose to have. During periods of optimism, intermediaries issue mortgages to support the securitization and sale of AAA-rated debt and additional profits. When neglected risks resurface, disgruntled investors start to sell, but now the supply of AAA-rated debt is too high and the demand for it is too low.

Illiquidity here relies not only on neglected downside risk but also on the intermediaries' optimism about future average conditions in the housing market, which raises their risk appetite.[9] This reminds us of the importance of understanding the full belief distribution, rather than just the left tail. Once again, the model in chapter 5 will allow us to address this issue.

Shadow Banking: Pooling and Tranching

So far we have shown that neglected risk can account for three central features of the crisis: overexpansion of intermediaries' assets, overexpansion of securitization in the form of AAA-rated debt issuance, and market illiquidity and fire sales during the crisis. In modeling securitization, we have not yet considered one essential feature discussed in chapter 1—the pooling of idiosyncratic risks to create collateral for safe debt. Here we show that this feature is important. While under rational expectations pooling reduces the risk of individual intermediaries, under neglected risk it creates an additional source of fragility by encouraging the overexpansion of the supply of AAA-rated debt.

To allow for pooling in our basic setup, we relax the assumption that all intermediaries receive the same cash flow $\tilde{X}$. We thus depart from a

---

9. This follows, for instance, when $h^\theta(\tilde{A})$ first order stochastically dominates $h(\tilde{A})$.

representative agent setting and denote by $\tilde{X}_i$ the cash flow of intermediary i. This cash flow is exposed to idiosyncratic risk, which creates a potential benefit from pooling risk among intermediaries. By reducing the riskiness of cash flows, pooling can expand the supply of AAA-rated debt. For simplicity, our formal analysis abstracts from endogenous lending, but the model with endogenous lending would be nearly identical to the analysis in the previous section.

To formalize idiosyncratic risk, assume that the cash flow from mortgages or loans of each intermediary i is given by

$$\tilde{X}\epsilon_i, \tag{3.12}$$

where ϵ_i is an i.i.d. shock distributed in $[\underline{\epsilon}, \overline{\epsilon}]$ with density $g(\epsilon)$ with unit mean $\int \epsilon g(\epsilon)\,d\epsilon = 1$. The cash flow factor $\tilde{X}$ is common across intermediaries and continues to be distributed according to the true density $f(\tilde{X})$. The shock ϵ_i creates an intermediary-specific risk, due for instance to intermediary-specific geographic specialization.

Denote by $f_i(\tilde{X})$ the cash flow distribution of intermediary i. Idiosyncratic risk as described in equation (3.12) fattens the left tail in the following sense.

Lemma 3.1. *If the density $f(\tilde{X})$ of the common cash flow factor $\tilde{X}$ is convex in $[0, \hat{X}]$, then the induced density $f_i(\tilde{X})$ of the intermediary-specific cash flow has a fatter left tail than $f(\tilde{X})$ in the sense that $\int_0^Z f_i(\tilde{X})\,d\tilde{X}_i > \int_0^Z f(\tilde{X})\,d\tilde{X}$ for all $Z \in [0, \hat{X}\underline{\epsilon}]$.*

Adding some idiosyncratic risk to a cash flow raises the probability that this cash flow falls in the unlikely left tail (i.e., in the leftmost interval where the original cash flow density is increasing). This is true under any cash flow distribution, be it the true one $f(\tilde{X})$ as explicitly considered in lemma 3.1 or the distorted one $f^\theta(\tilde{X})$, provided it is convex in $[0, \hat{X}]$.

The effect of idiosyncratic risk on the right tail does not matter for our purposes.

Equipped with this result, we can solve the model with neglected risk. In this case, market participants perceive the common factor $\tilde{X}$ to be distributed with a density function $f^\theta(\tilde{X})$ that satisfies definition 3.1 (idiosyncratic risk is however perceived correctly according to $g(\epsilon)$). We next compare the neglected risk case to rational expectations.

Idiosyncratic risk tightens the AAA constraint, reducing the supply of debt. Denote by $f_i^\theta(\tilde{X})$ the distorted distribution contaminated by idiosyncratic risk. The supply of AAA debt is then determined by the condition:

$$\int_0^{N_i^\theta} f_i^\theta(\tilde{X})d\tilde{X} = \delta^*. \tag{3.13}$$

Because $f_i^\theta(\tilde{X})$ has a fatter left tail than $f^\theta(\tilde{X})$, the probability of low cash flows is higher, which reduces the supply of AAA-rated debt. Formally, with equation (3.13) debt issuance is lower than the non-idiosyncratic risk benchmark of equation (3.6), $N_i^\theta < N^\theta$.

Pooling and Tranching with Neglected Risk

To avoid this cost of idiosyncratic risk, intermediaries can trade cash flows among themselves. Suppose that intermediary i sells a fraction α_i of its own cash flow $\tilde{X}_i$ and buys the same amount α_i of a pool of the other intermediaries' cash flows. Because the idiosyncratic shock ϵ has unit mean, the cash flow of the pool, which averages equation (3.12) across all intermediaries, is equal to $\tilde{X}$. As a consequence, the intermediary's overall cash flow becomes:

$$\tilde{X}_i = (1-\alpha_i)\tilde{X}\epsilon_i + \alpha_i\tilde{X}. \tag{3.14}$$

The intermediary's exposure to its idiosyncratic shock ϵ_i decreases with the extent of pooling α_i. When pooling is complete, $\alpha_i = 1$, the cash flow of the intermediary is given by the common cash flow actor $\tilde{X}$, just as in previous sections of this chapter.

We allow each intermediary to swap a share α_i of its idiosyncratic cash flow for an equivalent quantity of a pool of all other intermediaries' cash flows. One can think of loan pools as being assembled and sold by a firm, such as a mortgage originator, that faces competitive conditions, entailing zero profits. Because all cash flows are ex ante identical, they must fetch the same price, which is also—by the zero-profit condition—the price of the loan pool. For this reason, trading does not affect the average profit of the intermediary, but it changes its collateral: The intermediary can now pledge to outside investors its total $t = 1$ cash flow, which combines the repayment of its own retained loans and that of the pool acquired on the market.

Since intermediaries are identical, they all sell the same share of their own cash flows and purchase an identical share of the pool. The market equilibrium works as follows:

Proposition 3.4. *If $f^{\theta}(X)$ satisfies the conditions of lemma 3.1, then in the neglected risk equilibrium intermediaries fully diversify ($\alpha_i = 1$ for all i) and debt issuance is given by N^{θ}, as in the model where idiosyncratic risk is absent.*

In equilibrium, pooling is fully exploited. By swapping their own cash flows with a diversified pool, intermediaries make their cash flows safer. This, in turn, allows them to issue more AAA-rated debt using these cash flows as collateral and to raise issuance profits. The outcome with pooling is the same as that in the "Neglected Risk, Leverage, and the Crisis" section of this chapter.

The introduction of idiosyncratic risk in the background enables the model to explain some additional features of the precrisis period.

First, intermediaries originated and sold their loans, or perhaps simply bought mortgages from different originators. Idiosyncratic cash flows were not retained but rather sold in the market to the builders of loan pools. This is the growth in "originate and distribute" banking before the crisis.

Second, intermediaries purchased mortgage pools and then tranched a senior portion out of them to create AAA-rated debt for investors. While intermediaries shed idiosyncratic risk, the securities they sold were still exposed to systematic risk of the common cash flow $\tilde{X}$. Diversification and pooling reduce idiosyncratic, but not systematic, risk. To the extent that the latter was underestimated or incorrectly calculated, as Coval, Jurek, and Stafford (2009a, 2009b) show, extreme vulnerability remained, but was hidden by diversification.

Third, our model explains in a very standard way how pooling enables the joint growth of insurance and debt creation. Insurance takes the form of intermediaries trading their loans. The growth of debt creation occurs because the lower riskiness of loan pools allows intermediaries to manufacture a larger quantity of AAA-rated debt out of them. Adding mortgage lending to this model along the lines of the preceding section would also yield contemporaneous expansion of insurance, debt, and intermediary assets in the form of greater lending to marginal borrowers.

A key question is whether the effect of neglected risk is larger in an economy with pooling or without it. Under some conditions, pooling may actually exacerbate the consequences of neglected risk, and hence welfare losses relative to rationality. To see this, we compare the economy with neglected risk to the economy under rational expectations. Denote by $N^{\theta}(\alpha)$ and $N^{*}(\alpha)$ debt issuance under neglected risk and rationality when intermediaries pool cash flow share α. Recall that $f_i(\tilde{X})$ and $f_i^{\theta}(\tilde{X})$ denote the true and distorted cash flow distributions contaminated by idiosyncratic risk, when pooling is absent. We then establish:

Proposition 3.5. *Suppose that* $f(X) \geq f^\theta(X)$ *for* $X \leq N^\theta(1)/\underline{\epsilon}$ *and*

$f_i^\theta(N^*(0)) > f^\theta(N^\theta(1))$. *Then, if* $\left[f\left(\dfrac{X}{\epsilon}\right) - f^\theta\left(\dfrac{X}{\epsilon}\right) \right]\dfrac{1}{\epsilon}$ *is concave in* ϵ

for $X \leq N^\theta(1)/\underline{\epsilon}$, *cash flow pooling exacerbates overissuance due to neglected risk. Formally:*

$$N^\theta(1) - N^*(1) > N^\theta(0) - N^*(0).$$

The overissuance of AAA debt caused by neglected risk under full pooling, $N^\theta(1) - N^*(1)$, may be larger than the overissuance under no pooling, $N^\theta(0) - N^*(0)$. Pooling of mortgages boosts overissuance, exacerbating the consequences of neglected risk. Intuitively, even if investors neglect left-tail risk in the common cash flow component $\tilde{X}$, idiosyncratic risk limits debt issuance by enhancing tail risk and investor awareness of it. Pooling removes this effect, boosting debt creation. An excessively optimistic view about the aggregate economy encourages greater debt issuance when idiosyncratic risk is diversified away.[10]

There is a complementarity between risk pooling and debt expansion as a source of financial fragility: When investors neglect downside risk, insurance allows for an overexpansion of intermediary liabilities and risk-taking, rendering the financial sector more vulnerable to crises.

---

10. As proposition 3.5 shows, the result obtains when the difference between the truth and beliefs $(f - f^\theta)$ is concave enough in ϵ. Intuitively, in this case the random shock on average reduces the difference between the truth and beliefs, because by concavity the average value of $(f - f^\theta)$ across different idiosyncratic shocks ϵ is lower than the value obtained when the idiosyncratic shock is absent, thereby reducing overissuance of debt under neglected risk.

Securitization, Market Illiquidity, and Crises

By facilitating overissuance of safe debt, securitization renders the economy more vulnerable to crises. When neglected risks resurface, the quantity of AAA-rated debt in the system is so large, and this debt has become so much riskier than investors' risk tolerance δ^*, that downward price pressure in the secondary market is extremely strong.

We saw in "Neglected Risk, Leverage, and the Crisis" that the fall in market prices depends on the liquid wealth held by intermediaries. "Neglected Risk, the Supply of Loans, and Market Illiquidity" showed that neglected risk can itself generate illiquidity among intermediaries by encouraging overexpansion of lending. The pooling of mortgages considered here can reduce liquidity even further. We formally prove this result in the appendix, but the logic works as follows. When intermediaries do not pool their cash flows, some of them receive good idiosyncratic draws even as neglected risks about the aggregate cash flow $\tilde{X}$ resurface. These lucky intermediaries then have some liquidity to buy AAA debt in secondary markets, supporting its price. But when intermediaries pool their cash flows, they are all fully exposed to risk of the systematic cash flow $\tilde{X}$. As neglected risk resurfaces, all intermediaries bear losses and are illiquid at the same time, exacerbating fire sales. As in our account of fire sales in 2008, diversification causes intermediaries to be exposed to the same risks, creating massive illiquidity and fire sales when neglected risks resurface. In this sense, limits to pooling can be beneficial: They create ex post diversity among intermediaries, which enables the lucky ones to support demand for distressed assets and reduce fire sales. Neglected risk turns the role of diversification on its head.

We summarize the analysis of this chapter in figure 3.3.

The key source of fragility in the neglected risk model is financial sector overexpansion. Overexpansion of debt creation and lending causes

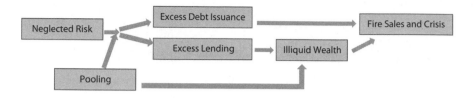

FIGURE 3.3. Pooling, Overexpansion, and Illiquidity.

illiquidity and severe fire sales in secondary markets when neglected risks resurface. This creates two inefficiencies that materialize during crises. First, the allocation of risk in the economy is inefficient. Second, the allocation of capital is also inefficient with too much investment in unprofitable projects.

Financial innovation, such as the pooling and tranching of mortgages to expand the supply of debt perceived to be safe, amplifies this mechanism. Ex ante, insurance improves the scope for intermediaries' assets and debt supply to overexpand. Ex post, insurance creates pervasive liquidity shortages because all intermediaries become illiquid at the same time.

The model we presented in this chapter accounts for several features of the 2008 financial crisis, including the expansion of mortgages to risky borrowers, the growth of securitization, the dramatic expansion of AAA-rated debt, the exposure of intermediaries to risky mortgages, and finally the extreme sensitivity of the financial system to bad news. Intermediaries end up taking too much risk not only in funding projects but also in holding mortgage pools, directly or indirectly. This renders the AAA-rated debt vulnerable: When neglected risks resurface, massive fire sales follow. Neglect of risk, such as that documented in chapter 2, yields these results under very standard mechanisms of risk-sharing.

As stressed from the outset, we do not rely on short-term funding mechanisms or bank runs to model financial fragility. Of course, we would expect to see such runs as a consequence of tremendous losses in MBS values if MBS was put into SIVs and funded with ABCP. These mechanisms exacerbated the financial crisis, but we abstract from them because we think they were its consequence, not its cause.

But the most important omission from the analysis in this chapter is the foundations of beliefs. Motivated by the evidence, we simply assumed that market participants neglect downside risk and examined the consequences of this assumption. This is insufficient for at least two reasons. First, the approach we pursued here cannot identify the conditions shaping the formation and evolution of incorrect beliefs. In the context of the 2008 crisis, this means that the current model explains neither how neglected risk depended on the pre-2007 economic trends, nor why it took so long for the crisis to climax after the initial bad news of 2007. A micro-founded model of beliefs can help shed light on these issues.

Second, the neglect of risk is one of the possible belief distortions that market participants may exhibit. As we saw in this chapter, understanding the link between neglect of risk and optimism about average conditions is key to establishing whether risk-taking was limited to the AAA segment of the market. A psychologically founded account of the full shape of beliefs can help identify conditions under which different biases go in the same or in opposite directions.

In the rest of the book we try to address these challenges. To begin, in chapter 4 we consider more broadly expectations of investors, managers, and professional forecasters in multiple contexts and try to assemble the facts that a more general model of expectations—not just tied to 2008 events—should seek to explain. In chapter 5, we present a general micro-foundation of beliefs based on Kahneman and Tversky's (1974, 1983) psychological principle of representativeness. This micro-foundation delivers what we call diagnostic expectations, a model that under some conditions can jointly predict overestimation of average returns after good news and underestimation of downside risks. We then use this model to shed light on the evidence in chapter 2. In chapter 6, we pull everything together and present a formal model of credit cycles that builds on our formulation of diagnostic expectations and several other empirical findings. This exercise shows that the diagnostic expectations model applies to a much broader set of phenomena related to financial volatility and instability than the 2008 crisis.

CHAPTER 4

Extrapolation in Financial Markets

I n previous chapters, we argued that errors in beliefs are central to
understanding the 2008 financial crisis. These errors are fundamental to understanding the housing bubble, the pricing of mortgage-
backed securities (MBS), and the choices made by policymakers in
2007–2008. But was this crisis an isolated episode, in which unusual growth
in home prices and financial innovation financing this growth disoriented
investors and policymakers? Alternatively, are errors in beliefs and expectations systematic, occurring in a broad range of circumstances? And
if so, are these errors responsible for financial fragility and economic
volatility more generally? Was the 2008 crisis one of a kind or similar to
others? Beginning with this chapter, we develop some evidence, as well as
a theoretical approach, to address these questions. Our basic theme is that
errors in expectations are systematic and that the credit cycle that ended
in the 2008 crisis shares essential features with other cycles and crises.

Our approach to answering these questions is to take survey data on
expectations reported by investors, corporate managers, analysts, and
professional forecasters, and integrate them into economic analysis. In
chapter 2, we used several examples of survey data, such as home price
expectations during the bubble and Fed macroeconomic forecasts prior

to the crisis, to document the errors in beliefs that we see as central to the origins of the crisis. Here we show how the evidence of similar errors in expectations shows up consistently across a range of financial markets.

The reliance on surveys of expectations to understand what people believe is a major departure from traditional economic analysis, which since the 1970s has been dominated by the Rational Expectations Hypothesis, originally proposed by Muth (1961). Under rational expectations, economic agents forecast the future by optimally using the true structure of the economy they operate in. This means that the structure of the economy itself dictates what beliefs they should hold. From the viewpoint of economic research, this implies that expectations data are redundant as long as the econometrician knows the model that economic agents rely on and can compute their statistically optimal expectations of future variables from that model. Economists also became skeptical about the quality of survey expectations data, especially when households are surveyed, because of doubts that respondents understand the questions or have the incentive to answer them accurately. According to Prescott (1977, 30), "Like utility, expectations are not observed, and surveys cannot be used to test the rational expectations hypothesis."

Survey expectations have not been used much in financial economics either, for reasons similar to those in macroeconomics.[1] The Efficient Markets Hypothesis—the proposition that market prices accurately reflect fundamental values of securities—implies that rational expectations

---

1. Some notable exceptions include Dominguez (1986); Frankel and Froot (1987); La Porta (1996); Vissing-Jorgensen (2004); Fuster, Laibson, and Mendel (2010); Bacchetta, Mertens, and van Wincoop (2009); Hirshleifer, Li, and Yu (2015); Malmendier and Nagel (2011); Ben-David, Graham, and Harvey (2013); Barberis et al. (2015); and Amromin and Sharpe (2014).

of asset returns directly follow from required rates of return implied by the economic model. In standard models such as Campbell and Cochrane (1999) or Lettau and Ludvigson (2001), the principal determinants of required returns are variations in wealth and consumption of investors. If wealth or consumption today is high, investors would like to save more in order to smooth consumption, which makes them willing to accept low returns on the stock market going forward. In a rational expectations equilibrium, expectations of returns should then be low and can be computed from the data on wealth and consumption. The stock market fluctuates as expected returns change because of this desire to consume now versus later. Because investor expectations are by assumption determined by the model, survey expectations data are not needed to test it.

The Rational Expectations Hypothesis (REH) and the closely related Efficient Markets Hypothesis (EMH) in finance are among the most important advances of twentieth-century economics. They brought elegance, order, discipline, and powerful empirical content to models on business cycles and financial markets. Perhaps as important, the REH unified microeconomic theory with macroeconomic models, since a researcher could start with assumptions on individual optimizing behavior, compute optimal choices for households and firms, and then aggregate them into macroeconomic models, which could be either tested or calibrated. The assumption that the economic model and expectations are consistent with each other delivered a lot of structure and predictive power, without measuring expectations directly.

Despite these benefits, the rejection of survey expectations data seems extreme. To begin, nearly all economic data come from surveys, and it is not obvious why surveys of expectations are any more problematic than those of, say, production. Nor is Prescott's analogy to utility valid. Preferences are not directly observed by economists, and even for consumers themselves it is hard to come up with a quantitative measure of their tastes. As a consequence, utility is difficult to elicit from surveys; inferring it from choices is easier. This is not a problem for expectations. These are already in the decision maker's mind. The number the surveyor asks for and probably gets back, such as the expectation of the return on the stock market, is exactly what one wants to measure. On this ground, it seems unjustified to discard the use of expectations data. In line with this view, Manski (2004) argues forcefully and convincingly that expectations data are necessary to distinguish alternative models in economics.

Whether survey expectations capture true beliefs that drive economic behavior or only reflect measurement error is an empirical question. In this chapter, we present evidence that provides some answers. This evidence shows that, far from being random noise, measured expectations are highly consistent across surveys that are conducted with different methodologies and using somewhat different questions. Furthermore, there is growing evidence that actual behavior of survey respondents is predicted more successfully by their responses than by some model-based predictors from a rational expectations model. People literally put their money where their mouth is.

Once it is shown that expectations data must be taken seriously as valid measures of beliefs, they can be used to evaluate belief rationality. The Rational Expectations Hypothesis holds that economic agents use all the information they have to make statistically optimal forecasts. As a consequence, forecast errors cannot be predicted from the information that the decision maker has at the time of making the forecast. Indeed, if some information could help predict forecast errors, rational decision makers would use the same information to improve their forecast, so as to avoid any predictable error. This observation suggests a test—in fact, a whole testing strategy—of the REH. A researcher can collect a time series of forecast errors and then ask whether these errors could have been anticipated, and therefore corrected, using information available at the time the forecasts were made. One can also examine the relationship between forecasts of asset returns and actual returns and check the accuracy of the forecasts.

In this chapter, we present some of this evidence. Generally speaking, the evidence rejects the Rational Expectations Hypothesis quite decisively: Forecast errors are systematically predictable. In the data, the reason for such predictable forecast errors appears to be extrapolation. Analysts, investors, and professional managers all ground their forecasts about the future in recent history. They are excessively optimistic about the future in good times and excessively pessimistic in bad times. Of course, the idea of investor extrapolation leading to the failure of the Efficient Markets Hypothesis is not new. Since Robert Shiller (1981) discovered excess volatility in the aggregate U.S. stock market, economists have produced a substantial amount of evidence documenting similar patterns of volatility and return predictability in many markets. In essence, the evidence shows that high asset valuations relative to estimated fundamental values are associated with low returns going forward, and conversely for low valuations. These patterns in the data look very much like a by-product of extrapolative beliefs, where good performance is projected too far into the future, leading to overvaluation and subsequent correction. In nearly all of this research, however, beliefs are inferred indirectly, from valuations, returns, and estimates of fundamentals. The measures of overvaluation that predict a correction going forward are either high past returns or high ratios of market value to estimated fundamental value (e.g., see De Bondt and Thaler 1985; Campbell and Shiller 1988; Cutler, Poterba, and Summers 1990; Lakonishok, Shleifer, and Vishny 1994). Our contribution to this evidence is to look at survey expectations directly.

We present the empirical evidence on expectations in four steps. We begin by summarizing the results of Greenwood and Shleifer (2014) on investor expectations about aggregate stock returns in the United States. These data are plentiful but not of the highest quality, yet they still allow us to address directly the question of whether survey expectations are noise or alternatively meaningful measures of beliefs that drive behavior. Even with all the concerns about the ability of individual investors to understand what they are being asked, these data show that expectations of aggregate market returns are highly consistent across surveys. The beliefs of individual investors are in fact highly correlated with those of professionals. Moreover, these beliefs predict actual investor behavior, such as flows of funds into equity mutual funds. Expectations data are definitely not noise.

Indeed, there is a lot of structure in these data. Across all the different surveys, expectations of stock returns are predominantly extrapolative: Expectations of future returns are strongly positively correlated with past returns. This is far from rational. In reality, when expectations of returns are high, realized future returns tend to be low. Nevertheless, high past returns encourage investors to be excessively optimistic about future returns. This is precisely the type of evidence of predictable forecast errors inconsistent with rationality.

We then turn to the evidence on the cross-section of stock returns in the United States, presenting results from Bordalo, Gennaioli, La Porta, and Shleifer (BGLS) (2017) on companies with extreme earnings growth expectations. Since the expectations data come from professional analysts, they are arguably of higher quality than individual investor surveys. Analysts surely know the meaning of expected growth in earnings, especially since the measure is defined in the survey instrument. Still, the data reject the Rational Expectations Hypothesis and show clear patterns of extrapolation and subsequent predictable disappointment. In addition, we present some evidence that extrapolation is not mechanical but rather takes the form of overreaction to news: Forecast revisions respond to news but excessively. This evidence gives us much more granular information about belief formation and revision and paves the way for the theoretical proposal in chapter 5 for how beliefs are formed.

Third, we summarize the results of Gennaioli, Ma, and Shleifer (2015) on the relationship between expectations of corporate chief financial officers (CFOs) about their firms' earning growth and the firms' investment plans and actual investment. We show again that expectations deviate from rationality. In addition, we find a strong relationship between expectations of earnings growth and actual investment. In fact, expectations predict investment much better than does the model-based measure of investment opportunities, Tobin's Q. As with the evidence on fund flows, behavior is driven by what expectations are, not what they ought to be in a rational expectations model.

Finally, we turn to credit markets, which after all are the principal subject of this book, and summarize the available evidence on credit cycles. In this part of the chapter, we consider broader evidence on systematic credit expansions, crises, and economic activity. Over the decade following the 2008 crisis, there has been tremendous progress in documenting these credit cycle facts. Various indicators of credit market frothiness, such as expansion of credit in general and household credit in particular, but also low credit spreads and a high share of risky debt in total issuance, predict financial trouble and economic slowdowns in the future. We bring in data on expectations to supplement these findings and show that credit markets as well witness systematic errors in expectations that look like extrapolation and in particular overreaction to news. Our broader goal is to show that, in a variety of ways, some of the main qualitative features of the 2008 episode find close parallels in historical data.

Expectations of Aggregate Stock Returns

Perhaps because the movements of the stock market engage so many people, from individual investors to managers to professional forecasters, there are multiple sources of data on expectations of aggregate stock market returns. Greenwood and Shleifer (2014) put together data on such expectations, some quantitative and some qualitative, from six different sources, with very diverse surveyed populations and different survey questions.

The first is the Gallup Survey of individual investors, with data from 1996 to 2012. For most of this period, this survey asked respondents where they are, ranging from "very optimistic" to "optimistic" to "neutral" to "pessimistic" to "very pessimistic," in their beliefs about stock market returns over the next year. One can then construct a qualitative indicator of return expected by Gallup respondents as the difference between the percentages of bullish and bearish investors. Between 1998 and 2003, the survey also asked for quantitative estimates of expected stock market return. Because during this overlap period the movements in the qualitative bullishness indicator and the quantitative expectations of returns are highly correlated, the overlap allows us to map the qualitative indicators into quantitative measures of expected return over the entire period from 1996 on.

The second source is the survey of CFOs of large U.S. companies, conducted since 1998 by John Graham and Campbell Harvey at Duke University. Here the respondents are asked for quantitative estimates of the expected stock market return over the next year. This is a more financially sophisticated pool of respondents than those in Gallup.

The third source is a member survey of investor sentiment conducted by the American Association of Individual Investors since 1987, which asks respondents whether they are bullish, neutral, or bearish on the stock market. Like Gallup, this is a qualitative survey, so one has to make do with the qualitative indicator of average bullishness that varies over time. Here the respondents might be more sophisticated than in Gallup, however, since they are involved in an association of investors.

The fourth source is a measure constructed by the editors of *Investor Intelligence* newsletter, going back to 1963, summarizing the investment outlook of more than 120 independent financial market newsletters. Each newsletter at a point in time is classified as bullish, neutral, or bearish, so one can produce an indicator of how many bullish newsletters there are relative to the bearish ones.

The fifth source is Robert Shiller's survey of individual investor confidence in the stock market. The survey is similar to Gallup, although the questions are somewhat different.

The sixth source is the Michigan survey of consumers, which goes back to 1946. During a brief period between 2000 and 2005, the survey asked respondents about their expectations of return on the stock market over the next two to three years.

Greenwood and Shleifer (2014) put these different data sources into comparable units and use average responses in each survey every month. They thus have monthly time series of expectations of returns on the stock market from six sources. Figure 4.1 presents pairwise correlations between these time series. With few exceptions, these correlations are positive, high, and highly statistically significant. At any given point in time, different financial market participants, regardless of their level of sophistication, have highly correlated levels of expectations or sentiment about future returns. In particular, measures of expected returns by individual investors are highly correlated with the quantitative expectation of returns by much more sophisticated CFOs of major companies. In light of the considerable heterogeneity of data collection procedures

	Gallup (N = 135)	Graham-Harvey (N = 42)	American Association (N = 294)	Investor Intelligence (N = 588)	Shiller (N = 132)	Michigan (N = 22)	Expectations Index (N = 294)
Graham-Harvey	0.77 [0.000]						
American Association	0.64 [0.000]	0.56 [0.000]					
Investor Intelligence	0.60 [0.000]	0.64 [0.000]	0.55 [0.000]				
Shiller	0.39 [0.000]	0.66 [0.000]	0.51 [0.000]	0.43 [0.000]			
Michigan	0.61 [0.003]	−0.12 [0.922]	0.60 [0.003]	0.19 [0.395]	−0.55 [0.020]		
Expectations Index	0.87 [0.000]	0.58 [0.000]	0.87 [0.000]	0.81 [0.000]	0.52 [0.000]	0.55 [0.008]	
Fund flow	0.69 [0.000]	0.71 [0.000]	0.42 [0.000]	0.20 [0.002]	0.51 [0.001]	0.40 [0.068]	0.45 [0.000]

FIGURE 4.1. Correlations between Measures of Investor Expectations. Survey expectations are not noise—financial market participants of different degrees of sophistication have highly correlated expectations about future returns. *Source*: Greenwood, Robin, and Andrei Shleifer. 2014. "Expectations of Returns and Expected Returns." *Review of Financial Studies* 27 (3): 714–46. Reprinted by permission of the authors.

across these surveys, this evidence decisively rejects the hypothesis that survey expectations are merely noise.

Figure 4.1 delivers an additional message. The last row shows the correlation of the six measures of expected returns with a measure of investor fund flows into equity mutual funds. The correlations are uniformly positive and statistically significant. When investors are optimistic about expected stock returns, they put money into equity mutual funds. This finding shows two things. First, it is an independent confirmation that expectations variables are not noise, for why would noise correlate with actual behavior? Second, the evidence shows that investors actually act on their beliefs. This is our first piece of evidence that survey expectations data can be used to predict economically relevant choices.

If these expectations are highly correlated across data sources and investor types, then what do they reflect? Figure 4.2 addresses this question

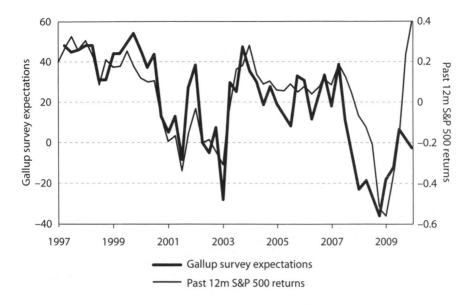

FIGURE 4.2. **Expectations of Future Stock Returns and S&P 500 Past Returns.** Investors expect future stock returns to be high when past stock returns have been high. *Source*: Gennaioli, Nicola, Yueran Ma, and Andrei Shleifer. 2015. "Expectations and Investment." *NBER Macroeconomics Annual* 30 (1): 379–431. Reprinted by permission of the authors.

by plotting, on the same graph, Gallup expectations of the next twelve-month return and the past twelve-month return on the S&P 500. The two series practically lie on top of each other. Gallup investors, as well as participants in other surveys, expect high future returns precisely when the last year's stock market return has been high. They appear to extrapolate past returns into the future.

Is such extrapolation an effective return forecasting strategy? The answer is no. The correlation between the same Gallup expected return we saw in figure 4.2 and the S&P return for the next—as opposed to the past—twelve months is negative though statistically insignificant. This finding is consistent with well-known evidence in finance that high market valuations, which would typically follow high returns, are associated with lower returns going forward (Campbell and Shiller 1987,

1988). In fact, in these data, high past returns predict expectation errors: When past returns are high, expected future returns are on average higher than realizations. Similar patterns obtain for other expectations series and not just Gallup. A quick summary of what the data say is that when stock market returns have been high, investors expect high returns to continue, but in reality the returns are, if anything, on average low.

As a final point, Greenwood and Shleifer (2014) also compare this evidence to several rational expectations models of the expected return on the stock market, such as those of Campbell and Cochrane (1999) and Lettau and Ludvigson (2001) mentioned earlier. They find that expected returns dictated by the rational expectations models are strongly and statistically significantly *negatively* correlated with the actual survey expectations of returns. According to these efficient markets models, stock prices are high when investors are willing to accept low returns going forward because their wealth or consumption is high today. With extrapolation, in contrast, stock prices are high precisely because, by extrapolating past returns, investors incorrectly expect future prices to become even higher, bidding up current prices. This evidence explains, in the clearest way, how the rational expectations models get it wrong: The models need investors to expect low returns in good times, the opposite of what they say they expect.

Expectations in a Cross-Section of Stock Returns

An important advantage of aggregate stock market return forecasts is that they are available from several very different sources, so one can test and reject the hypothesis that these forecasts are noise. But this advantage comes at a cost: The forecasts are collected in different ways, in different units, and typically from very different populations. An alternative is to look at a much more uniform population of forecasters. For individual stocks, the standard population for this purpose is financial analysts whose job is to forecast earnings, earnings growth, and stock prices of companies. Looking at this population in fact may provide a deeper insight into how expectations are formed.

In 1996, Rafael La Porta published an intriguing finding. He compared companies with the most optimistic and most pessimistic long-term earnings growth forecasts made by financial analysts. He found that stocks with most optimistic analysts earn sharply lower returns than those with most pessimistic ones. It is not just that when analysts are extremely optimistic, the true long-term earnings growth is slower than they expect. Their optimism also infects prices, perhaps because they influence investors or perhaps because investors hold similar beliefs, and leads to overvaluation and low subsequent returns on the stocks whose growth prospects they find most favorable.

Together with Pedro Bordalo and Rafael La Porta (BGLS 2017), we revisited La Porta's finding with twenty additional years of data and took a much closer look at how expectations are formed, how they are revised, and how earnings, beliefs, and prices co-evolve. As figure 4.3 shows, the La Porta initial finding still holds: A portfolio of High Long-Term Growth or HLTG stocks (those with the top 10 percent most optimistic earnings growth forecasts) returns 3 percent on average in the year after formation during the 1981–2015 sample period. In contrast, a portfolio of Low Long-Term Growth or LLTG stocks (those with the bottom 10 percent most pessimistic earnings growth forecasts) returns 15 percent on average in the year after formation. The latter stocks are a much better investment, on average.

So, why are HLTG stocks such a bad investment? First, as figure 4.4 shows, analyst expectations of long-term earnings growth are at their peak at the time of portfolio formation for HLTG firms. These expectations have been rising, along with earnings, for several years prior to

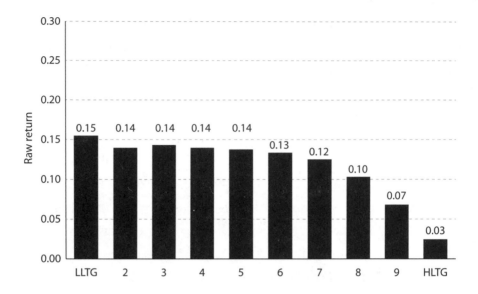

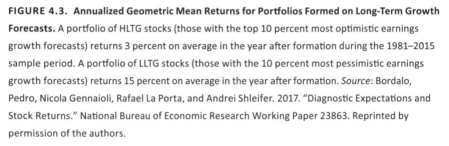

FIGURE 4.3. Annualized Geometric Mean Returns for Portfolios Formed on Long-Term Growth Forecasts. A portfolio of HLTG stocks (those with the top 10 percent most optimistic earnings growth forecasts) returns 3 percent on average in the year after formation during the 1981–2015 sample period. A portfolio of LLTG stocks (those with the 10 percent most pessimistic earnings growth forecasts) returns 15 percent on average in the year after formation. *Source*: Bordalo, Pedro, Nicola Gennaioli, Rafael La Porta, and Andrei Shleifer. 2017. "Diagnostic Expectations and Stock Returns." National Bureau of Economic Research Working Paper 23863. Reprinted by permission of the authors.

portfolio formation and decline in the years right after. Analysts learn that they are too optimistic about HLTG firms and revise their beliefs accordingly. The opposite pattern holds for LLTG firms: Analysts revise their views of these firms down prior to portfolio formation, but subsequently recognize that long-term earnings growth will not be as bad as they anticipated and correct their beliefs upward. Portfolio returns follow forecast revisions: As analysts curb their earlier enthusiasm, returns are poor; as they cheer up, returns are high.[2]

---

2. The fact that expectations on earnings growth three to five years down the road exhibit a boom-bust pattern is not per se symptomatic of distorted expecta-

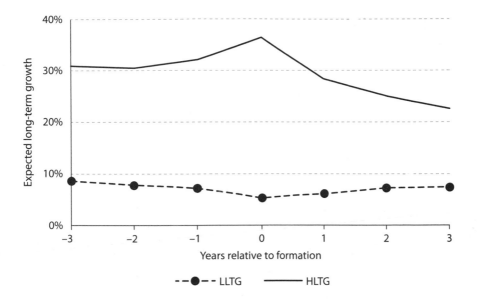

FIGURE 4.4. Expected Long-Term Growth for LLTG and HLTG Portfolios. Analysts are at peak optimism when HLTG portfolios are formed and at the deepest pessimism when LLTG portfolios are formed. *Source*: Bordalo, Pedro, Nicola Gennaioli, Rafael La Porta, and Andrei Shleifer. 2017. "Diagnostic Expectations and Stock Returns." National Bureau of Economic Research Working Paper 23863. Reprinted by permission of the authors.

We can see similar trends in the earnings data: HLTG firms bring positive earnings surprises on the way up, yet disappoint looking forward from the peak. LLTG firms disappoint on their way down, but turn out not to be as bad as expected looking forward from the bottom. To put this differently, analysts extrapolate past performance and become excessively optimistic about HLTG firms and excessively pessimistic about

---

tions. It could be due to fundamental mean reversion in earnings growth, which explains why—after reaching its peak—expected earnings growth monotonically declines with the horizon. What indicates that this boom-bust pattern of expectations is due to departures from rationality is the evidence on predictable returns and forecast errors (see BGLS 2017 for a detailed analysis of this issue).

LLTG firms. And critically, these extreme beliefs are reflected in valuations as well, leading to sharp differences in returns as analysts and others correct their mistaken extreme beliefs.

This evidence raises perhaps a deeper question about how analysts form beliefs in the first place. Do they mechanically extrapolate past earnings growth trends, or is there more to their belief formation? BGLS (2017) suggest that belief formation is not mechanical but takes a particular form of sophisticated yet not entirely rational learning. The study finds that among HLTG firms, there are in fact some whose earnings continue to grow spectacularly—they are the future Googles. It is just that most HLTG firms do not turn out to be Googles, but slow down instead. Analysts form average expectations for HLTG firms as if there are more future Googles among them than there actually are in reality.

Figure 4.5 illustrates this finding. It shows the distribution of long-term earnings growth rates from HLTG (solid curve) and the rest (dashed curve). As the figure shows, HLTG firms do have a fat right tail of performance outcomes relative to all firms. There are indeed more Googles among them. But if you look at expectations and how they are corrected going forward, there are not nearly as many Googles as analysts think. Analysts use information about past performance but overreact by predicting too many high performers. This observation will be central to our theory of belief formation in chapter 5.

So we see that, in the cross-section of stocks, there are some very similar phenomena to those we saw in the aggregate. Good performance leads to predictions of good performance in the future, and the opposite for bad performance. Forecasters extrapolate, but not mechanically. They use some forward-looking logic. Analysts understand correctly that extremely high earnings growth portends extremely high continued growth for some firms; there is indeed information in high past earnings

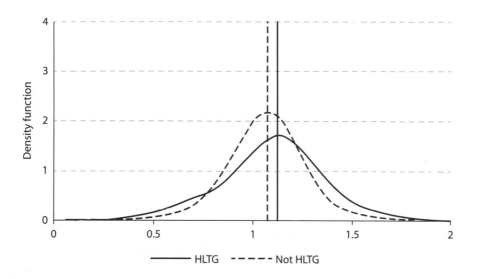

FIGURE 4.5. Kernel Density Estimates of Growth in Earnings per Share for LTG Portfolios.
Source: Bordalo, Pedro, Nicola Gennaioli, Rafael La Porta, and Andrei Shleifer. 2017. "Diagnostic Expectations and Stock Returns." National Bureau of Economic Research Working Paper 23863. Reprinted by permission of the authors.

growth for future earnings growth. Among the HLTG firms, there actually are some remarkable performers going forward, many more than among LLTG firms. Unfortunately, such performers tend to be relatively few, yet the forecasts become overoptimistic by expecting too many of them. Analysts react to the good news of high earnings growth, but excessively. Extrapolation is caused by overreaction to information.

Expectations and Investment

Do survey expectations predict actual behavior? We have already mentioned that expectations of aggregate stock returns shape the flow of money into equity mutual funds. Likewise, we showed that expectations about real estate prices influence home buying decisions. But do they shape corporate decisions as well?

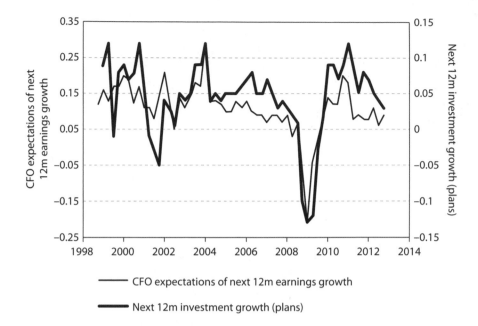

FIGURE 4.6. CFO Earnings Growth Expectations and Investment. CFO earnings expectations and investment plans move together. *Source*: Gennaioli, Nicola, Yueran Ma, and Andrei Shleifer. 2015. "Expectations and Investment." *NBER Macroeconomics Annual* 30 (1): 379–431. Reprinted by permission of the authors.

Together with Yueran Ma (Gennaioli, Ma, and Shleifer 2015), we have explored this question for corporate investment. For this project, we used the Duke Survey of Chief Financial Officers (CFOs) of large U.S. companies already mentioned as a source of data on expected stock returns. These CFOs also report their expectations of earnings growth and investment plans for their own companies. The Duke Survey has a variety of privacy issues in how data are reported. Accordingly, not all the analysis can be done using individual firm data. Even so, we can aggregate the data to look at the basic patterns without knowing firm names.

Figure 4.6 presents the basic evidence. It shows in the same graph CFO earnings growth expectations and investment plans for the next year, aggregated over the firms in the Duke sample. It shows that the two

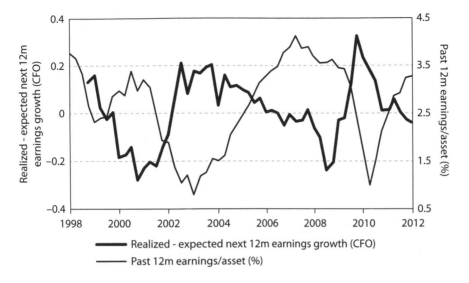

FIGURE 4.7. Errors in Earnings Expectations and Past Profitability. Expectations errors are predictable. Realized earnings growth falls short of expectations when past earnings are high and exceeds expectations when past earnings are low. *Source*: Gennaioli, Nicola, Yueran Ma, and Andrei Shleifer. 2015. "Expectations and Investment." *NBER Macroeconomics Annual* 30 (1): 379–431. Reprinted by permission of the authors.

follow each other closely. The collapse of earnings growth expectations following the Lehman bankruptcy, for example, is accompanied by the collapse of investment plans. The two recover together in 2009–2010 as well. Actual investment is very close to investment plans, so CFO beliefs go hand in hand with economic activity. The study also shows that CFO earnings growth expectations are a much stronger predictor of investment plans (as well as realizations) than Tobin's Q, the preferred indicator of investment opportunities in a standard rational expectations investment framework.

But are CFO expectations rational? In figure 4.7, we look at the predictability of forecast errors of CFO predictions of their own firms' earnings growth. The figure graphs the forecast error (dark line) as well as a measure of past year profitability of the firm (light line). It shows that

CFOs are excessively optimistic about their firms' earnings growth when past profitability has been high, and conversely when it has been low. The predictability of forecast errors is inconsistent with the REH. The evidence again points to extrapolation: The CFOs expect the profitability of their firms to be more persistent than it turns out to be, on average. We do not have enough data to conduct the kinds of tests on CFO expectations that we performed with stock market analysts for HLTG firms, but the pattern of overreaction seems closely related.

Evidence from Credit Markets

The evidence presented so far comes mostly from the stock market and from firms. It suggests that market participants and corporate managers hold extrapolative expectations that in some circumstances lead to the overvaluation of stocks, both in the aggregate and for individual companies, and that such overvaluation leads to predictable low returns and downward revisions of expectations. These expectations also influence corporate investment.

But the story of the 2008 crisis is not one of the stock market, but of the housing and credit markets. This raises the question of whether and how broadly the narrative of extrapolative expectations and overvaluation applies to these markets as well. We have already discussed in chapter 2 the importance of extrapolative expectations in 2008, but is the evidence more general? The answer appears to be yes. Since the financial crisis, economists have put together a substantial amount of evidence on credit cycles. In brief, this evidence reaches four conclusions. First, expansion of credit predicts future financial crises and recessions. Second, the rising share of risky credit is a central and especially worrisome part of credit overexpansion. Third, some kinds of credit expansions, such as those funding household spending on housing and consumption, are especially potent predictors of crises and recessions. And fourth, critically for our analysis, excessively optimistic expectations are an important driver of credit growth. We next highlight some of this evidence, finishing up with its connection to the expectations data.

The hypothesis that credit expansion increases the risk of financial crises and recessions has a long history in economics. It is usually associated with the writings of Minsky (1977) and Kindleberger (1978). Some of the earliest theoretical work on the risks of credit expansion for financial fragility is by John Geanakoplos (1997, 2010). Empirically, these ideas have received a considerable boost in the historical work of Reinhart and Rogoff (2009) and, more recently, Schularick and Taylor (2012). The latter authors in particular investigate the hypothesis that credit expansions predict economic crises and recessions, using a historical data set for fourteen developed countries over 140 years. They find strong supportive evidence.

Baron and Xiong (2017) take this evidence one step further and examine the effects of bank credit growth on bank shareholder returns for twenty developed countries between 1920 and 2012. Bank credit expansion here is growth in loans to households and nonfinancial corporations. Baron and Xiong present dramatic evidence that high bank credit expansion predicts both a high probability of a crash and low average returns on bank stocks. Figure 4.8, taken from their paper, presents the main findings of shareholders first rewarding the credit expansion with unusually high returns on the bank stocks, and then being severely disappointed as revealed by the bank's share prices collapse. Baron and Xiong interpret their findings as evidence of neglect of risk during credit expansion, since predictably negative returns are clear evidence of systematic surprise, and hence systematic forecast error. Research by Fahlenbrach, Prilmeier, and Stulz (2017) on the cross-section of U.S. banks between 1973 and 2014, as discussed in chapter 2, is broadly consistent with these findings.

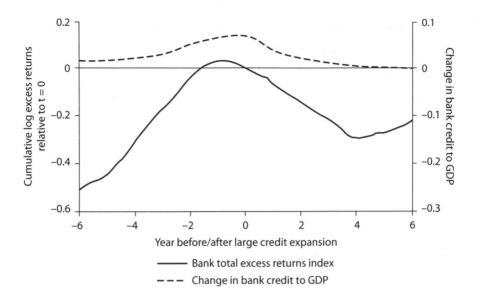

FIGURE 4.8. Bank Equity Prices and Bank Credit before and after Large Credit Expansions.
The dashed line tracks credit expansion. Bank equity prices rally leading up to the peak of a credit boom and decline afterward. *Source*: Baron, Matthew, and Wei Xiong. 2017. "Credit Expansion and Neglected Crash Risk." *Quarterly Journal of Economics* 132 (2): 713–64. Reprinted by permission of the authors.

The evidence from both Baron and Xiong (2017) and Fahlenbrach, Prilmeier, and Stulz (2017) suggests that when bank credit expands rapidly, the loans that banks make are risky, but neither analyst forecasts nor asset prices incorporate this higher risk. Another perspective on these issues, also highly relevant given the centrality of subprime mortgages in the 2008 crisis and the Great Recession, comes from public debt markets rather than banks. In a pioneering paper using U.S. data, Greenwood and Hanson (2013) found that credit spreads, defined as the difference between the cost of risky and safe debt, as well as the share of risky debt issuance in the total debt issuance, are effective barometers of credit market sentiment. Perhaps not surprisingly, the risky debt share tends to be unusually high when credit spreads are particularly low, suggesting that

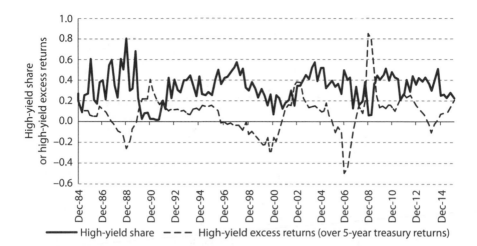

FIGURE 4.9. Issuer Quality and Subsequent High-Yield Excess Returns. When the share of risky corporate debt in total is high, corporate bonds have low excess returns moving forward. *Source*: Greenwood, Robin, and Samuel G. Hanson. 2013. "Issuer Quality and Corporate Bond Returns." *Review of Financial Studies* 26 (6): 1483–525. Reprinted by permission of the authors.

both are driven by optimism about returns on risky debt. But Greenwood and Hanson also find, as figure 4.9 illustrates, that such frothy risky debt conditions predict low returns on risky debt going forward: Investors buying risky debt at relatively low yields compared to safe debt are disappointed. Put differently, when credit spreads are extremely low and risky debt markets are buoyant, these credit spreads tend to rise in the future, leaving debt investors with losses. This evidence is quite suggestive of possible overexcitement, reflected both in the pricing of risky debt and in the quantities of such debt being issued.

López-Salido, Stein, and Zakrajšek (LSZ 2017) take this discovery further and connect it to the credit cycle. They confirm the finding of Greenwood and Hanson (2013) that measures of credit market sentiment based on the risky share and the credit spread predict future returns. But they also predict recessions. A buoyant risky debt market forecasts a slowdown in aggregate economic activity over the next two to three years

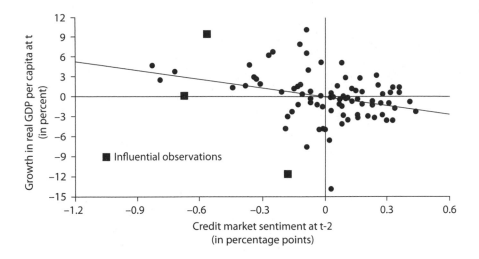

FIGURE 4.10. Credit Market Sentiment and Economic Growth. Exuberant credit market sentiment is followed by slower economic growth. *Source*: López-Salido, David, Jeremy C. Stein, and Egon Zakrajšek. 2017. "Credit-Market Sentiment and the Business Cycle." *Quarterly Journal of Economics* 132 (3): 1373–426. Reprinted by permission of the authors.

measured by either output growth or unemployment. Figure 4.10 illustrates their finding of the negative relationship between credit market sentiment in year t-2 and economic growth in year t. This gets us closer to the narrative of the 2008 crisis, in which the collapse of the housing bubble and of prices of risky debt that paid for it undermined both financial institutions and consumers, causing the Great Recession. The authors also find, interestingly, that credit market sentiment predicts future economic growth much more successfully than measures of stock market valuation.

Kirti (2018) extends LSZ's evidence by constructing a high-yield share in bond issuance for thirty-eight countries. He finds that a high level of this share is correlated with survey indicators of looser lending standards, but also predicts slower economic growth going forward. All the evidence appears to fit together: Credit expansions, particularly of risky credit, increase financial fragility and the chances of a recession.

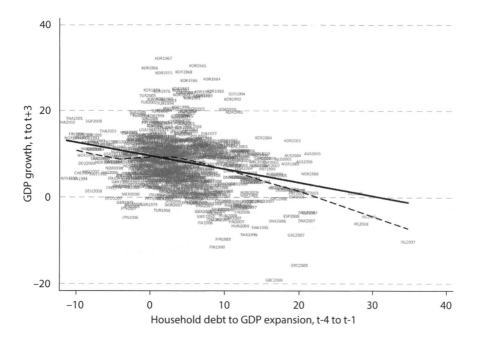

FIGURE 4.11. **Household Debt to GDP Expansion and Growth.** Rapid household credit growth is followed by slower economic growth. *Source*: Mian, Atif, Amir Sufi, and Emil Verner. 2017. "Household Debt and Business Cycles Worldwide." *Quarterly Journal of Economics* 132 (4): 1755–817. Reprinted by permission of the authors.

Such evidence raises the question of what kinds of credit expansions are most closely associated with the expansion of risky borrowing. In 2008, the expansion of mortgage debt played a central role, not just for the financial crisis but also, as Mian and Sufi (2009, 2014b) have shown convincingly, for the Great Recession. Mian, Sufi, and Verner (2017) take this evidence further and show, using a panel of thirty countries between 1960 and 2012, that growth in household debt relative to GDP predicts subsequent recessions. Figure 4.11 presents their central finding of a negative correlation between household credit growth and subsequent GDP growth. Mian, Sufi, and Verner (2017) take a strong view that household debt is more important than corporate or bank debt for predicting recessions, since household debt overhang is particularly detrimental to consumption spending and economic activity. Jordà, Schularick, and Taylor (2015) find, in a related vein, that the growth of mortgage debt is a successful predictor of crises.

But how do expectations enter this picture? Recall that the central finding of Greenwood and Hanson (2013) is that frothy conditions in the risky debt markets lead to reversals. One can then ask whether these frothy conditions are reflected not just in low credit spreads, but also in the expectations of continued low credit spreads. If investors in risky debt believe that good times will continue into the future (as they seem to have felt before the 2008 crisis), then the Greenwood and Hanson evidence on subsequent low returns can be seen as that of disappointment. This can be tested by looking at the expectations of the credit spread and relating the forecast error in these expectations to the prevailing credit spreads at the time forecasts are made, as we have done with Pedro Bordalo (Bordalo, Gennaioli, and Shleifer 2018). Figure 4.12 presents this evidence covering only the relatively short period for which the data on expectations from the Blue Chip Survey of professional forecasters are available.

Figure 4.12 is broadly consistent with the Greenwood and Hanson (2013) evidence. When credit spreads are low, forecasters expect them to remain low relative to what turns out to be the case. As we saw in other settings (such as earnings), forecasters underestimate the extent of mean reversion in credit spreads, leading to disappointment and, as LSZ (2017) show, economic slowdowns. To the extent that forecast errors are predictable, forecaster expectations are not rational. Similar findings appear in Glaeser's (2013) analysis of housing bubbles in U.S. history and in Greenwood and Hanson's (2015) research on cycles in the ship-building industry.

Figure 4.13 reports an econometric test of predictability. Column 1 estimates an AR(1) process for the BAA-10Y spread; column 2 regresses

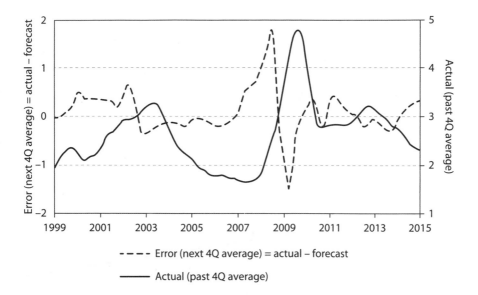

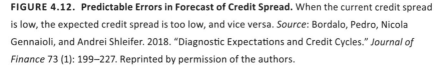

FIGURE 4.12. Predictable Errors in Forecast of Credit Spread. When the current credit spread is low, the expected credit spread is too low, and vice versa. *Source*: Bordalo, Pedro, Nicola Gennaioli, and Andrei Shleifer. 2018. "Diagnostic Expectations and Credit Cycles." *Journal of Finance* 73 (1): 199–227. Reprinted by permission of the authors.

the analysts' forecast on the current spread; and column 3 regresses the future forecast error on the current spread. The table confirms the message of figure 4.12. In column 3, the higher the current spread, the higher the forecast is relative to the realization. This may occur because analysts see excessive persistence in current conditions: In column 1, the estimated persistence of the actual BAA-10Y spread is about 0.4, but in column 2, forecasts follow the current spread with a coefficient of about 0.6.

This evidence as well is consistent with the narrative of 2007–2008, which is in fact part of this sample. During the period of expanding credit and rising risky debt share prior to the crisis, credit spreads were extremely low, and forecasters expected low spreads to stay. As defaults started to mount, the spreads widened considerably, leading to massive

	BAA-10Y spread		
	Actual	Forecast	Error
Average spread past year	0.3927 [1.67]	0.6519 [4.62]	−0.2592 [−2.20]
Constant	1.6280 [2.56]	0.8596 [2.25]	0.7684 [2.40]
Observations	64	64	64
R^2	0.158	0.472	0.161

FIGURE 4.13. **Actual, Forecast, and Forecast Error of Next Year Average BAA-10Y Credit Spread.** (Forecast Error = Actual − Forecast, Newey West t-statistics in brackets.) *Source*: Bordalo, Pedro, Nicola Gennaioli, and Andrei Shleifer. 2018. "Diagnostic Expectations and Credit Cycles." *Journal of Finance* 73 (1): 199–227. Reprinted by permission of the authors.

losses for mortgage and MBS holders and eventually a crisis and the Great Recession. By 2009, Fed interventions managed to calm markets and the actual spread dropped again. But now forecast errors are large and negative, indicating that in 2008, after the Lehman events, forecasters were too pessimistic about the future. Such extremely adverse outcomes might not be universal, but the broader patterns in the data suggest that the sequence of events in the 2000s was not an exception. Errors from extrapolating the safety of risky debt are a broader phenomenon.

Summary

Our brief overview of the evidence on survey expectations and on credit cycles points to several conclusions.

First, survey expectations are not noise. They are consistent across different survey instruments and predict actual behavior of both investors and corporate managers. Survey expectations are a useful tool for evaluating economic models, insofar as they reflect what market participants believe and act on. They are as important an economic variable as any other, and economic models should be judged by their consistency with survey expectations data, just as they are judged by their consistency with other economic data.

Second, once we begin to take survey expectations seriously and subject them to the tests of statistical rationality, the rational expectations hypothesis is rejected. In financial markets at least, both expectations errors and subsequent revisions of expectations can be predicted at the time the original expectations are reported. This cannot happen if expectations are statistically optimal. The Rational Expectations Hypothesis can of course be rejected in other ways, such as the predictability of future stock returns, as in the Baron-Xiong (2017) study of banks. In fact, there are now decades of evidence along these lines. But the expectations evidence is more direct and free from the objections to inferring beliefs indirectly. Findings such as Greenwood and Shleifer (2014), which show that survey measures of expected returns are strongly *negatively* correlated with model-based expected returns, are not a good sign for the standard theory and present a challenge that needs to be addressed.

Third, investors, analysts, and managers appear to make systematic expectations errors by extrapolating the past into the future. In some situations, they extrapolate changes in security prices or economic conditions; in other situations, they presume that certain variables, such as profitability, are more persistent than they really are. Such behavior is consistent with the evidence of excess volatility and return predictability that has been central to economic research on financial market efficiency. We also presented some evidence that, in the context of the cross-section of stock returns, extrapolation is not entirely mechanical or naïve. Forecasters react to information but too strongly, neglecting the possibilities they are not thinking about. Such sophisticated extrapolation will be central to our proposal for modeling expectations in chapters 5 and 6.

Fourth, expectation errors appear to be central for understanding credit cycles. Credit expansions, particularly those of risky credit, forecast economic crises and recessions, both in the United States and in other countries. Such credit expansions are supported by excessive optimism about the debt being issued, as one can see from the evidence on stock returns of banks making the loans, and critically for us, from the revisions in expectations. Beliefs are central to understanding credit markets as well.

Finally, the evidence suggests that the credit cycle leading to the financial crisis of 2008, while surely characterized by several financial innovations, in many respects was not exceptional. Like other episodes, the expansion of the 2000s developed along with a housing bubble and the growing leverage of households and banks that this bubble encouraged. Like other episodes, this expansion was supported by extraordinary optimism—in the form of both high expected appreciation and low risk of a price decline—about home prices and the safety of securities, including mortgages and MBS, which financed these homes. Like other episodes, this one saw a relative increase in the share of risky loans in total lending, most conspicuously represented by subprime mortgages, as well as growth of household leverage. Like other episodes, this credit boom made financial institutions including banks as well as households extremely vulnerable to the deflation of the bubble. And as with many other episodes, the bubble collapsed, causing both the 2008 crisis and the Great Recession that followed.

In sum, extrapolative beliefs offer a promising strategy for understanding fluctuations in credit markets, equity markets, and real activity. To make progress, in the next chapter we seek to understand at a deeper level how expectations are formed and offer a psychological foundation for extrapolation. In chapter 6, we apply this analysis to credit and investment cycles.

CHAPTER 5

Representativeness and Diagnostic Beliefs

I n the last several decades, behavioral economics and behavioral finance became integral parts of economic analysis. Early work in these fields identified major inconsistencies between the predictions of standard economic models based on rational actors and data. Behavioral finance, for example, began as a field with Shiller's (1981) remarkable finding that the stock market fluctuates much more than the present value of corporate dividends, inconsistent with the central prediction of the Efficient Markets Hypothesis. It was followed by several demonstrations that stock returns are predictable, some of which we already described in chapter 4, again contrary to the basic model of efficient financial markets. In behavioral economics, Daniel Kahneman, Amos Tversky, and Richard Thaler came up with striking experimental findings of systematic departures of probabilistic judgments and choice under risk from the predictions of Bayesian rationality and Expected Utility Theory.

But how to deal with this evidence theoretically? Kahneman and Tversky followed a somewhat informal approach by suggesting that human judgment is subject to a number of shortcuts or heuristics, which save on cognitive costs and generally lead to good assessments, but occasionally lead to errors. Economists took a more formal approach. Following the early empirical evidence, they incorporated into standard economic models specific failures of rationality motivated by experimental and field evidence in order to analyze particular economic problems. For example, in an early attempt to explain empirical patterns of stock returns, Barberis, Shleifer, and Vishny (1998) used psychological notions such as representativeness and conservatism to motivate their assumptions, but then built a specialized model of belief under- and overreaction tailored to a specific financial market setting. There are many other notable models of heuristics and cognitive biases, including the law of small numbers and the hot-hand fallacy (e.g., Rabin and Vayanos 2010), probability weighting (Barberis and Huang 2008), overconfidence (e.g., Daniel, Hirshleifer, and Subramanyam 1998), and wishful thinking (Brunnermeier and Parker 2005), among others. These models typically do not go as far as we do here to apply the same idea across contexts, including experiments, field evidence on beliefs, and financial markets.

Chapter 3 offered one example of this customized approach to models of beliefs. We modeled a particular belief distortion, neglect of downside risk, assuming that market participants underestimate the frequency of events in the left tail. We then analyzed a competitive market in which participants depart from rationality in this way. Chapter 4 offered another example. Here we presented evidence of extrapolative beliefs, which are typically formalized using adaptive expectations. In that framework, expected price changes mechanically depend on past price changes:

$$\Delta_t p^e_{t+1} = (1-\lambda)\Sigma_{s\geq 0}\lambda^s \Delta p_{t-s}, \tag{5.1}$$

where the expectation $\Delta_t p^e_{t+1}$ held at time t about the next period's price growth depends on past price growth Δp_{t-s}, and $\lambda \in (0, 1)$ captures the extent of extrapolation. Such an adaptive rule can be incorporated into models of asset prices, investment, and so on. Adam, Marcet, and Beutel (2017) and Barberis et al. (2018) are recent applications of this approach.

These context-specific models of beliefs provide several important insights, but they have two main shortcomings. First, they abstract from the relationship between different biases. In the context of the previous chapters, this raises several questions. What is the relationship between neglect of tail risk and extrapolation of average future conditions? Are they two separate belief distortions or just one? If relatively few biological processes, such as attention and memory, shape beliefs, we should expect some relationship between different biases. Memory retrieval, for instance, is an essential part of belief construction, which arguably shapes our beliefs about future average conditions, our perception of tail risks, and our interpretation of incoming news. But then, as the product of the same retrieval mechanisms, how are these features of beliefs related to each other? By treating biases as separate, the current approach in behavioral finance—and behavioral economics more generally—cannot address this question.

A second shortcoming of many available models is that mechanical rules for beliefs do not allow researchers to predict when certain belief distortions are present. For instance, the neglect of downside risk described in chapter 3 may be valid in the pre-2008 period, but it may have been reversed into a panic after the Lehman bankruptcy. The probability of unlikely events, including presumably of downside risks, is actually exaggerated in Kahneman and Tversky's (1979) Prospect Theory. So, when should we expect low probability events to be neglected, as in Taleb (2007) or chapter 3, and when do we expect them to be overweighted in judgment? Barberis (2013) summarizes the available evidence but suggests no answer. One might need to dig deeper to reconcile contrasting cases.

Likewise, chapter 4 presented evidence of extrapolative inference. However, the adaptive formula in equation (5.1) is probably not the best way forward. The Lucas (1976) critique of mechanical rules such as equation (5.1) holds that they cannot account for the flexibility of beliefs across different (e.g., policy) regimes or information shocks. For that, decision makers need to look forward, not backward. The Rational Expectations Hypothesis assumes too much about the capabilities and flexibility of our minds, but it validly stresses—relative to adaptive expectations—that beliefs adjust to the reality around us. Accurate models of belief formation should incorporate such flexibility and use it to predict when biases come and go.

The survival of the customized approach to modeling biases may be due in part to a resistance to unification. Behavioral economics developed originally as a collection of tests and rejections of the predictions of neoclassical theory, whose point of pride is precisely a unified approach to human behavior. Unification was not the point of these daring and effective hit-and-run attacks on the colossus. In recent years, however, a vast amount of systematic evidence on belief distortions has been collected in economics, psychology, and cognitive sciences. Several cognitive principles have emerged. Trying to organize, distill, and unify this knowledge seems increasingly realistic but also essential for economics to make progress.

This chapter describes some of our research with Pedro Bordalo and other collaborators that seeks to unify several departures from belief rationality using a simple cognitive foundation. We build on a formalization of Kahneman and Tversky's representativeness heuristic that was proposed by Gennaioli and Shleifer (GS 2010) and applied to stereotype formation in Bordalo, Coffman, Gennaioli, and Shleifer (BCGS 2016a). This formalization is closely related to a fast-growing movement in cognitive science that views selective memory and attention as central to judgment. Our model captures only some of the belief distortions considered in behavioral finance, but it nonetheless accounts for a number of empirical findings, including many of those on expectations described in chapter 4. We see it as a first step to address the methodological shortcomings of some of the earlier work, and to illustrate the benefits of moving on.

In reference to chapters 3 and 4, our model yields neglect of risk and extrapolation as special cases and describes the conditions in which these distortions arise. It therefore explains when extrapolation and neglect of downside risk go hand in hand and when they do not. For the 2008 crisis, the model offers an account of beliefs before the initial tremors in 2007, during the relatively quiet period between these tremors and Lehman, as well as after Lehman. In chapter 6, we show that a dynamic version of the same model can shed light on the evidence on credit cycles, including beliefs, documented in chapter 4. The model we describe here is widely applicable outside of specific finance settings. It accounts for several experiments in psychology, but also sheds light on such diverse phenomena as macroeconomic forecasts and social stereotypes. We see cross-context applicability as crucial to validating our approach.

Our model of belief formation is forward-looking and in fact nests rational expectations as a special case. This means that, unlike mechanical rules, expectations in our model respond to regime changes and news about the future. They are not vulnerable to the Lucas critique. Most important, the forward-looking nature of beliefs delivers the "kernel of truth" property: Representativeness causes biases by exaggerating real patterns in the data. We saw some evidence for the kernel of truth in chapter 4 when we discussed Bordalo, Gennaioli, La Porta, and Shleifer's (BGLS 2017) work on extreme analyst forecasts that seem to reflect an exaggeration of the incidence of Googles in the sample of rapidly growing firms. Kernel of truth allows us to characterize departures from rationality in terms of features of the real world, making the model empirically testable.

This chapter proceeds as follows. First, we review the concept of representativeness in psychology. The concept was introduced by Kahneman and Tversky in 1974 and over the years refined by them and others (e.g., Kahneman and Tversky 1983). It was criticized as ill-defined (Gigerenzer 1996), formalized in a number of ways, some closely related to ours (Tenenbaum and Griffiths 2001), but also extensively tested and confirmed in both experiments and field data (e.g., Chen, Moskowitz, and Shue 2016). Second, we present our formalization and briefly discuss how it can shed light on the evidence from psychology and on the phenomenon of social stereotypes. Third, and crucial for our current purpose, we apply it to the finance model of chapter 3. We first analyze the implications of representativeness for neglected risk. In chapter 6, we analyze the model's implications for the evidence in chapter 4.

Representativeness

Starting from the early 1970s, psychologists Daniel Kahneman and Amos Tversky put together a collection of laboratory findings of systematic departures of human judgment from Bayesian inference. They explained these departures by suggesting that humans use a few judgment heuristics: representativeness, availability, and anchoring (Kahneman and Tversky 1974). Heuristics are rules of thumb. They may have emerged from adaptive processes: They speed up cognition and often yield good approximate answers. But they produce incorrect answers in some situations.

Kahneman and Tversky describe the representativeness heuristic as our tendency to judge likelihood by similarity. For instance, when thinking about a shy person called Steve, who is described as having a need for order and a passion for detail, we may think that he is more likely to be a librarian than a farmer because his attributes are similar to those of a typical librarian. The problem here is that likelihood and similarity do not always go together. Very few men work as librarians, and millions do as farmers, which makes it much more likely in reality that Steve is a farmer. Similarity causes us to neglect how many male farmers there are relative to librarians. Representativeness is a powerful heuristic. It accounts for disparate phenomena, including the conjunction fallacy and base rate neglect.

The conjunction fallacy refers to the mistake of judging an event $A \cap B$ to be more likely than either A or B alone. This behavior is inconsistent with the axioms of probability theory. Kahneman and Tversky documented a robust tendency of subjects to commit the conjunction fallacy in several experiments, the most famous of which is Linda.

Linda is thirty-one years old, single, outspoken, and very bright. She majored in philosophy. As a student, she was deeply concerned with issues of discrimination and social justice, and also participated in antinuclear demonstrations.

The respondents are asked to assess Linda's occupation today by ranking several options in order of their likelihood. The options include "Linda is a social worker," "Linda is a school teacher," as well as the following two:

1. Linda is a bank teller.
2. Linda is a bank teller and active in the feminist movement.

Most subjects report that option 2 is more likely than option 1. This is a big mistake, because option 1 includes both feminist and nonfeminist bank tellers. With standard notions of probability, option 1 contains option 2 and thus it must be at least as likely as 2. The logic of similarity explains why people get this wrong. The population of Lindas consists of leftists, and a feminist bank teller is more similar to a leftist than the *stereotypical* bank teller, who is probably less political. By conflating probability with similarity, subjects mistakenly conclude that option 2 is more likely than option 1.

Base rate neglect refers to the tendency for individuals to react too strongly to information, as we already saw in the case of Steve the librarian, where the subjects overreact to the information that Steve is orderly and detail-oriented. Another classic example is provided by Casscells, Schoenberger, and Graboys (1978), who analyze inference by physicians. Doctors are asked to assess the health status of a patient in light of a positive medical test of imperfect precision. The study shows that doctors tend to attach too high a probability of the patient being sick conditional on a positive test, particularly if the disease is rare. This is a puzzle because according to Bayes' rule:

$$Pr(sick \mid positive) = \frac{Pr(positive \mid sick) \, Pr(sick)}{Pr(positive)}.$$

If the disease is rare (i.e., its base rate *Pr(sick)* is small), the patient is unlikely to be sick even if the test is positive. Intuitively, when the disease is rare, a positive test is very likely to be a false positive. In reality, however, doctors overreact to a positive test. Because a sick patient is similar to someone who tested positive, representativeness leads to such overreaction. The representativeness heuristic can thus account for base rate neglect as well.

A Formal Model of Representativeness

Gennaioli and Shleifer (2010) model the representativeness heuristic by building on the following definition given by Kahneman and Tversky

(1983): "An attribute is representative of a class if it is very diagnostic, that is, if the relative frequency of this attribute is much higher in that class than in a relevant reference class."

Representativeness is defined to be relative, not absolute, likelihood. The virtue of this definition is that it can be implemented in a standard probabilistic model and is applicable to any probabilistic judgment. Before discussing its relationship to similarity, consider its formalization.

Suppose that there is a group G and a decision maker assesses the distribution of types T in it. Types T could be standardized test scores and G a social group (e.g., women). Or T could be the future stock return of a firm in sector G. Or T could be the future performance of the economy and G its past performance. The true distribution of types follows the conditional probability $h(T = \tau \mid G)$. This distribution reflects the true frequency of test scores in a group, or the rational expectation about the firm's or the economy's future performance. A group can also be defined by past history, including all types that share the same past performance. This connection is important because it links representativeness to the dynamic inference problems that are important in finance and macroeconomics.

In light of what Kahneman and Tversky wrote, we define the representativeness $R(\tau, G)$ of a type $T = \tau$ for group G by its relative probability:

$$R(\tau, G) \equiv \frac{h(T = \tau \mid G)}{h(T = \tau \mid -G)}, \tag{5.2}$$

where $-G$ is a comparison group. Here $-G$ captures a natural context in which group G is assessed. Consider our previous examples. When assessing the test scores of women, group G, the comparison $-G$ is naturally pinned down by men. When assessing the future performance of a firm in sector G, the comparison $-G$ is naturally given by firms in other sectors. When assessing whether a patient is sick after a medical test outcome G, the comparison −G is naturally given by the health status of untested people. In a similar vein, when assessing the future state of the economy in the current state G, the comparison −G is plausibly given by the state of the economy before recent news is received. As in the above definition, then, a type τ is more representative if it is *relatively* more frequent in G than in −G.

To see how this works, consider the example from BCGS (2016a) in which an individual assesses the distribution of hair color among the Irish. The trait *T* is hair color, the conditioning group *G* is the Irish. The comparison group −G is the world at large. The true frequency distribution of hair color in different groups is reported below.

	Red	Light/Brown	Dark
Irish	10%	40%	50%
World	1%	14%	85%

On the basis of the data alone, it is hard to make sense of the tendency of people to report a large incidence of red hair in the Irish population. In this group, just as in the rest of the world, red-haired people are a small minority and dark-haired people are the absolute majority. Why, then, is red hair viewed as common and even stereotypical of Irish people?

Representativeness offers an explanation: Because red is the distinctive hair color of the Irish, in the precise sense of equation (5.2), this hair color indeed has the highest likelihood ratio:

$$\frac{Pr(red \mid Irish)}{Pr(red \mid World)} = 10 > \frac{Pr(light / brown \mid Irish)}{Pr(light / brown \mid World)}$$

$$= \frac{40}{14} > \frac{Pr(dark \mid Irish)}{Pr(dark \mid World)} = \frac{50}{85}.$$

While rare in absolute terms, red hair is relatively much more common among the Irish. As a result, red hair is representative of Irish people.

But how does one go from representativeness to beliefs? In line with Kahneman and Tversky's original intuition, we view representativeness as influencing probability assessments through limited and selective memory. Representative types quickly come to mind, so that their probability is inflated in judgments. This mechanism can be traced to memory research (Kahana 2012), which has identified two principles of recall: It is associative and subject to interference. Recall is associative in that seeing a sequence of pairs (A, B) induces subjects to later retrieve A when cued with B. Recall is subject to interference in that seeing a sequence of pairs (A, B) and (A, C) together with other sequences such as (A′, B) reduces the extent to which subjects, after being cued with B, recall A. This phenomenon, which is called the *fan effect*, arises because the association of A with B is interfered with by the association of the same A with C. This effect also makes it more likely that after seeing B one recalls A′, because A′ is distinctively associated with B and hence faces no interference.

The formalization of representativeness in equation (5.2) captures this memory mechanism. When primed with the task of assessing group G, a person is more likely to recall a type more associated with this group, in the sense of its frequency $h(T = \tau \mid G)$ being higher. At the same time, though, the strength of association of the same type τ with other groups—in the sense of the frequency $h(T = \tau \mid -G)$ being higher—interferes with the recall of τ after cue G. In the hair color example, when primed with the group $G = Irish$, the type "dark hair" is suppressed because it faces strong interference. In fact, dark hair is much more strongly associated with other groups $-G$. Due to such interference, memory oversamples the distinctive traits of the Irish, the red hair, even if these traits are unlikely in absolute terms. Oversampling of red-haired memories in turn leads to an inflated probability assessment of this hair color.

This principle can be connected to similarity, which is at the heart of the original Kahneman and Tversky's intuition. Taking the frequency of association $h(T = \tau|G)$ as a measure of similarity between type τ and group G, equation (5.2) says that recall of τ is interfered with when this type is also similar to other groups $-G$, namely, when $h(T = \tau|-G)$ is high. Due to interference, recall favors the types that are relatively more similar to G than to the comparison group $-G$. Representativeness and similarity are by-products of the same basic recall processes.

We formalize this distorted recall process by assuming that the probability of types that score high in $R(\tau, G)$ is inflated. Because these types come to mind quickly, they are overweighted in judgment. In contrast, the probability of types that score low in $R(\tau, G)$ is deflated or outright neglected. These types are harder to recall, which makes us underweight them. In BCGS (2016a) and Bordalo, Gennaioli, and Shleifer (BGS 2018) we propose a tractable formalization by assuming that probability judgments are formed using the representativeness-distorted density:

$$h^{\theta}(T = \tau|G) = h(T = \tau|G) \left[\frac{h(T = \tau|G)}{h(T = \tau|-G)} \right]^{\theta} Z, \qquad (5.3)$$

where $\theta \geq 0$ captures the extent of probability distortions and Z is a constant ensuring that the distorted density $h^{\theta}(T = \tau|G)$ integrates to 1. In equation (5.3), the decision maker inflates the probability of highly representative types and discounts the probability of unrepresentative ones. BCGS (2016a) show that the key properties of our model hold under a more general weighting function. Here we stick to the above functional form because it yields convenient closed-form solutions.

GS (2010) show that this model of belief distortion due to oversampling of representative types from memory accounts for many biases associated with representativeness, including the conjunction fallacy and base rate neglect. We next explain the logic of this result.

Representativeness and the Conjunction Fallacy

Begin with the Linda experiment. Our explanation of this puzzle builds on the intuition that subjects do not assess option 1, "Linda is a bank teller," as an abstract logical statement. They instead fill in details from memory, and the filling is tainted by representativeness.

When thinking about the broad category "bank teller," subjects recall specific bank tellers who may differ in their political orientation. For instance, they could be "feminist" or "nonfeminist." Here the type is $T = \{$ feminist, nonfeminist$\}$, the group that is assessed is $G = $ bank teller, while the comparison group includes other occupations Linda might have, such as $-G = $ social worker or school teacher. Critically, when thinking about bank tellers, the type "feminist" faces strong interference. The "feminist" type is arguably more strongly associated with other candidate occupations, such as social worker, implying a low likelihood ratio:

$$\frac{Pr(\,feminist \mid bank\ teller)}{Pr(\,feminist \mid social\ worker)}.$$

In contrast, the "nonfeminist" type faces much lower interference because nonfeminists are relatively more prevalent among bank tellers, implying a high likelihood ratio:

$$\frac{Pr(nonfeminist \mid bank\ teller)}{Pr(nonfeminist \mid social\ worker)}.$$

Interference implies that the category "bank teller" is represented with its stereotypical nonfeminist type. The possibility that "bank teller" includes the feminist types is forgotten. As a result, subjects assess option 1 by judging the probability of Linda, with her radical past, being a "nonfeminist bank teller." The true probability of this narrow event is of course very low, and lower than the probability of Linda being "a feminist bank teller." Subjects commit the conjunction fallacy because representativeness causes them to represent option 1 in a stereotyped way.

Representativeness and Base Rate Neglect

Consider next base rate neglect. Once again, our model delivers this phenomenon very naturally through the logic of selective recall. Formally, doctors assess $T = \{healthy, sick\}$ in the group of positively tested patients $G = +$. The test is assessed in the context of patients who have not been subject to it ($-G = untested$). By equation (5.2), then, when primed with the positive test result $G = +$, the "sick" type is representative if and only if:

$$\frac{Pr(T = sick \,|\, G = +)}{Pr(T = sick \,|\, -G = untested)} > \frac{Pr(T = healthy \,|\, G = +)}{Pr(T = healthy \,|\, -G = untested)},$$

which holds if and only if the test is even minimally informative of health status. When the test is informative, sick types are relatively more prevalent among patients who tested positive. This makes "sick" representative after a positive test. The resulting judgment is particularly inaccurate if the disease is rare. In this case, the most likely outcome is that the patient is healthy, even after a positive test. But this type faces strong interference, because healthy patients are even more prevalent among untested people. As the positive test brings "sick" to mind, the doctor inflates its probability relative to the truth.

In the rest of the chapter, we show how the same logic can be applied to belief distortions in finance, including neglected risk, extrapolation, and overreaction to news. To motivate the transition to finance, we first illustrate how the logic of representativeness can be applied to the analysis of stereotypes of social groups. The discussion stresses the generality and broad applicability of the representativeness-based model of judgment.

Representativeness and Social Stereotypes

As we show in BCGS (2016a), our model offers a foundation for stereotypes as described in social psychology. In the words of Hilton and Von Hippel (1996), stereotypes are "mental representations of real differences between groups . . . allowing easier and more efficient processing of information. Stereotypes are selective, however, in that they are localized around group features that are the most distinctive, that provide the greatest differentiation between groups, and that show the least within-group variation."

These traits of stereotypes arise naturally from the principle of selective recall in which representative population members are overweighted while unrepresentative ones are underweighted or forgotten. One key property of this theory is that, in line with social psychology, stereotypes are mental representations of *real* differences. The example of the red-haired Irish illustrates this point: The frequency of red hair is inflated because this hair color is in reality much more prevalent among the Irish than in the rest of the world. This idea that stereotypes exaggerate real differences between groups is referred to as "the kernel of truth."

Using data from the Moral Foundations Questionnaire of Graham, Nosek, and Haidt (2012), BCGS (2016a) show that the kernel of truth principle helps shed light on beliefs about members of political parties in the United States. In particular, survey respondents (both liberals and conservatives) universally exaggerate the polarization of the views between liberals and conservatives relative to true differences.

In BCGS (2016b), we conduct a laboratory experiment in which men and women answer trivia questions in different domains, some of which are generally viewed as female gendered (art) and others as male gendered (sports). We assess both the subjects' performance in different domains and beliefs about the performance of others. The same kernel of truth principle characterizes beliefs about gender as well: The confidence held by men and women about their own ability and the ability of others in different domains exaggerates real performance differences between genders. Compared to men, women are under-confident relative to their own true ability in domains where men on average do better. Likewise, when judging others, men are perceived to be better than they really are in male-gendered domains and worse than they really are in female-gendered domains. In this sense, our theory allows us to characterize distortions on the basis of the measurable reality.

In the Bordalo, Gennaioli, La Porta, and Shleifer (2017) example of analyst expectations described in chapter 4, we saw the same phenomenon: Analysts react in the right direction about extremely good performance news, but too strongly relative to Bayesian norms. The kernel of truth appears to be a fairly universal property of beliefs across extremely diverse domains and types of respondents.

Representativeness and Beliefs in Finance

We now apply representativeness to modeling beliefs about future cash flows, such as a portfolio of mortgages or mortgage-backed securities (MBS), in the setting of chapter 3. The kernel of truth logic allows us to view phenomena usually considered separate, such as neglected risk and extrapolation, in a coherent and unified way. We also analyze debt issuance, leaving a complete dynamic model with security prices and investment (but not fire sales) to chapter 6.

In the context of the model of chapter 3, the most natural way to formulate diagnostic beliefs is to think in terms of information arriving about the future payoff on mortgages $\tilde{X}$. Market participants observe developments in the economy, in the financial sector, and in policy, and revise their beliefs about $\tilde{X}$ accordingly. This setting is similar to the medical test example, in which representativeness affects how beliefs react to information (the medical test) relative to a baseline condition (the untested patients). And just as in the medical test example, interference is at play. Future mortgage payoffs that are likely both after the news and under the baseline conditions are interfered with and hence underweighted. In contrast, future mortgage payoffs $\tilde{X}$ that are disproportionately more likely after the news relative to the baseline conditions are quickly recalled and hence overweighted in beliefs.

These ideas can be formalized as follows. At $t=0$, before issuing safe debt, the true distribution of the intermediary's future cash flow from mortgages is $f(\tilde{X}\,|\,I_0)$. It is conditional on the information set I_0 held at the time of issuance $t=0$, which includes news about housing prices, future economic conditions, the effectiveness of securitization, and so on. These initial conditions are compared to those prevailing in the previous period, say $t=-1$, characterized by the information I_{-1}. This formulation captures a normal state of affairs in which the housing market is growing but not yet booming and banks are not yet embracing securitization. The true conditional distribution in this baseline state is denoted by $f(\tilde{X}\,|\,I_{-1})$.

Consider how representativeness is applied to this setup. The object of inference T is the cash flow $\tilde{X}$. To make the parallel transparent, in the medical test example the object of inference T was the health status of the patient. The target distribution that agents seek to represent is $f(\tilde{X}|I_0)$. That is, the group assessed by investors is the set of future cash flow realizations sharing the same news, $G = I_0$. In the medical test example, the assessed group was similarly the set of health status types sharing the same positive test outcome, $G = +$. Finally, in the current setting the comparison group is specified by the previous period $t = -1$, which pins down the group of cash flows sharing the same past normal conditions $-G = I_{-1}$. Likewise, in the medical test the comparison group was identified by the health status types before the test is taken, $-G = untested$. In chapter 6 we show how these groups arise naturally in a dynamic setting with recurrent information arrival.

We can apply equation (5.2) mechanically to this setup. The representativeness of a certain future cash flow realization $\tilde{X}$ at $t = 0$ is given by:

$$R(\tilde{X}, I_0) = \frac{f(\tilde{X}|I_0)}{f(\tilde{X}|I_{-1})}.$$

The most representative cash flows in light of I_0 are those whose likelihood has increased the most on the basis of recent news. The least representative cash flows are those whose likelihood has decreased the most on the basis of recent news. For instance, growth of home prices increases the probability that mortgage repayments will be high, causing high cash flows to become more representative and low cash flows unrepresentative.

By equation (5.3), the distorted density of cash flow $\tilde{X}$ is given by:

$$f^\theta(\tilde{X}|I_0) = f(\tilde{X}|I_0)\left[\frac{f(\tilde{X}|I_0)}{f(\tilde{X}|I_{-1})}\right]^\theta Z. \tag{5.4}$$

Cash flow realizations that have become more likely in light of news are overweighted, while cash flow realizations that have become less likely are underweighted. Note again the effect of interference: Cash flow realizations highly likely under normal times I_{-1} face strong interference. They are unrepresentative and hence underweighted, even if they are quite likely under current conditions I_0. In contrast, cash flow realizations that are much more likely under current conditions than in the past face little interference. They are highly representative and hence overweighted, even if they are quite unlikely in absolute terms.

In this way, shifting representativeness shapes reaction to news. Favorable news about housing markets enhances the perceived probability $f^\theta(\tilde{X}|I_0)$ of high payoffs from mortgages in two ways. First, it makes such good return objectively more likely, increasing $f(\tilde{X}|I_0)$. Second, it makes the same high payoff more representative, facilitating its recall. The second effect, captured by the term in square brackets in equation (5.4), boosts expectations even further. This boost is responsible for overreaction to news that is central to our findings.

Equation (5.4) yields convenient closed-form solutions when the target and comparison distribution belong to the same exponential or power class. In particular, suppose that $\tilde{X}$ is lognormally distributed. We then obtain the following result:

Proposition 5.1. *Suppose that* $\ln\tilde{X}|I_0 \sim N(\mu_0,\sigma_0^2)$ *and* $\ln\tilde{X}|I_{-1} \sim N(\mu_{-1},\sigma_{-1}^2)$. *Then, provided* $(1+\theta)\sigma_{-1}^2 - \theta\sigma_0^2 > 0$, *the distorted density* $f^\theta(\tilde{X}|I_0)$ *is also lognormal with mean* $\mu_0(\theta)$ *and variance* $\sigma_0^2(\theta)$ *given by:*

$$\mu_0(\theta) = \mu_0 + \frac{\theta\sigma_0^2}{\sigma_{-1}^2 + \theta(\sigma_{-1}^2 - \sigma_0^2)}(\mu_0 - \mu_{-1}), \qquad (5.5)$$

$$\sigma_0^2(\theta) = \sigma_0^2 \frac{\sigma_{-1}^2}{\sigma_{-1}^2 + \theta(\sigma_{-1}^2 - \sigma_0^2)}. \qquad (5.6)$$

When the true target and comparison distributions are lognormal, the distorted distribution is also lognormal, but with distorted mean and variance. We call "diagnostic" the mean and variance obtained by over-weighting representative states, because they overemphasize diagnostic news. When $\theta = 0$, diagnostic beliefs coincide with rational expectations: The mean in equation (5.5) and the variance in equation (5.6) are assessed correctly.

When instead representative future cash flows are oversampled from memory, $\theta > 0$, diagnostic beliefs are distorted. The diagnostic mean in equation (5.5) is inflated relative to the true mean, $\mu_0(\theta) > \mu_0$, if and only if there is good news of higher average cash flow, $\mu_0 > \mu_{-1}$. Likewise, the diagnostic variance in equation (5.6) is lower relative to the true variance, $\sigma_0^2(\theta) < \sigma_0^2$, only after good news for reduced cash flow volatility, $\sigma_0^2 < \sigma_{-1}^2$.

Proposition 5.1 illustrates the kernel of truth logic: The diagnostic mean and variance move in the direction of news, but too much. Because diagnostic beliefs specify a distribution over the entire outcome range, they can also be used to describe perception of downside risk. The diagnostic lognormal distribution of proposition 5.1 implies the following.

Proposition 5.2. *Agents neglect downside risk in the sense of definition 3.1 if and only if cash flow volatility has not increased relative to the past, $\sigma_0^2 \leq \sigma_{-1}^2$. When this is the case, diagnostic beliefs neglect downside risk below the threshold $\underline{X}$ given by:*

$$\underline{X} = \mu_0 + \theta \varphi \left(\frac{\sigma_{-1}}{\sigma_0} \right) (\mu_0 - \mu_{-1}), \qquad (5.7)$$

where $\varphi(\cdot)$ is a positive function that decreases in σ_{-1} / σ_0 such that

$$\lim_{\frac{\sigma_{-1}}{\sigma_0} \to 1} \varphi \left(\frac{\sigma_{-1}}{\sigma_0} \right) = +\infty.$$

A necessary condition for the appearance of neglected downside risk is that at $t=0$, cash flow variance has not increased relative to the past. A more volatile environment would render extreme realizations very representative and hence overweighted, including those in the left tail.

We can use proposition 5.2 to illustrate neglect of downside risk during the mid-2000s. To do so, we first abstract from changes in volatility by assuming that $\sigma_0^2 = \sigma_{-1}^2$. In this case, equation (5.7) implies that neglect of downside risk arises if and only if good news about average cash flow is received at $t=0$, with $\mu_0 > \mu_{-1}$.[1]

This condition captures salient features of the U.S. economy in the mid-2000s. Sustained economic growth after the 2001 recession, an accommodative monetary policy, and the continuing increase in home prices all brought good news about the expected return from real estate investments $\mu_0 > \mu_{-1}$. In our model, these developments have two effects. In line with proposition 5.1, they encourage excessive optimism about average cash flow of mortgages, $\mu_0(\theta) > \mu_0$. In line with proposition 5.2, they also cause neglect of downside risk. This mechanism can jointly account for the exaggerated expectations about home price growth, as in the data from Case, Shiller, and Thompson (2012), and for the neglect of downside risk in the housing market documented in figure 2.1. The reduced form model of chapter 3 did not tie neglect of downside risk and overly optimistic expectations to prevailing economic conditions. Diagnostic expectations establish this link, which depends on the true cash flow distribution.

---

1. In this case, one can show that $\underline{X}$ in equation (5.7) diverges to $+\infty$. As a result, under these special conditions one obtains a version of definition 3.1 of neglected risk in chapter 3, where the believed density first order stochastically dominates the true one.

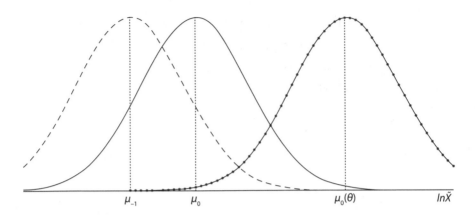

μ_{-1} μ_0 $\mu_0(\theta)$ $ln\tilde{X}$

FIGURE 5.1. Cash Flow Distributions under Rational and Diagnostic Expectations.

Figure 5.1 illustrates the intuition for this result. The central curve is the true cash flow distribution at $t=0$. The left curve is the true cash flow distribution before good news is received at $t=-1$. The representativeness of a given cash flow is the ratio of the central to the left distribution at this cash flow. Intuitively, the arrival of good news shifts the true cash flow distribution to the right, increasing the probability of high cash flows and reducing that of low cash flows. High cash flows become more representative and more heavily weighted in expectations than low ones. The right curve then captures the resulting diagnostic distribution: It shifts to the right relative to the truth, featuring both an inflated mean and a thinner left tail.

The initial chapters highlighted another important development in the mid-2000s, the growth of insurance mechanisms such as the pooling of mortgages and their distribution across investors. As we showed in chapter 3, this innovation amounts to reducing cash flow risk by diversifying idiosyncratic risk. Banking-sector risks in this period were also reduced by financial engineering and a less volatile economic environment, the Great Moderation.

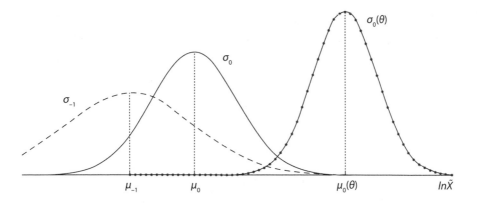

$\sigma_0(\theta)$

σ_0

σ_{-1}

μ_{-1} μ_0 $\mu_0(\theta)$ $ln\tilde{X}$

FIGURE 5.2. Perceived Safety of Cash Flows with Rational and Diagnostic Expectations.

In our model, these changes are captured by the case in which not only the average cash flow improves, but also volatility declines, $\sigma_0^2 < \sigma_{-1}^2$.[2] This has two effects. First, in line with proposition 5.1, the decline causes an exaggerated perception of cash flow safety, $\sigma_0^2(\theta) < \sigma_0^2$. Second, in line with proposition 5.2, it reinforces neglect of downside risk by reducing even further the weight attached to the left tail in beliefs. The kernel of truth logic exacerbates the neglect of downside risk: Insurance mechanisms expand, but their effect exaggerates the perception of safety. This also helps to account for the neglect of downside risk in housing, as reported in figure 2.1.

Figure 5.2 describes the joint effects of good news about cash flow mean $\mu_0 > \mu_{-1}$ and variance $\sigma_0^2 < \sigma_{-1}^2$. After the news, the true cash flow distribution (the middle curve) moves to the right and becomes tighter than the original cash flow distribution (the left curve). Due to the

---

2. The model of pooling in chapter 3 yields exactly this setting by assuming that both the common cash flow factor $\tilde{X}$ and the idiosyncratic noise ϵ are lognormally distributed.

actual reduction in risk, cash flows on both the right and left tails become less likely and hence less representative. Both the right and left tails are then neglected, reducing the perceived variance.[3] Due to the higher mean, however, left-tail cash flows become especially unlikely. This effect inflates the mean of the diagnostic distribution. The end beliefs are the rightmost curve, which exhibits an exaggerated increase in the mean and an exaggerated reduction in the variance relative to the truth.

In sum, diagnostic expectations offer an account for precrisis beliefs described in chapter 2 as a function of underlying fundamentals. In this account, optimistic expectations and neglect of downside risk are not universal features of beliefs. Rather, they are a product of economic conditions and of the psychology of representativeness. Under different economic conditions, different outcomes emerge. For instance, propositions 5.1 and 5.2 imply that bad cash flow news $\mu_0 < \mu_{-1}$ induces excess pessimism and exaggeration of downside risk, and the latter effect is reinforced by an increase in volatility $\sigma_0^2 > \sigma_{-1}^2$. Increases in risk during bad economic conditions cause an exaggerated perception of the left tail, inducing an overweighing of left tail risk. In this precise sense, our model predicts when tail risks are overweighted or neglected depending on economic conditions. These predictions naturally follow from the kernel of truth logic, which generates biases in beliefs shaped by fundamentals. As we show next, due to this feature, our model can account for beliefs both during the quiet period in 2007–2008 and after Lehman.

---

3. This case yields the GSV modeling shortcut (Gennaioli, Shleifer, and Vishny 2012) that all low probability cash flows are neglected. When the mean does not change and the variance shrinks, tail risk is neglected but mean beliefs are correct. This is one example in which neglect of risk and optimism about average conditions do not go hand in hand.

Debt Issuance and the Pre-Lehman Quiet Period

It is helpful at this point to look at AAA debt issuance in the setting of chapter 3, which helps us account for financial market outcomes around the crisis. As in chapter 3, we denote the equilibrium issuance of safe debt attained under distorted beliefs by N_0^θ. Under the lognormal distribution of proposition 5.1, we obtain the following result.

Proposition 5.3. *Denote by $z^* < 0$ the δ^*-percentile under a standard normal distribution. With diagnostic expectations, the AAA constraint takes the form:*

$$lnN_0^\theta = \mu_0(\theta) + \sigma_0(\theta)z^*. \tag{5.8}$$

In equilibrium, safe debt issuance is excessive if $\mu_0 > \mu_{-1}$ and $\sigma_0^2 < \sigma_{-1}^2$.

Excess debt issuance and thus hidden risks in the financial sector are particularly severe when two changes occur at the same time: Mean conditions improve and expected cash flow volatility declines.[4] Equation (5.8) captures these effects. When market participants perceive a higher mean and a lower variance, they are optimistic about the average return on mortgages and they neglect tail risk. As a result, they are willing to absorb a larger supply of debt N_0^θ.

Good economic news and financial innovation such as pooling of risks led investors before 2007 both to hold optimistic expectations and to neglect downside risks, as captured by the inflated mean $\mu_0(\theta)$ and a deflated variance $\sigma_0(\theta)$. These beliefs in turn supported the massive issuance of AAA-rated securitized debt that we documented in chapter 1.

---

4. The condition is only sufficient. Debt issuance can be excessive even if mean cash flows increase enough relative to volatility or if volatility decreases enough relative to cash flows.

At the same time, our model can account for the initial tremors of 2007 and the continued neglect of downside risks until Lehman. The deflation of the housing bubble, which was already apparent in the summer of 2007, caused a reduction in the mean future cash flow μ_0. This bad news reduced or reversed the initial excess optimism $\mu_0(\theta)$ about mean conditions. It thus reduced the market's willingness to absorb AAA-rated MBS and tightened the AAA constraint in equation (5.8). As we saw in chapter 1, new issuance of asset-backed commercial paper (ABCP) came to a halt, but the bad shock was dealt with successfully through extremely effective liquidity interventions by the Fed. As we saw in figure 1.7, these policies prevented the initial tremors from turning into a full-blown crisis.

The quieting down of markets that followed can be explained by continued neglect of downside risk due to an exaggerated perception of safety $\sigma_0(\theta)$. Markets still felt securitization was working so that banks were not so exposed to risk, and the Fed stood ready to help out the financial sector. Investors' belief in low risk to the financial system remained in place. Even assuming that by early 2008 investors held realistic expectations about home price growth μ_0, they still held an excessive faith in insurance mechanisms such as pooling of risks, financial engineering, and Fed interventions. In fact, the Fed itself might have felt calmer in this respect precisely because the interventions were so successful. Diagnostic expectations account for the believed stability during 2007–2008 because they allow us to separate neglected tail risk from optimism about mean conditions or extrapolation.

Why, then, was Lehman so devastating? We see the bankruptcy of Lehman as news about risk σ_0. This news only needed to be significant enough to make a financial meltdown representative. Put differently, after seeing Lehman collapse, market participants realized that the entire financial system was vulnerable. It was exposed to severe systemic risk, and the government was not ready to save it. Fire sales and asset price dislocations were massive, and much stronger than investors expected, because the pooling of risks exposed the entire financial sector to the same neglected risk. The debunking of the "diversification myth" destroyed the excessive confidence in risk management. The failure of Lehman showed that a black swan event was not only possible but actually representative, so that diagnostic beliefs exaggerated the assessment of risk $\sigma_0(\theta)$. Even if the objective probability of witnessing a total financial meltdown remained low, as massive government bailouts would have followed, the perception of systemic risk turned extreme. This perception became a lethal shock to a system built entirely on the manufacture of safe assets from risky collateral. In equation (5.8), an increase in perceived variance has drastic consequences for such assets, which are characterized by a very low δ^* and hence a very negative z^*.

When bad states become representative, as they do after news pointing to black swan events, even investors holding AAA assets perceive large risks, encouraging liquidation. In this sense, diagnostic beliefs accelerate fire sales and price collapses during crises. This mechanism is different from the specification in chapter 3, in which we assumed that at some point neglect of risk just disappeared and market participants became rational. The same psychology that generates excess optimism and financial sector overexpansion in the precrisis period also accounts for a slow reaction to bad news and can magnify fragility during the crisis, when neglected risks are laid bare. Consistent with this view, we saw in figure 4.12 that right after Lehman forecasts of credit spreads were too pessimistic.

Overreaction to crises in the form of strong risk aversion is a recurrent theme in theories of financial fragility (e.g., Caballero and Simsek 2013). This phenomenon is typically explained by assuming that crises create ambiguity and that investors are ambiguity averse (Gilboa and

Schmeidler 1989; Hansen and Sargent 2001). An alternative account is that the flight to safety that we saw, for example, in figure 1.6 is due to the representativeness heuristic, which contributes both to an over-expansion of the financial sector during booms and an excess contraction during crises. This mechanism is at the heart of our analysis of credit cycles in chapter 6.

Summary

This chapter shows that our model, built from general assumptions on selective memory and recall, offers a unified account of beliefs around 2007 and 2008. The kernel of truth logic of diagnostic beliefs can help explain why before the summer of 2007 there was both neglected downside risk and optimism about average future conditions, why between 2007 and 2008 optimism about average future conditions went down but neglect of downside risk remained, and finally why after the failure of Lehman Brothers downside risk was no longer neglected, and if anything exaggerated, leading to massive fire sales.

These dynamics cannot all be accounted for by using ad hoc modeling approaches that incorporate a single bias such as neglect of downside risk or mechanical extrapolation of mean conditions. The model of chapter 3 accounts for beliefs before 2007 but cannot explain why it took markets so long before recognizing financial sector risks or excessive pessimism after Lehman. Excessive pessimism during crises is typically explained with some form of uncertainty or ambiguity aversion, but this cannot in turn explain why market participants were so overly optimistic before 2007. Mechanical extrapolation of housing prices also has a hard time fitting the evidence: It does not yield neglect of downside risk in general, and in particular before Lehman, when it became clear that the real estate bubble had started to deflate.

Diagnostic beliefs accommodate different features of the data precisely because they adjust to new economic arrangements. For instance, neglect of risk changes with the use of risk-reducing financial innovations, such as securitization. By exaggerating their insurance benefits, market participants neglect the extent to which these arrangements expose everyone to the same risk. As a consequence, they neglect the extent of fire sales when left-tail events become representative. This general logic can also account for the evidence on fragility following the introduction of financial innovations such as portfolio insurance and index options (Coval, Pan, and Stafford 2014).

This chapter also shows that diagnostic beliefs are not just a modeling strategy designed to explain the boom-bust episode culminating in the 2008 crisis but have a deeper foundation and broader applicability. They can account for classical laboratory puzzles on judgment under uncertainty, as well as shed light on social stereotypes. Such cross-context applicability suggests that the model captures a broad psychological force.

In chapter 6 we show that the same model can be used to shed light on the systematic evidence of belief distortions presented in chapter 4, where we argued that extrapolation is systematic. Market participants regularly extrapolate in dynamic contexts, when repeated observations of stock returns, firms' earnings, house prices, and credit spreads are available. Credit markets regularly experience boom-bust cycles, even though most are not as dramatic as the one in 2008. Diagnostic beliefs can deal with fully dynamic environments and incorporate overreaction to information, offering a theory for credit and investment cycles. This provides an additional step of putting extrapolation on a more solid psychological foundation.

CHAPTER 6

Diagnostic Expectations and Credit Cycles

D iagnostic beliefs can account for the evidence on survey expectations and credit cycles, which were both presented in chapter 4. It is worth rehearsing the salient facts.

With respect to expectations, we saw a common thread across different domains: extrapolation from the recent past. Expectations of aggregate stock returns by both professionals and unsophisticated investors are too optimistic when recent returns have been high. Expectations of a firm's earnings growth, especially in the long term, by both professional analysts and by the firm's own CFO, are too optimistic when recent earnings have been high (in levels or growth rates). Analysts' expectations of future earnings actually exhibit a kernel of truth property: After good past performance, it is objectively more likely that the firm is a superstar, but analysts exaggerate this likelihood. Finally, analysts expect future credit spreads to be too low when current spreads are low, again extrapolating recent conditions into the future.

In this chapter we show that diagnostic expectations generate such extrapolative behavior because they entail overreaction to information. To do so, we draw on results from Bordalo, Gennaioli, and Shleifer (BGS

2018) and Bordalo, Gennaioli, La Porta, and Shleifer (BGLS 2017). Once again, the driving force is the kernel of truth logic: In dynamic environments, beliefs change on the basis of news, but representativeness amplifies this response. As a foundation of the kernel of truth, representativeness reconciles the qualitative features of beliefs around 2008, and in particular neglect of risk, with repeated extrapolation of recent conditions. We show that this approach fits the survey evidence considerably better than the more conventional models of mechanically adaptive expectations.

The ability of the model to explain fluctuations in expectations, and in particular to generate excess volatility of beliefs, also sheds light on credit cycle facts. As we discussed in chapter 4, there is growing evidence that rapid credit expansions forecast declines in real economic activity (e.g., Schularick and Taylor 2012; Mian, Sufi, and Verner 2017). Parallel findings emerge from the examination of credit markets. Greenwood and Hanson (2013) show that credit quality of corporate debt issuers deteriorates during credit booms and that a high share of risky bonds in total bond issuance forecasts low, and even negative, corporate bond returns. That paper uses a model of representativeness related to Barberis, Shleifer, and Vishny (1998) to explain its findings. López-Salido, Stein, and Zakrajšek (LSZ 2017) find that low credit spreads, a strong correlate of the high risky share, predict both a rise in credit spreads and low economic growth afterward.

These boom-bust dynamics can be generated by overreaction of expectations to good news and subsequent predictable reversals. In this spirit, we present a model developed by BGS (2018) that introduces diagnostic expectations into an otherwise standard economy with borrowing and lending. This model yields many of the credit cycle facts, including systematic reversals in spreads and risky debt share, predictability of bond returns, and investment cycles. Critically, this model also matches the evidence on systematic extrapolative errors by market participants, particularly in predicting credit market outcomes such as spreads. This is not the case for rational expectations models or even for some leading alternatives (such as rational inattention), suggesting that fluctuations in expectations due to overreaction to news may be an important determinant of credit cycles.

Representativeness, Overreaction, and Extrapolation

To begin, we describe diagnostic expectations for a basic stochastic process. In the next section, "Diagnostic Expectations and Credit Cycles," we incorporate these expectations into a dynamic model economy with borrowing and lending. Time is infinite, and at each date $t = 0, 1, \ldots$, the decision maker is forecasting a variable $\hat{X}_{t+1}$ that follows an AR(1) process with persistence parameter ρ:

$$\hat{X}_{t+1} = \rho \hat{X}_t + \epsilon_{t+1}, \tag{6.1}$$

where ϵ_{t+1} is an i.i.d. normal shock with mean zero and variance σ^2. For simplicity, we consider the case with a constant σ^2. This implies that the current analysis cannot yield the joint dynamics of beliefs about average conditions and risk considered in chapter 5.[1] Here $\hat{X}_{t+1}$ could capture a variety of economic indicators, such as the price of a financial

---

1. To capture the changes in volatility described in chapter 5, we can allow for stochastic volatility, but here we stick to a simpler formulation in which variance is constant.

asset (e.g., the S&P 500 index), the earnings of a firm, credit spreads, or a macroeconomic indicator such as inflation or GDP.

The rational expectation of $\hat{X}_{t+1}$ at time t is given by:

$$\mathbb{E}_t(\hat{X}_{t+1}) = \rho \hat{X}_t.$$

How does representativeness influence beliefs for $t+1$? Once again, we approach this dynamic setting from the vantage point of reaction to information, as in the medical test example. After observing news, the agent easily recalls representative outcomes that such news renders much more likely than in the past. These outcomes quickly come to mind and get overweighted in judgments. In contrast, the agent does not as easily recall unrepresentative outcomes that were also likely under past conditions. These outcomes are then underweighted in judgments.

Let us formally map this problem to the setting of chapter 5. Now the target variable T is the future realization $\hat{X}_{t+1}$. The group to be assessed is the set of these realizations sharing the same current state, $G = \hat{X}_t$. In this setting, the target distribution $h(t \mid G)$ is the true distribution $\hat{X}_{t+1}$ at time t, which is normal with mean $\rho \hat{X}_t$ and variance σ^2. Consider now the reference distribution $h(t \mid -G)$. As in chapter 5, the comparison group $-G$ is described by past conditions. To capture those, we use the state that would occur today in the absence of news, namely $\rho \hat{X}_{t-1}$.[2] Under this assumption, the comparison distribution $h(t \mid -G)$

---

2. Our results go through if, in equation (5.4) of chapter 5, the comparison distribution $h(t \mid -G)$ is taken to be the true conditional distribution of $\hat{X}_{t+1}$ at $t-1$. In this specification, the comparison distribution has higher variance than the target distribution $((1+\rho^2)\sigma^2 > \sigma^2)$. Thus, diagnostic beliefs also compress the variance of the true distribution. Despite this difference, the diagnostic expectation takes

is the true distribution of $\hat{X}_{t+1}$ conditional on the current state being $\rho\hat{X}_{t-1}$. This distribution is also normal, with mean $\rho^2\hat{X}_{t-1}$ and variance σ^2.

To gauge the implications of representativeness, denote by $f(\hat{X}_{t+1}|\cdot)$ the density of $\hat{X}_{t+1}$ conditional on the realized state at time t. The representativeness of $\hat{X}_{t+1}$ at time t is then captured by the likelihood ratio:

$$R(\hat{X}_{t+1}, t) = \frac{f(\hat{X}_{t+1}|\hat{X}_t)}{f(\hat{X}_{t+1}|\rho\hat{X}_{t-1})}. \qquad (6.2)$$

The most representative future states $\hat{X}_{t+1}$ are those whose true likelihood has increased the most on the basis of recent news. With normal distributions, the most representative states are in one of the two tails.[3] In equation (6.2), representativeness is shaped by the recent news received between $t-1$ and t. Because of slow memory decay, it may be more realistic to compare current conditions to a moving average of past realized

---

the form of equation (6.3) except that parameter θ is replaced by an increasing transformation $\hat{\theta}(\theta)$. We formally analyze this case in the proof of proposition 6.1.

3. The most representative realizations are in the tail because the normal distribution satisfies the monotone likelihood ratio property. This property captures the interference mechanism at play in the red-haired Irish example, where the least likely category "red hair" is most representative. Upon receiving good news, the current state $\hat{X}_t$ is above $\rho\hat{X}_{t-1}$. Thus, recall of the rational expectation $\rho\hat{X}_t$ is inhibited. In fact, this realization is also very likely with past information (i.e., at $\rho\hat{X}_{t-1}$). If $\rho > 0$, realizations in the right tail are recalled after good news because, while unlikely in absolute terms, they are now much more likely. Hence, their recall is not interfered with.

states, leading to a slow adaptation of the reference $-G$.[4] BGS (2018) show how our model can be extended to this case.

Because both the target and the comparison distributions are normal, proposition 5.1 can be applied. The diagnostic distribution is also normal, with distorted mean and variance. Proposition 6.1 characterizes diagnostic expectations in this dynamic setting.

Proposition 6.1. *The believed distribution at t for $\hat{X}_{t+1}$ is normal, with variance σ^2 and expectation:*

$$\mathbb{E}_t^\theta(\hat{X}_{t+1}) = \rho\hat{X}_t + \rho\theta(\hat{X}_t - \rho\hat{X}_{t-1}). \qquad (6.3)$$

Diagnostic expectations distort the rational expectation $\rho\hat{X}_t$ in the direction of current news $\hat{X}_t - \rho\hat{X}_{t-1}$. If the process is positively auto-correlated, $\rho > 0$, diagnostic expectations look extrapolative. After good news, the most representative states are those on the right tail, and expectations are too optimistic. After bad news, the most representative states are those on the left tail, and diagnostic expectations are too pessimistic. Extrapolation however is not universal. If the process exhibits a negative serial correlation, $\rho < 0$, diagnostic expectations exaggerate reversals of current conditions. This is yet another implication that distinguishes the kernel of truth from mechanical extrapolation.

The general and distinguishing property of diagnostic expectations, which holds regardless of ρ, is overreaction to information. One way to see this is to correlate the diagnostic forecast revision with the diagnostic forecast error. As argued by Coibion and Gorodnichenko (2015), the forecast revision is an empirically observable measure of news. Under rational expectations, news is optimally incorporated into forecasts, so

---

4. The memory-based intuition here is that news about the past realized states $\hat{X}_{t-s}$ are kept track of, and therefore integrated into a comparison distribution.

the correlation between forecast errors and forecast revisions should be zero. The same is true in models of rational inattention such as Sims (2003) and Woodford (2003), in which forecasters receive a noisy signal of the state but use it optimally.[5] In contrast, when forecasters overreact to news, the correlation between their forecast revisions and forecast errors should be negative.

Suppose in fact that the forecaster receives good news, so that the forecast revision $\mathbb{E}_t^\theta(\hat{X}_{t+1}) - \mathbb{E}_{t-1}^\theta(\hat{X}_{t+1})$ is positive. Overreaction then means that the forecaster is too optimistic, which implies that the forecast error $\hat{X}_{t+1} - \mathbb{E}_t^\theta(\hat{X}_{t+1})$ is negative on average. Underreaction to news implies conversely that forecast error and forecast revision should be positively correlated.

Formally, from equation (6.3) we can compute:

$$cov(\hat{X}_{t+1} - \mathbb{E}_t^\theta(\hat{X}_{t+1}), \mathbb{E}_t^\theta(\hat{X}_{t+1}) - \mathbb{E}_{t-1}^\theta(\hat{X}_{t+1})) = -\theta(1+\theta)\rho^2\sigma^2, \quad (6.4)$$

which is negative because individual forecasts overreact, $\theta > 0$. This is again due to the kernel of truth logic: Representativeness induces forecasters to recall extreme consequences of their information, causing overreaction. As in chapter 5, such overreaction in turn causes neglect of downside risk when news is good and exaggeration of downside risk when news is bad.

Because overreaction to information is a source of extrapolation, it can account for the evidence of chapter 4. Suppose that $\hat{X}_t$ captures the

---

5. As shown by Coibion and Gorodnichenko (2015), in models of rational inattention the forecast error of an individual forecaster should be uncorrelated with the forecast revision by that same forecaster. When different forecasters receive different noisy signals, however, the consensus forecast error is positively correlated with the consensus forecast revision.

current value of the stock market index and $\rho = 1$, in line with the random walk hypothesis. The investor's diagnostic expectation of the future stock index $\mathbb{E}_t^\theta(\hat{X}_{t+1})$ entails an assessment of future stock returns given by:

$$\mathbb{E}_t^\theta(\hat{X}_{t+1}) - \hat{X}_t = \theta(\hat{X}_t - \hat{X}_{t-1}).$$

In line with the survey evidence, past stock returns are projected into the future. Intuitively, current price growth makes high future prices representative, inflating their probability. Under rational expectations, with $\theta = 0$, this does not occur because returns are i.i.d.[6]

The overreaction of diagnostic expectations also yields the extrapolative features of firms' earnings forecasts discussed in chapter 4. Suppose that $\hat{X}_t$ is the current level of earnings in a given firm. The covariance of forecast errors with current earnings is then negative, in line with the evidence of chapter 4:

$$cov\left(\hat{X}_{t+1} - \mathbb{E}_t^\theta(\hat{X}_{t+1}), \hat{X}_t\right) = -\theta\rho\sigma^2, \tag{6.5}$$

because earnings are positively auto-correlated, $\rho > 0$. Intuitively, high current earnings are on average associated with good past news. Overreaction to such good news creates excessive optimism and hence negative forecast errors in the future. Overreaction and extrapolation both follow from the kernel of truth feature of judgment by representativeness.

This model can also account for the evidence on analyst expectations about individual firms and stock returns (BGLS 2017). Suppose that $\hat{X}_t$

---

6. As we previously discussed, one can have slow decay of past news with a slow moving $-G$ (see BGS 2018). Even in this case, diagnostic expectations differ from adaptive expectations due to their forward-looking nature.

is a given firm's earnings, which follow an AR(1) process. After receiving good news, high future earnings become objectively more likely and hence more representative compared to the past estimate. The probability that the firm is a future Google in the right tail is exaggerated, and its average future growth is inflated as well.[7]

Finally, diagnostic expectations generate systematic reversals of expectation errors. This feature plays an important role in accounting for credit cycles. To see this, consider the diagnostic beliefs held on average next period about $\hat{X}_{t+2}$:

$$\mathbb{E}_t[\mathbb{E}^\theta_{t+1}(\hat{X}_{t+2})] = \mathbb{E}_t(\hat{X}_{t+2}) = \rho^2 \hat{X}_t.$$

Because extrapolation emerges from overreaction to news, expectations errors systematically disappear in the future. Since *on average* there is no news in the future, expectations systematically revert to rationality, causing a failure of the law of iterated expectations. In a financial market context, this implies automatic correction of mispricing and predictability of returns.[8]

We can compare diagnostic expectations and adaptive expectations of the form:

$$\mathbb{E}^a_t(\hat{X}_{t+1}) = \hat{X}_t + \mu[\hat{X}_t - \mathbb{E}^a_{t-1}(\hat{X}_t)],$$

---

7. In BGLS (2017), we obtain similar results by modeling expectation formation as a signal extraction problem in which forecasters receive noisy signals of a firm's persistent future earnings potential.

8. The law of iterated expectations holds with respect to the diagnostic distribution, $\mathbb{E}^\theta_t[\mathbb{E}^\theta_{t+1}(\hat{X}_{t+2})] = \mathbb{E}^\theta_t(\hat{X}_{t+2})$, but it fails with respect to the true data-generating process, $\mathbb{E}_t[\mathbb{E}^\theta_{t+1}(\hat{X}_{t+2})] \neq \mathbb{E}^\theta_t(\hat{X}_{t+2})$.

which are frequently used to describe extrapolation. With adaptive expectations, a negative correlation between $\hat{X}_t$ and the future forecast error of equation (6.5) arises only for processes with low persistence, when $\mu > \rho$. In the data, however, we observe a negative correlation even for highly persistent variables such as interest rates (Bordalo, Gennaioli, Ma, and Shleifer 2018).

Furthermore, for mechanical adaptive expectations the serial correlation ρ of the data-generating process does not affect beliefs, which are only shaped by the fixed coefficient μ. In contrast to this prediction, Bordalo, Gennaioli, Ma, and Shleifer (2018) using professional forecast data, and Landier, Ma, and Thesmar (2017) using a lab experiment, show that expectations are systematically influenced by the true persistence ρ of the process.[9] In particular, Bordalo, Gennaioli, Ma, and Shleifer (2018) show that, for given current news, updating about future outcomes is more aggressive in macroeconomic series characterized by higher persistence ρ. This property does not arise under mechanical updating and lends support to the kernel of truth property of diagnostic expectations. As we already showed, in the extreme case of a negatively autocorrelated process with $\rho < 0$, diagnostic expectations imply that high levels of $\hat{X}_t$ should induce excessive pessimism. With mechanical adaptive expectations, in contrast, agents would be excessively optimistic in this context as well.

In sum, diagnostic expectations yield a psychologically founded theory of extrapolation based on selective memory. With representativeness-based thinking, good news causes agents to oversample good future states from memory, inducing excessive optimism. The reverse occurs

---

9. The Landier, Ma, and Thesmar (2017) paper cannot be directly mapped to our setting because the subjects do not know the true persistence ρ of the data-generating process and learn about it during the experiment.

after people get bad news. Overreaction to news parsimoniously accounts for several findings for financial markets, such as neglect or exaggeration of downside risk, extrapolation of past changes, predictability of forecast errors, and reversals in expectations. These properties are obtained from a theory that has explanatory power in different contexts such as laboratory experiments and social stereotypes.

Diagnostic Expectations and Credit Cycles

We now apply diagnostic expectations to investigate the properties of credit cycles documented in chapter 4. To this end, we incorporate the previous model of diagnostic expectations into a repeated economy with borrowing and lending, whose main features are taken from chapter 3. Compared to chapter 3, we allow for both safe and risky debt, where the latter stands for debt instruments that are significantly riskier than AAA, such as junk bonds. By so doing, we capture the dynamics of the so-called junk share, which plays a leading role in credit market facts. The second main departure from the model of chapter 3 is that we do not consider fire sales, and in particular we rule out re-trading of debt.

We first show that when this setting is repeated over many periods, the dynamics of debt issuance follow expectations-driven cycles that match the facts discussed in chapter 4. To account for additional facts about credit spreads and investment, we enrich the model with two standard ingredients: risk aversion (see "Cycles in Credit Spreads" later in this chapter) and production (see "Investment Cycles").

As in the model of chapter 3, there are two types of agents: borrowers and savers. Here we use broader terms than intermediaries and investors, because we want the model to describe credit cycles more broadly and not just the 2008 crisis. Borrowers play the same role as do the intermediaries in chapter 3: They are risk neutral, impatient—as captured by their low discount factor β_l—and issue debt against their future income. They could be firms borrowing against their future earnings or households borrowing against their future wages.

Savers, who play the same role as investors in chapter 3, are also risk neutral, but they are more patient than borrowers, as captured by a high discount factor $\beta_h > \beta_l$. Critically, savers have a preference for debt defaulting with probability less than δ^*, which captures their preferred habitat. Savers value debt that is either entirely safe or risky up to δ^* in a risk neutral way. Because we now consider risky debt such as junk bonds (and not AAA as in chapter 3), the threshold riskiness is higher—e.g., $\delta^* \approx 0.03$.

Beyond the level of risk δ^*, savers are much less willing to hold risky debt. Once again, we assume that they discount the risky debt's future cash flow by $\epsilon \beta_h$, with $\epsilon \ll 1$. In chapter 3, the parameter ϵ played an important role during fire sales episodes. Here, this parameter will not play as important a role because there is no re-trading of debt. Still, the preferred habitat δ^* continues to conveniently pin down the quantity of risky debt issued.

In each period $t = 0, 1, \ldots$, each borrower optimally issues N_t units of new debt. This debt matures in one period and has a face value of 1, so that N_t is the total face value promised at $t + 1$. At the same time, the borrower receives a perishable cash flow $\tilde{X}_t$, which he uses to pay off the N_{t-1} one-period debt issued in the previous period. As in chapter 3, the past N_{t-1} claims are paid with the current cash flows, while the currently issued N_t claims are pledged next period's cash flow $\tilde{X}_{t+1}$. If $\tilde{X}_t$ is insufficient to repay the past N_{t-1} claims, there is default and the losses are borne by savers. Savers buy debt using the endowment they receive in each period.

To capture cycles in the risk-composition of credit, we allow some borrowers to be completely safe and others to be risky (in chapter 3 all borrowers were risky). A share $s \in (0, 1)$ of borrowers is safe, while the remaining $1 - s$ are risky. Each safe borrower receives a deterministic cash flow equal to 1 in every period. Each risky borrower receives a stochastic cash flow, the logarithm of which follows the AR(1) process:

$$ln\tilde{X}_t = \rho ln\tilde{X}_{t-1} + \epsilon_t, \tag{6.6}$$

where ϵ_t is i.i.d. normal with mean zero and variance σ^2. To focus on aggregate conditions, we assume that risky cash flows are identical for all risky borrowers. By defining $\hat{X}_t = ln\tilde{X}_t$, we can apply to the risky cash flows the previous analysis of diagnostic expectations.

In every period, each safe borrower issues an amount $N_t^s = 1$ of debt that never defaults, adding up to a total measure s of safe debt. Each risky borrower, in turn, issues debt until the risk threshold δ^* is reached. Given the stochastic process for cash flow, denote by $f^\theta(\hat{X}_{t+1}|t)$ the diagnostic distribution at t of the logarithm of next period cash flow. By equation (6.6), $\hat{X}_{t+1}$ is normally distributed so that $f^\theta(\hat{X}_{t+1}|t)$ is also normal. Each risky borrower then issues N_t^θ claims implicitly defined by:

$$\int_{-\infty}^{lnN_t^\theta} f^\theta(\hat{X}_{t+1}|t)d\hat{X}_{t+1} = \delta^*.$$

In line with chapter 3, higher debt issuance means a higher probability of default. Debt is then issued until the probability of default is δ^*, so that debt can still be placed in the market. The total amount of risky debt issued at time t is equal to $(1-s)N_t^\theta$.

Using the diagnostic distribution of the future cash flows that we characterized in proposition 6.1, debt issuance satisfies the condition:

$$lnN_t^\theta = \mathbb{E}_t^\theta(\hat{X}_{t+1}) + \sigma z^*,$$

where $z^* < 0$ denotes the first δ^* quantile under the standard normal distribution. Using the expression for diagnostic expectations, one can compute that debt issuance at t is given by:

$$lnN_t^\theta = \rho\hat{X}_t + \rho\theta(\hat{X}_t - \rho\hat{X}_{t-1}) + \sigma z^*. \qquad (6.7)$$

Under diagnostic expectations, with $\theta > 0$, the issuance of risky debt overreacts to news. As the economy improves, $\hat{X}_t > \rho\hat{X}_{t-1}$, high future cash flows become representative in savers' minds and their probability is exaggerated, while the risk of low cash flows is neglected. This extrapolation of good news causes excessive issuance of risky debt. When in contrast bad news arrives, $\hat{X}_t < \rho\hat{X}_{t-1}$, low future cash flows become representative and their probability is exaggerated, leading to excessively low debt issuance.

This mechanism has important implications for debt dynamics. After some calculations, we can establish that, by equation (6.7), risky debt follows the law of motion:

$$lnN_t^\theta = (1-\rho)\sigma z^* + \rho lnN_{t-1}^\theta + \rho(1+\theta)\epsilon_t - \rho^2\theta\epsilon_{t-1}. \qquad (6.8)$$

Given that the quantity of safe debt issued is constant at s in each period, equation (6.8) describes the dynamics of i) total debt in the economy, as well as ii) the risky debt share, or "junk share," which is the share of risky debt in total debt.

Under rational expectations, with $\theta = 0$, the logarithm of the quantity of risky debt and the junk share evolve according to an AR(1) process with persistence ρ. Debt tracks fundamentals—namely, risky cash flows. Under diagnostic expectations, in contrast, fluctuations in savers' beliefs also influence total debt and the junk share, which follows an ARMA(1,1) process.

There are two departures from rational expectations. First, debt issuance overreacts to current news ϵ_t by a factor $\rho\theta$. This is the third term on the right side of equation (6.8). After good news, risky debt expands too much. After bad news, it contracts too much. Second, there is systematic reversal of past news ϵ_{t-1}: good news at $t-1$, and hence high issuance in the same period predicts a contraction of risky debt issuance at t. This is the last term on the right in equation (6.8). This correction does not reflect future bad news. It reflects the cooling off of current optimism.

More generally, equation (6.8) yields the following result.

Proposition 6.2. *Under diagnostic expectations $\theta > 0$, risky debt (and hence both total debt and the junk share) exhibits the following properties:*

i) It expands too much after good news, $cov\left(lnN_t^\theta, \epsilon_t\right) = \rho(1+\theta)\sigma^2$.

ii) It displays stronger reversals than fundamentals,

$$\frac{cov\left(lnN_t^\theta, lnN_{t-1}^\theta\right)}{var\left(lnN_{t-1}^\theta\right)} = \rho - \frac{\rho(1+\theta)\theta(1-\rho^2)}{[1+(1-\rho^2)\theta(2+\theta)]}.$$

iii) It is excessively volatile, $var\left(lnN_t^\theta\right) = \dfrac{\rho^2\sigma^2\left[1+(1-\rho^2)\theta(2+\theta)\right]}{1-\rho^2}.$

iv) Forecasts of future debt issuance are too optimistic after good news and too pessimistic after bad news, $\mathbb{E}_t\left[lnN_{t+1}^\theta - \mathbb{E}^\theta\left(lnN_{t+1}^\theta \mid t\right)\right] = -\rho^2\theta\epsilon_t.$

Our model captures the findings on credit cycles in Greenwood and Hanson (2013) and LSZ (2017), summarized in chapter 4. First, according to property *(i)* total debt expands after good news and contracts after bad news, due to fluctuations in expectations about future cash flows. The risky debt share mimics this pattern. Procyclicality of risky debt issuance obtains also under rational expectations (i.e., $\theta = 0$), but the pattern is stronger when $\theta > 0$ because expectations are revised more aggressively based on the news.

Second, as stated in property (*ii*), periods of debt expansion are followed by reversals. Mean reversion in debt issuance would also occur under rational expectations due to the stationarity of fundamentals, $\rho < 1$. This can be seen by noting that, with $\theta = 0$, we have:

$$\frac{cov\left(lnN_t^\theta, lnN_{t-1}^\theta\right)}{var\left(lnN_{t-1}^\theta\right)} = \rho < 1,$$

so that debt reverts to its long-run level. Because economic conditions are stationary, rational expectations of future conditions are also stationary, and debt issuance inherits this stationarity. Under diagnostic expectations, however, this mean reversion is stronger due to the fact that expectations errors get corrected on average. After good news, expectations of future conditions are too optimistic and debt issuance expands a lot. Because, on average, optimism cools off in the next period, expectations revert toward rationality, as described previously. This reversion of expectations errors causes strong reversion of future debt levels because it adds to fundamental mean reversion.

Third, as illustrated by property (*iii*), debt issuance is more volatile than is warranted by the fundamental shock ϵ_t alone. This is due to a combination of overreaction to incoming news and subsequent reversal. Both forces contribute to excess volatility.

Fourth, diagnostic expectations lead to systematic predictability of forecast errors. After good news, market participants become too optimistic about the future. As a result, they overpredict future debt issuance. After bad news, market participants become too pessimistic about the future, and underpredict future debt issuance.[10] This implication of

---

10. Although forecast errors are predictable, the average forecast error is zero (because the average shock ϵ_t is zero). In this sense, agents holding diagnostic expectations cannot be systematically fooled.

the model is consistent with the evidence on extrapolative errors of chapter 4. Just like excess volatility and excess reversals, it cannot be accounted for under rational expectations.

Procyclicality of risky debt issuance, strong mean reversion after financial booms, and overall excess volatility of financial conditions are consistent both with the evidence on U.S. credit markets and the international evidence on the debt cycles reviewed in chapter 4. In our model, these booms and busts are generated on the supply side: Savers' expectations become inflated in good times and are met with excess debt issuance, but then systematically deflate, leading to a bust.

Existing research recognizes the importance of credit supply shocks but typically models them in a reduced form way, by assuming, for instance, fluctuations in the risk premium demanded by lenders. This approach does not have a theory of where such fluctuations in risk premiums come from. For instance, a financial bust in this framework requires a sharp increase in risk premiums. However, it is not obvious what may account for such a shock since credit markets often revert in the absence of significant fundamental news. Diagnostic expectations offer a theory of a negative credit supply shock as a correction of initially overly optimistic expectations. They link the boom phase of a cycle with its eventual demise.

Another distinctive prediction of our model concerns the time-variation of realized returns on debt. The average realized return of risky debt issued at t is the average repayment at $t+1$, computed using the true distribution, divided by the debt's market price at t:

$$\frac{\mathbb{E}_t\left[min(\tilde{X}_{t+1}, N_t^\theta)\right]}{\beta_h \mathbb{E}_t^\theta\left[min(\tilde{X}_{t+1}, N_t^\theta)\right]}.$$

Proposition 6.3. *After positive news* $\epsilon_t > 0$ *the average realized return is lower than the riskless return* β_h^{-1}; *after negative news* $\epsilon_t < 0$ *it is higher than the riskless return* β_h^{-1}.

Under rational expectations, the average realized return of risky debt every period is given by its expected return, which is in turn equal to the riskless rate β_h^{-1}. This is due to the fact that, conditional on meeting the risk threshold δ^*, savers in our model are risk neutral. Under diagnostic expectations, this equivalence between the expected and the average realized return on debt breaks down. The expected return continues to be equal to the riskless rate β_h^{-1}, but the mean conditional realized return deviates from this benchmark due to errors in expectations.

After good news, savers are too optimistic. Although they expect to obtain the riskless return, they are on average disappointed and obtain less. After bad news, savers are too pessimistic. They are positively surprised on average and obtain more. This prediction of the model accounts for the finding of Greenwood and Hanson (2013) that the junk share negatively predicts the realized returns on risky debt (and that sometimes junk debt yields less than riskless debt). In our model, as in the data, in good times debt expands, the junk share is high, and the average return going forward is low. In bad times, debt contracts, the junk share is low, and the average return going forward is high.

In sum, diagnostic expectations generate cycles in the quantity of debt, in the junk share, and in realized returns that track those documented in the data. We have so far abstracted from the analysis of credit spreads. By assuming risk neutrality, we have not considered changes in spreads due to changes in the credit risk premium, defined as expected return differences between safe and risky debt. The next section extends the model to explore the behavior of credit spreads over time.

Cycles in Credit Spreads

We assume that savers have concave utility $u(c_t) = ln\ c_t$. They still exhibit preferred habitat preferences in that they are only willing to buy debt that is safer than δ^*, but they now value it according to their risk averse utility. The price of one unit of risky debt issued at time t and satisfying the preferred habitat condition is determined by the Euler equation:

$$P_t^r = \beta_h \mathbb{E}_t^\theta \left[min \left(\frac{\tilde{X}_{t+1}}{N_t^\theta}, 1 \right) \cdot \left(\frac{c_t}{c_{t+1}} \right) \right]. \qquad (6.9)$$

The price of one unit of safe debt is in turn given by:

$$P_t^s = \beta_h \mathbb{E}_t^\theta \left[\frac{c_t}{c_{t+1}} \right]. \qquad (6.10)$$

Since debt has a face value of 1, the price of each unit is equal to the inverse of the return required to hold it. The interest rate spread between risky and safe debt at time t can then be approximated by the difference between the prices of safe and risky debt from equations (6.9) and (6.10), or $P_t^s - P_t^r$.

To characterize the spread, we need to pin down the marginal utility of consumption of savers in equilibrium. The complication here is that savers' consumption depends on many factors, including risky and safe debt they bought in the past, debt they currently purchase, and their endowment. To make this analysis tractable, we take two shortcuts. First, we price assets by using the marginal utility of consumption of a fictitious representative agent who consumes a constant fraction α of the risky cash flow, $c_t = \alpha \tilde{X}_t$. This scenario would arise in an economy in which the supply of safe debt is negligible, $s \rightarrow 0$, and agents share their income so that consumption is proportional to the risky cash flow $\tilde{X}_t$.[11] This simplification allows us to keep the analysis tractable while preserving the standard intuition that the marginal utility of consumption falls as the state of the economy gets better.

The second simplifying assumption is that the supply of risky debt continues to be determined by the risk constraint, so that N_t^θ follows equation (6.8). In general, concave utility may affect the quantity of debt issued, but for simplicity we abstract from this effect.

Under these assumptions, we can characterize the behavior of the spread. We measure the spread as the natural logarithm of the excess price of one unit of safe debt $P_t^s - P_t^r$, and we analyze the dynamics of the deviation of this measure of the spread from its long-run value. We denote this variable by φ_t. We then obtain the following result.

Proposition 6.4. *The measure φ_t of the spread of risky debt issued at t satisfies the law of motion:*

$$\varphi_t = \rho\varphi_{t-1} + \rho^2\theta\epsilon_{t-1} - (\rho(1+\theta)-1)\epsilon_t. \tag{6.11}$$

Under diagnostic expectations, $\theta > 0$, the behavior of the spread—just like the behavior of the quantity of debt—is characterized by overreaction to current news and a future reversal. After good news $\epsilon_t > 0$ expectations are too optimistic. Provided economic conditions are persistent enough, $\rho(1+\theta) > 1$, the supply of capital expands too much,

---

11. Savers' consumption is equal to the payoff of the safe and risky debt bought in the past minus the expenditure incurred to purchase the newly issued debt. The assumption $s \to 0$ implies that consumption is only a function of the risky payoff, while the sharing rule implies that savers and borrowers bear the same income risk (which may arise due to the presence of a government redistributing income).

which inflates the price of risky debt. The spread falls more than it would under rational expectations, and the quantity of debt and the junk share overexpand. This is the credit boom phase. Subsequently, overreaction to good news systematically wanes. The cooling off of investor optimism increases the future spread and causes both the quantity of debt and the junk share to contract. This phenomenon is captured by the term $\rho^2 \theta \epsilon_{t-1}$ in equation (6.11).

The excess volatility of credit spreads obtained under diagnostic expectations offers an expectations-based account of the excess volatility documented by Collin-Dufresne, Goldstein, and Martin (2001). Systematic reversals of credit spreads documented by LSZ (2017) are also consistent with diagnostic expectations. Our model additionally matches the evidence on the predictability of errors in predicting credit spreads that we documented in chapter 4. The one-step-ahead predictable forecast error is given by:

$$\mathbb{E}_t \left[\varphi_{t+1} - \mathbb{E}_t^\theta (\varphi_{t+1}) \right] = \theta \rho (\rho(1+\theta) - 1) \epsilon_t,$$

where we continue to assume that the process is persistent enough, $\rho(1+\theta) > 1$.

After good times, when $\epsilon_t > 0$, the forecast error is positive, in the sense that market participants are excessively optimistic about the persistence of low spreads. This occurs because beliefs and credit markets are overheated. During bad times, when $\epsilon_t < 0$, the opposite error is made: Market participants are too pessimistic and are systematically surprised by the future reductions in the spread. These patterns line up with the errors made by professional forecasters when predicting credit spreads around Lehman and more generally with the evidence of extrapolation reported in chapter 4.

Investment Cycles

We next trace the implications of these results for investment and production, seeking to explain the LSZ (2017) facts from chapter 4. In addition to documenting mean reversion in credit spreads, which we have already discussed, LSZ show that such mean reversion predicts future economic growth. To account for this finding, we introduce production into our model. We use the extension from chapter 3 in which the cash flow of risky firms is produced from investment according to technology $\tilde{X}_t = A_t q(I_{t-1})$, where $q(I)$ is a concave Cobb Douglas production function $q(I) = I^\alpha$ with $\alpha \in (0, 1)$.

Because of time to build, current investment influences output the next period. For simplicity, the capital stock fully depreciates after one period. Production is affected by a contemporaneous productivity shock that follows an AR(1) process in logs:

$$lnA_t = \rho \, lnA_{t-1} + \epsilon_t.$$

Productivity shocks make cash flows stochastic, and for simplicity there is no safe production. Finally, we assume that savers and borrowers are very patient, $\beta_l = \beta_h = 1$. The only reason for issuing debt, then, is to raise revenues to invest, not to profit from creating savings vehicles for the more patient savers.

In this model, investment I_t is shaped by both demand and supply factors. On the demand side, borrowers are more eager to invest when expected productivity is high because their profits are higher. On the supply side, savers are willing to buy more debt when expected productivity is high because default is perceived to be less likely.

When borrowers' desired investment is lower than the maximum amount of debt that savers are willing to buy (i.e., when the δ^* constraint is not binding), the level of investment is determined by equating the expected marginal product of investment to one:

$$I_t = \left[\alpha e^{\mathbb{E}_t^{\theta}\left(\ln A_{t+1}\right)+\frac{\sigma^2}{2}} \right]^{\frac{1}{1-\alpha}}.$$

Optimal investment today increases in future expected productivity (the term in square brackets). When this investment level cannot be entirely financed by issuing debt, actual investment is determined by the total value of risky debt the firm can issue:

$$I_t = q(I_t)\int_0^{\frac{N_{t+1}^{\theta}}{q(I_t)}} A h_t^{\theta}(A) dA + N_{t+1}^{\theta}(1-\delta^*),$$

where the term on the right-hand side is the total debt payment that can be pledged to savers when the debt constraint is binding. Savers receive the face value N_{t+1}^{θ} if debt does not default, which occurs with probability $1-\delta^*$. They receive the entire cash flow (the integral) if default occurs. Because the debt constraint is binding, in this regime the total face value N_{t+1}^{θ} of issued debt is determined by the risk constraint $\int_0^{\frac{N_{t+1}^{\theta}}{q(I_t)}} h_t^{\theta}(A) dA = \delta^*$.

As we show in the appendix, the behavior of investment over time is similar in both cases, precisely because higher expected productivity increases both borrowers' desired investment level and savers' willingness to buy debt.

Proposition 6.5. *Within each of the two regimes described above, a linear approximation of investment around the steady state expected productivity* $\mathbb{E}_t^{\theta}(\ln A_{t+1})=0$ *yields the following law of motion:*

$$I_t \approx a_0(1-\rho) + \rho I_{t-1} - a_1\rho^2\theta\epsilon_{t-1} + a_1\rho(1+\theta)\epsilon_t, \qquad (6.12)$$

where a_0, a_1 *are positive constants.*

Just like the quantity of debt and credit spreads, productive investment exhibits boom-bust dynamics that are created by overreaction and reversal of expectations. The booms and busts in economic activity here mimic those documented by LSZ (2017). During good times, when spreads are low and the junk share is high, there is a boom in investment and production. This boom is followed by a systematic reversal of credit market conditions, with tightening of spreads and reduction in the junk share, which leads to a drop in investment and production two periods later. These output reversals also account for the finding by Mian, Sufi, and Verner (2017) that booms in household debt predict subsequent declines in GDP growth, as described in chapter 4.

In our model, this phenomenon is due to overreaction and the reversal in the optimism of firms (borrowers) and households (savers). Critically, these investment and production cycles are due to the combination of both demand and supply forces. On the demand side, good news about productivity increases the willingness to borrow. On the supply side, good news about productivity increases the willingness to lend because of the reduction in perceived default risk. On both sides of the market, overreaction implies that the investment boom is excessive and followed by a disappointing profitability of investment, in line with the waves in housing construction documented by Glaeser (2013) and in shipbuilding documented by Greenwood and Hanson (2015).

Summary

This chapter shows that a model of diagnostic expectations can account for the evidence of extrapolation in chapter 4, yielding a theory of credit cycles that mimics the booms and busts in the issuance of risky debt, the dynamics of credit spreads, as well as waves in investment and production. One important feature of this approach is its promise to match not only the quantity variables of interest, but also the beliefs that market participants hold.

The analysis has only one nonstandard ingredient: expectations that overreact to news. This is a natural by-product of the model of diagnostic expectations presented in chapter 5. It yields both extrapolative beliefs, which help account for excess expansions or contractions of credit, and systematic reversals in expectations, which help account for the documented reversals in spreads and economic activity. In this way, the model delivers a parsimonious theory of credit supply shocks that can explain why busts follow booms in prices, debt issuance, and investment even in the absence of bad fundamental shocks.

CHAPTER 7

Open Problems

The theme of this book is the centrality of beliefs and expectations for financial stability. We developed this theme in three related directions. First, we argued that expectations of investors, and in particular errors in expectations, are central to understanding the 2008 financial crisis, as well as credit cycles more generally. Second, we summarized considerable evidence that beliefs and expectations can be measured with survey data, and when they are, they exhibit systematic patterns of predictable errors inconsistent with the widely accepted view that expectations are rational. Third, we proposed a model of expectations, called diagnostic expectations, micro-founded using well-established features of human memory and judgment. We showed that this model can be used to account both for the central features of credit cycles and for several empirical findings about survey expectations.

In this chapter, we briefly summarize our findings along these three directions, but then turn to the many open problems that need to be solved. Our book is only an early step in the vast open agenda of studying beliefs and integrating them into mainstream economic analysis. Further explorations in these domains look extremely promising.

Understanding Credit Cycles

We began this book with a description of the 2008 financial crisis and argued that expectations of market participants are extremely helpful for understanding what happened. They shed light on the housing bubble whose deflation was the fundamental cause of the crisis; they account for the quiet period between the initial tremors in financial markets in the summer of 2007 and the Lehman bankruptcy; and they help us understand why this bankruptcy precipitated the meltdown of the financial system. Expectations during this period can be measured from surveys of professional and government forecasters, but also to some extent from speeches of government officials. The data on beliefs informs a story of the crisis broadly consistent with movements in financial markets and the real economy.

We also argued that in many critical respects, the 2008 crisis and the ensuing Great Recession were not exceptional. As demonstrated by extensive recent evidence, credit cycles are often preceded by periods of good economic news, financial bubbles, and credit expansions. These measurable periods of euphoria are characterized by low credit spreads between risky and safe debt and increases in the share of risky debt in total issuance. They are also consistently accompanied by optimistic expectations, yet systematically lead to disappointment. One can use indicators of euphoria to predict rising credit spreads, financial crises, and slowdowns in economic activity. Economists have returned to and confirmed the fundamental insights of Kindleberger (1978) and Minsky (1977) of credit overexpansions leading to crises, but with much better data.

In chapter 6, we presented an economic model of credit cycles in which the fundamental driving force is movement in expectations. To this end, we constructed a model of diagnostic expectations based on the representativeness heuristic that incorporates the kernel of truth principle:

People tend to overweight economic outcomes that become more likely in light of incoming data. We showed that when incorporated into a very standard dynamic macroeconomic model, diagnostic expectations deliver many of the stylized facts about credit cycles. These include periods of excessive optimism and credit expansion in response to good news, with neglected risk building up in credit markets, and predictable disappointment and economic slowdown afterward as investors learn that their optimism was excessive. The expectations in this model are not rational, but the model's predictions on the behavior of financial markets and the real economy, including the predictability of returns and real outcomes, are broadly consistent with the available evidence.

Our analysis of credit cycles remains incomplete in many important dimensions. Perhaps at the most basic level, our model is qualitatively consistent with broad credit cycle facts but is not yet at the level of full quantification. One important missing piece is the value of the parameter θ that controls how representativeness distorts the true probability distribution. In Bordalo, Gennaioli, and Shleifer (2018), we calibrated θ by matching the predictability of errors in credit spread forecasts from the model with the empirical counterpart computed from Blue Chip professional forecasts. In Bordalo, Gennaioli, La Porta, and Shleifer (2017), we calibrated θ to match predictability of errors in long-term earnings growth rate predictions of U.S.-listed firms with the empirical counterpart computed using actual forecasts by financial analysts. Despite the different market settings and data, the calibrated value of θ most consistent with the evidence on fundamentals, expectations, and returns falls in the range between 0.7 and 1.0. It remains an open question whether θ is shaped by some universal psychological force that makes it stable across contexts, or whether it will turn out to be context-specific.

The model we presented is highly stylized and omits at least four potentially important components. First, while diagnostic expectations lead to overreaction, we do not have a model of market bubbles per se. The most recent generation of expectations-based models of market bubbles still relies on mechanical extrapolation of past price trends (e.g., Barberis et al. 2018). A key feature of actual bubbles, stressed as far back as Kindleberger (1978), is that while they get started with overreaction to good fundamental news, they keep going through investor reaction to price increases themselves. This feature is not in our current model, in which people learn about the future exclusively from fundamental news. An important agenda item for research on diagnostic expectations is to consider a more realistic model in which investors learn from both fundamental news and market prices. This can perhaps lead to much more aggressive and long-lasting extrapolation than we have in chapter 6.

Second, the model of credit cycles we presented is entirely symmetric. After an initial overreaction to good news, beliefs and markets on average revert to reality. The data, however, point to an asymmetry in credit cycles, with credit expansions predicting with some accuracy deep and long-lasting crises, such as the one we saw in 2008. To deal with crises, we need to add financial frictions to the model in chapter 6. One way to do it is by incorporating some version of fire sales (along the lines of chapter 3), as we did in Bordalo, Gennaioli, and Shleifer (2018). Another way to make progress is to introduce financial frictions as a driver of real consequences of financial volatility, as demonstrated in the work of Bernanke (1983), Bernanke, Gertler, and Gilchrist (1999), and Kiyotaki and Moore (1997). These studies typically assume rational expectations, which we do not see as a realistic framework for studying credit cycles. Understanding the interaction between market participant expectations, financial frictions, and financial fragility remains a key open problem.

Third, our model has a very simple real sector, and more generally the book has stayed away from studying the business cycle consequences of nonrational beliefs. One aspect to this challenge is understanding the role of financial frictions. But expectation errors might also help account for other macroeconomic problems, such as sectoral spillovers. The 2008 crisis after all centered around the housing bubble and its deflation, which devastated the financial system as well as the households that borrowed to buy homes. But the housing crisis also translated into a general recession, with sharp declines in output and investment across the board and unemployment reaching 10 percent of the labor force. Proposed explanations of these spillovers rely on Keynesian aggregate demand mechanisms as in Eggertsson and Krugman (2012) and Mian and Sufi (2014a), or rigidities in sectoral reallocation of resources as in Rognlie, Shleifer, and Simsek (2018). Can expectations mechanisms themselves add to these effects, creating a broad overreaction to news such as the bursting of a housing bubble and the Lehman bankruptcy?

Fourth, in chapters 3 and 5, we showed that financial innovation can be an important source of instability for two reasons. First, activities in which risks are neglected tend to overexpand because new financial instruments are invented to capitalize on such neglect. Neglect of the possibility of housing crashes led to the production of vast amounts of falsely safe assets backed by mortgages. Second, innovative products themselves create neglected risks. Pooling and tranching of mortgages, for instance, created additional safety, but as we saw in chapter 5, it may also have encouraged an exaggerated perception of safety, as per the kernel of truth principle. Portfolio insurance is another example of the same mechanism. Of course, financial innovation can create large social gains by completing asset markets. Understanding its role in causing instability when risks are neglected and considering policies to reduce the scope of such misperceptions (e.g., stress testing of new financial products or consumer protection) are important open problems.

These considerations lead us to the last item on this list. We have not explored economic policy in the world where volatility is driven by expectations. A central question is this: If policymakers see something that looks like a bubble, with rising market prices, expanding credit, narrowing credit spreads, and highly optimistic investor expectations, what should they do? Although there are many essential operational issues that shape the answers, in our view there are three broad approaches to this problem.

The first approach holds that policymakers should do nothing. After all, it is very hard to tell whether a price increase in a major credit class is really a bubble or just good fundamentals. It is equally hard to tell whether credit expansion is speculative or supportive of authentic economic growth. From the vantage point of 2005–2006, was the housing expansion a bubble or an opportunity for millions of Americans to own their own homes? Policymakers are unlikely to know much more than sophisticated investors, so who are they to tell? Should the crisis erupt, it is of course important to intervene to stabilize the financial system, but ex ante policy should be passive. Policymakers are firefighters, not policemen.

A second approach holds that precisely because it is so hard to identify bubbles and to measure risks to financial stability, a wise policy should require financial institutions to meet higher capital requirements and to otherwise keep themselves better able to withstand market meltdowns. The stress tests introduced by President Barack Obama's treasury secretary, Tim Geithner, which check the vulnerability of banks to severe market shocks, are an example of this policy. Diagnostic expectations present a potentially useful take on this issue. To the extent that they produce information about tail risks, stress tests can reduce the neglect of such risks by both intermediaries and investors. Greater transparency can also relieve exaggerated concerns about tail risks and restore confidence, as the U.S. stress test in the spring of 2009 showed. At the same time, from an ex ante perspective, surprising stress test results may generate overreaction and excess market movements. Assessing these effects and their implications for optimal stress testing procedures is an interesting open problem.

A third approach, advocated by Anil Kashyap and Jeremy Stein (Stein 2012, 2014; Kashyap and Stein 2012; Gourio, Kashyap, and Sim 2017), holds that authorities should lean against the wind by increasing capital requirements, raising interest rates, and otherwise interfering with rapid growth of prices and credit when economic conditions look frothy. Some central bank governors do not like this approach because they feel that central banks should use the instruments they control, such as interest rates, to influence output and inflation, not financial markets.

The research presented in this book is too stylized to take a decisive stand on these issues, but it does move the needle toward the Kashyap-Stein view. Credit cycles and business cycles often occur in tandem. Credit expansions, as well as other measures of frothiness, are predictors of slowdowns to come. Of course, the policymakers are vulnerable to the same expectations errors as investors. And it is clearly politically dangerous to interfere with the economic improvements during a general euphoria. However, the criminal bar that policymakers should only lean against the wind when it is clear beyond reasonable doubt that the economy is overheated seems too high. In light of all the evidence of predictability of economic and financial instability from credit market indicators, some leaning against the wind seems like a good idea.

As we showed in chapter 4, a growing collection of economic indicators, from credit growth to lowered credit spreads, help identify market frothiness. Our analysis suggests that monitoring the expectations of market participants can also help in this task. To the extent that expectations display predictable errors, expectations data may help policymakers to anticipate future market corrections. Several central banks already survey the expectations of market participants, but such data could be collected much more extensively, from a broader range of borrowers, lenders, and investors. Although we do not believe there is one magic variable on which all policy should turn, expectations data can be used along with price and quantity variables for more systematic policy analysis.

A deeper question is how markets would react to a leaning against the wind policy or to direct monitoring and use of expectations data by policymakers. Diagnostic expectations are forward-looking, so—just as under rational expectations—a new policy regime would be incorporated into beliefs. Understanding the role of policy in managing expectations is another open problem for future work.

Expectations

Throughout the book, we argued that expectations can be both measured and modeled. They can be and have been measured via surveys of households, investors, corporate managers, and professional forecasters. The answers are generally consistent across surveys, but also predict the behavior of those reporting expectations. Surveys are a valid and extremely useful source of data on beliefs. We also showed that expectations and beliefs can be modeled because they derive from universal psychological mechanisms of how people process information. Expectations are not rational, but they are far from arbitrary. We focused on one key psychological mechanism shaping beliefs: representativeness. The resulting diagnostic beliefs exaggerate statistically correct patterns in the data—the kernel of truth property. Such beliefs can account for some dumbfounding experimental evidence on judgment under uncertainty and social beliefs such as stereotypes, and can also unify seemingly unrelated patterns of economic and financial expectations such as overreaction to news, neglect of risk, and extrapolation.

Here as well we have only started to make progress. Perhaps at the most basic level, we do not yet know how far the kernel of truth property goes in explaining the data. It implies that economic agents are forward-looking and respond to information but not by the right amount. It further implies that the magnitude of the reaction to information is not mechanical but rather shaped by the objective features of the environment that agents operate in, including the economic model and the stochastic process of the shocks. In these respects, diagnostic expectations are close to rational expectations yet allow for what appears to be the empirically accurate overreaction.

We have pointed to some evidence supportive of this idea in the Bordalo, Gennaioli, La Porta, and Shleifer (2017) study of analyst forecasts, in which the analysts respond to high earnings growth in the right direction by updating their estimates of future earnings growth but go too far in their assessments of how likely these firms are to continue growing rapidly. Some of the evidence on stock returns as well as on credit spreads is also consistent with the kernel of truth property of beliefs.

At the same time, existing work in finance and macroeconomics shows that overreaction to news is not universal. In financial economics, even though overreaction to news is the dominant theme since Shiller (1981), there is also evidence of slow incorporation of some information into prices. For stock returns, this phenomenon is known as momentum (e.g., Hong and Stein 1999) and looks more like underreaction. In macroeconomics, there is an even stronger commitment to underreaction to information as a source of price rigidity—for instance, in studies of rational inattention (Sims 2003). The study of consensus macroeconomic forecasts by Coibion and Gorodnichenko (2015) employs an ingenious test to look at this question. They examine the relationship between forecast revisions of macroeconomic variables, which they take to be a proxy for unobserved news, and forecast errors. The positive errors (reality exceeds the forecast) after positive revisions would point to underreaction to news, while the negative errors (reality falls short of the forecast) after positive revisions would point to overreaction. For the consensus macroeconomic forecasts, Coibion and Gorodnichenko find consistent evidence of underreaction.

This body of work stressing the relevance of underreaction raises two questions. First, what is the dominant mechanism for expectations error, underreaction or overreaction? Second, is it possible to identify the conditions under which overreaction and underreaction to information occur, perhaps within a more general psychological model allowing for both? Bordalo, Gennaioli, Ma, and Shleifer (2018) address the first question in the domain of macroeconomic forecasts. They look at similar macroeconomic forecast data as Coibion and Gorodnichenko. They focus on individual and not just consensus forecasts because the finding of underreaction by Coibion and Gorodnichenko might be due to aggregation, since individual forecasters do not react to information received by others (Woodford 2003). Consistent with this conjecture, in individual forecaster data overreaction is much more common than underreaction. In fact, there is evidence that the kernel of truth property holds: The reaction of expectations to news is stronger in series with stronger persistence. In a related study of time-series forecasts made by experimental subjects, Landier, Ma, and Thesmar (2017) find strong evidence of overreaction as well, but also of some rigidity in revisions. As of this writing, understanding the fundamental conditions under which people over- and underreact to news remains an open problem.

A related and critical problem is the neglect of risk, the starting point of this book. We emphasized its centrality for understanding the growth of leverage prior to the financial crisis, as well as for the pricing of mortgage-backed securities. It is of course a broader issue, famously described by Nassim Taleb (2007) as the black swan. Coval, Pan, and Stafford

(2014) suggest that financial markets often misprice new products because some risks remain unforeseen until they surface. This, for example, was the case when stock index options were first introduced or when portfolio insurance became popular. After neglected risks resurface, perhaps with a bang leading to major price movements as in the 1987 stock market crash, markets learn and reprice securities. Diagnostic expectations offer one formalization of substantial underappreciation of low probability unrepresentative risks. In cases of financial (or other) innovation, the outright neglect of remote adverse contingencies might be a closely related phenomenon, but one that relies on a more drastic failure of memory. In this book we provided some direct evidence on neglected risk, such as figure 2.1 based on the beliefs of Lehman analysts, but much remains to be done. Survey data on higher moments of beliefs can be used to this effect and might allow us to study the connection between expectations about the mean and the neglect of risk.

Foundations

As soon as the data on survey expectations are taken seriously as measuring beliefs, the Rational Expectations Hypothesis loses its potency. To better match expectations data and improve economic analysis, we offered an approach based on Kahneman and Tversky's (1974) representativeness heuristic. Their work identifies several other important heuristics such as anchoring—the idea that people adjust their beliefs to whatever information they started with in their heads, regardless of relevance. Anchoring would seem to be a natural source of underreaction, even though formalizing it faces the challenge of accounting for outright irrelevant information serving as an anchor. Integrating anchoring in diagnostic expectations may be a promising way to unify under- and overreaction to news.

Reliance on heuristics is perhaps a deeper way of understanding expectations than rationality, but it is not deep enough. After all, heuristics are summaries of how the more fundamental brain mechanisms, such as attention, perception, and memory, process information. Eventually, to develop accurate models of how humans form beliefs, we need to use knowledge of how these basic biological systems operate and matter.

From our perspective, the most important system for understanding belief formation is likely to be memory, and foundational models of beliefs will build on the basic mechanisms of memory. Memory research sees selective recall as operating via two principles: similarity and interference (Kahana 2012). We discussed the role of interference and its potential to offer a foundation for the representativeness heuristic in chapter 5. The similarity principle can lead us to recall future scenarios similar to the current one, offering a potential foundation for anchoring and underreaction.

These, of course, are the least well charted waters for economists to swim in. But to get to the bottom of beliefs and expectations, we might need to take a dive.

As a final note, we would suggest that the various problems and challenges we have outlined in this chapter are not just isolated questions but part of a broader goal. Neoclassical economics in the twentieth century built a remarkable scientific synthesis by starting with the foundations of preferences and endowments for households, technology for firms, and markets to coordinate them. From these foundations, it built a theory of choice by firms and households, of market equilibrium, and eventually of macroeconomic growth and fluctuations as an aggregation of these outcomes. The unifying assumption that glues these elements together is rationality of choice and expectations. Without it, things fall apart.

But maybe they don't. We agree entirely that economics must aim for a unified theory of micro and macro. But the assumption of rational expectations is a high cost of unification and could well be a lethal one when it comes to explaining the evidence. It might not be the only way forward. Economists and especially other social scientists over the last several decades have come up with considerable evidence and some underlying theories on where beliefs come from. There are ways to put these theories into the language of economics, as well as to construct new ones. These theories of beliefs, we expect, would need to follow all the same rules as those that have come to constitute good economics. In particular, they would need to be formalized, incorporated into models of decisions by households and firms, and finally aggregated to market and economy-wide outcomes. But they would start with biological reality rather than rationality.

Our book is an early and highly tentative step in this direction. Other steps are likely to be different and might take research in different directions. But eventually, and we suspect sooner rather than later, it will all come together, especially as we understand more and more about human nature. We will then have realistic and scientifically founded models of expectations, so the inaccurate though aesthetically attractive ones can be honorably retired. This would be, indeed, a crisis of beliefs.

Proofs

Chapter 3

Proposition 3.1. *Provided $\underline{X} > N^*$ in definition 3.1, neglected downside risk boosts the issuance of safe debt relative to rational expectations, $N^\theta > N^*$.*

Proof. As we showed in the text, in equilibrium, the AAA constraint must be binding, which implies:

$$\int_0^{N^\theta} f^\theta(\tilde{X})d\tilde{X} = \delta^* = \int_0^{N^*} f(\tilde{X})d\tilde{X}.$$

Given definition 3.1 and provided $\underline{X} > N^*$, the above equality implies $N^\theta > N^*$.

Proposition 3.2. *When neglected risk resurfaces, the secondary market outcomes are as follows:*

a) *If $\sigma \geq p_{inv}^{crisis}/p(N^\theta)$, all debt is bought back by intermediaries and the market price of debt is given by $min(\sigma p(N^\theta), p_{int}^{crisis})$.*

b) *If $\sigma < p_{inv}^{crisis}/p(N^\theta)$, intermediaries can buy only some debt ($\sigma N^\theta p(N^\theta)/ p_{inv}^{crisis}$), investors retain the rest of it, and the secondary market price of debt is given by p_{inv}^{crisis}.*

Proof. Because $\beta_l > \epsilon\beta_h$, we have that, in a crisis, intermediaries have a higher reservation price for the debt issued at $t=0$ than investors: $p_{inv}^{crisis} < p_{int}^{crisis}$. As a result, intermediaries are willing to buy debt back from investors. The market outcome depends on intermediary wealth. There are two cases:

a) If $\sigma p(N^\theta)N^\theta > p_{inv}^{crisis}N^\theta$, the wealth of intermediaries is large enough to purchase all claims held by investors at investors' reservation price. In this case, two subcases can occur. First, if $\sigma p(N^\theta) \geq p_{int}^{crisis}$, intermediaries are wealthy enough to absorb the entire supply at their own reservation price. In this case, the secondary market price is $p = p_{int}^{crisis}$. Second, if $\sigma p(N^\theta) < p_{int}^{crisis}$, the price settles at the level at which intermediaries can afford to purchase the entire supply: $p = \sigma p(N^\theta)$. As a result, in this regime all debt is bought back by intermediaries at the equilibrium price $p = min(\sigma p(N^\theta), p_{int}^{crisis})$.

b) If $\sigma p(N^\theta)N^\theta \leq p_{inv}^{crisis}N^\theta$, the wealth of intermediaries is not high enough to purchase all claims held by investors at investors' reservation price. The secondary market price must be equal to p_{inv}^{crisis} and the amount of debt bought back by intermediaries is equal to $\sigma N^\theta p(N^\theta)/p_{inv}^{crisis}$.

Proposition 3.3. *With neglected risk:*

i) *The level of lending is higher than under rationality: $I^\theta > I^*$.*

ii) *If the perception of average economic conditions $\int_0^\infty \tilde{A}h^\theta(\tilde{A})d\tilde{A}$ is sufficiently above the truth $\int_0^\infty \tilde{A}h(\tilde{A})d\tilde{A}$, the intermediary does not carry any liquid wealth: $I^\theta = p(N^\theta(I^\theta))N^\theta(I^\theta)$.*

Proof. The maximization problem of the representative intermediary under neglected risk is:

$$\max_{(N,I)} (\beta_h - \beta_l) \left[N - \int_0^{\frac{N}{q(I)}} (N - \tilde{A}q(I)) h^\theta(\tilde{A}) d\tilde{A} \right]$$

$$+ \beta_l q(I) \int_0^{+\infty} \tilde{A} h^\theta(\tilde{A}) d\tilde{A} - I,$$

$$s.t. \int_0^{\frac{N}{q(I)}} h^\theta(\tilde{A}) d\tilde{A} = \delta^*,$$

$$I \le q(I) \int_0^{\frac{N}{q(I)}} \tilde{A} h^\theta(\tilde{A}) d\tilde{A} + N(1 - \delta^*),$$

which already incorporates the fact that at the optimum, the AAA constraint is binding and includes the intermediary's liquidity constraint.

The AAA constraint implicitly identifies a default threshold A^θ such that $\int_0^{A^\theta} h^\theta(\tilde{A}) d\tilde{A} = \delta^*$. Because of neglected downside risk, this threshold is higher than under rational expectations: $A^\theta > A^*$. In equilibrium, then, the amount of debt issued is equal to $N^\theta = A^\theta q(I)$. By substituting the constraint into the objective function, we can eliminate one choice variable and restate the intermediary's problem as:

$$\max_I (\beta_h - \beta_l) \left[A^\theta q(I) - \int_0^{A^\theta} (A^\theta q(I) - \tilde{A}q(I)) h^\theta(\tilde{A}) d\tilde{A} \right]$$

$$+ \beta_l q(I) \int_0^{+\infty} \tilde{A} h^\theta(\tilde{A}) d\tilde{A} - I.$$

The first order condition equalizing marginal benefit and marginal cost of investment reads:

$$q'(I^\theta) \left[(\beta_h - \beta_l) \left(\int_0^{A^\theta} \tilde{A} h^\theta(\tilde{A}) d\tilde{A} + A^\theta (1 - \delta^*) \right) \right.$$

$$\left. + \beta_l \int_0^{+\infty} \tilde{A} h^\theta(\tilde{A}) d\tilde{A} \right] = 1. \tag{A.1}$$

The same condition under rational expectations would read:

$$q'(I^*) \left[(\beta_h - \beta_l) \left(\int_0^{A^*} \tilde{A} h(\tilde{A}) d\tilde{A} + A^* (1 - \delta^*) \right) \right.$$

$$\left. + \beta_l \int_0^{+\infty} \tilde{A} h(\tilde{A}) d\tilde{A} \right] = 1.$$

There are two cases to consider:

i) Consider first the case in which the optimal investment I^θ is determined by the first order condition (A.1) so that the liquidity constraint is slack. As long as the perception of average economic conditions $\int_0^{+\infty} \tilde{A} h^\theta(\tilde{A}) d\tilde{A}$ is at least as optimistic as under rational expectations $\int_0^{+\infty} \tilde{A} h(\tilde{A}) d\tilde{A}$, investment I^θ under neglected risk is larger than investment I^* under rationality. In this case, in fact, the term in square brackets in equation (A.1) is larger than its counterpart under rationality. Thus, $q'(I^\theta) < q'(I^*)$, where I^* is the unconstrained investment under rational expectations. This in turn implies, given concavity of $q(I)$, that $I^\theta > I^*$ (this is a fortiori true if rational investment is constrained).

ii) Suppose now that optimal investment I^θ is determined by the binding liquidity constraint, which at the optimum can be rewritten as:

$$\frac{I}{q(I)} \leq \left[\int_0^{A^\theta} \tilde{A} h^\theta(\tilde{A}) d\tilde{A} + A^\theta(1 - \delta^*) \right],$$

where the left-hand side increases in I given that the marginal product of capital is decreasing and that $q(0) = 0$. For any given investment level I, this constraint is more slack under neglected risk than under rationality, because $A^\theta > A^*$. If the liquidity constraint is binding both for neglected risk and rationality, investment is larger under neglected risk. But even if the liquidity constraint is binding for neglected risk but not for rationality, it must be that investment under rationality is lower than under neglected risk. If not, the liquidity constraint under rationality should also be binding, leading to contradiction. At the optimum, the liquidity constraint under neglected risk is binding—so that the intermediary carries no liquidity—if the investment level satisfying equation (A.1) entails $p(N(I))N(I) - I < 0$. Conditional on a certain value of A^θ and of $\int_0^{A^\theta} \tilde{A} h^\theta(\tilde{A}) d\tilde{A}$, the liquidity constraint is more likely to be binding provided $\int_0^{+\infty} \tilde{A} h^\theta(\tilde{A}) d\tilde{A}$ is sufficiently in-flated relative to the truth. In this case, in fact, the unconstrained level of investment is large enough to violate the liquidity constraint.

Lemma 3.1. *If the density $f(\tilde{X})$ of the common cash flow factor $\tilde{X}$ is convex in $[0, \hat{X}]$, then the induced density $f_i(\tilde{X})$ of the intermediary-specific cash flow has a fatter left tail than $f(\tilde{X})$ in the sense that $\int_0^Z f_i(\tilde{X}) d\tilde{X}_i > \int_0^Z f(\tilde{X}) d\tilde{X}$ for all $Z \in [0, \hat{X} \underline{\epsilon}]$.*

Proof. Recall the initial assumption that $f(\tilde{X})$ is increasing in the left tail. Recall also that ϵ is a shock distributed in the positive support $[\underline{\epsilon}, \bar{\epsilon}]$ with density $g(\epsilon)$ with unit mean $E[\epsilon] = \int \epsilon g(\epsilon) d\epsilon = 1$. Consider a new random variable, $Z = \tilde{X} \epsilon$, which is the product of two statistically independent variables. Given the positive support of ϵ, the support of Z is again $[0, +\infty]$. Deriving the joint distribution and marginalizing, we obtain the product density

$$h(Z) = \int_{\underline{\epsilon}}^{\bar{\epsilon}} f\left(\frac{Z}{\epsilon}\right) \frac{g(\epsilon)}{\epsilon} d\epsilon,$$

which yields:

$$\int_0^X h(Z) dZ = \int_0^X \int_{\underline{\epsilon}}^{\bar{\epsilon}} f\left(\frac{Z}{\epsilon}\right) \frac{g(\epsilon)}{\epsilon} d\epsilon \, dZ.$$

This distribution has a fatter left tail in the sense of definition 3.1, provided there is an $\underline{X}$ such that:

$$\int_0^X h(Z) dZ > \int_0^X f(Z) dZ \text{ for all } X \le \underline{X}.$$

This inequality surely holds if $h(X) > f(X)$ for all $X \le \underline{X}$. This can be rewritten as:

$$h(X) = \int_{\underline{\epsilon}}^{\bar{\epsilon}} f\left(\frac{X}{\epsilon}\right) \frac{g(\epsilon)}{\epsilon} d\epsilon \ge f(X).$$

Given that the mean value of ϵ is equal to one, Jensen's inequality implies the above inequality provided $f\left(\dfrac{X}{\epsilon}\right)\dfrac{1}{\epsilon}$ is a convex function of ϵ for all $X \leq \underline{X}$. This is equivalent to requiring:

$$\frac{d^2}{d\epsilon^2} f\left(\frac{X}{\epsilon}\right)\frac{1}{\epsilon} = \frac{1}{\epsilon^2}\left[4X\frac{1}{\epsilon^2}f'\left(\frac{X}{\epsilon}\right) + X^2\frac{1}{\epsilon^3}f''\left(\frac{X}{\epsilon}\right)\right.$$

$$\left. +2\frac{1}{\epsilon}f\left(\frac{X}{\epsilon}\right)\right] \geq 0 \ \text{for } X \leq \underline{X}. \tag{A.2}$$

A sufficient condition for the above inequality to hold is that $f''\left(\dfrac{X}{\epsilon}\right) \geq 0$ in the relevant range $[0, \underline{X}]$. Given that $f''(X) \geq 0$ for all $X < \hat{X}$, condition (A.2) is guaranteed provided $\dfrac{X}{\epsilon} \leq \hat{X}$, which is satisfied in the entire range of ϵ provided $X < \hat{X}\underline{\epsilon}$. Convexity is sufficient because of the assumption that, on the left tail, $f'(X) \geq 0$.

Proposition 3.4. *If $f^\theta(X)$ satisfies the conditions of lemma 3.1, then in the neglected risk equilibrium intermediaries fully diversify ($\alpha_i = 1$ for all i) and debt issuance is given by N^θ, as in the model where idiosyncratic risk is absent.*

Proof. Intermediaries are given the option to swap their idiosyncratic cash flow for a diversified pool. Intermediary i chooses to swap a share α_i of its own cash flow. Because the price of the cash flows of different intermediaries are identical, each intermediary makes neither profit nor loss in choosing different levels of α_i. The only consequence is that α_i changes the cash flow to:

$$\tilde{X}_i = \tilde{X}[1 + (1 - \alpha_i)(\epsilon_i - 1)].$$

The cash flow is the product of the systematic component $\tilde{X}$ and a statistically independent, idiosyncratic, mean one component $[1 + (1 - \alpha_i)(\epsilon_i - 1)]$. The idiosyncratic density function is:

$$f_i^\theta(X) = \int_{\underline{\epsilon}}^{\overline{\epsilon}} f^\theta\left(\frac{X}{1+(1-\alpha_i)(\epsilon_i-1)}\right)\frac{g(\epsilon)}{1+(1-\alpha_i)(\epsilon_i-1)}d\epsilon.$$

The key aspect is that for $\alpha_i = 1$, the intermediary's cash flow distribution only depends on the systematic component: $f_i^\theta(X) = f^\theta(X)$. Under the assumptions of lemma 3.1, then, setting $\alpha_i = 1$ allows the intermediary to reduce the probability mass on the left tail.

The intermediary's profit maximization problem is:

$$max_{N_i,\alpha_i}(\beta_h - \beta_l)\left[N_i - \int_0^{N_i}(N_i - X)f_i^\theta(X)dX\right] + \beta_l\int_0^{+\infty}X f_i^\theta(X)dX,$$

$$s.t. \int_0^{N_i}f_i^\theta(X)dX \leq \delta^*,$$

where changes in α_i affect the distribution $f_i^\theta(X)$. The first order condition with respect to N_i is:

$$(\beta_h - \beta_l)\left[1 - \int_0^{N_i}f_i^\theta(X)dX\right] - \gamma f_i^\theta(N_i) = 0,$$

where γ is the multiplier of the AAA constraint. Because $(\beta_h - \beta_l) > 0$, this constraint is binding.

Consider now the optimal choice of α_i. Setting $\alpha_i < 1$ implies choosing a cash flow distribution that has a fatter left tail relative to setting $\alpha_i = 1$. This is a consequence of lemma 3.1. It is therefore optimal for intermediaries to choose $\alpha_i = 1$. This choice does not affect the expected cash flow, the second term of the intermediary's objective. It however exerts two positive effects. First, it increases debt issuance revenues. After integrating by parts, one can see that the second (negative) term in square brackets can be written as:

$$\int_0^{N_i}(N_i - X)f_i^\theta(X)dX = \int_0^{N_i}\left[\int_0^X f_i^\theta(Z)dZ\right]dX.$$

By setting $\alpha_i = 1$ the term $\int_0^X f_i^\theta(Z)dZ$ is minimized at any $X < N_i$, reducing the expected shortfall and hence boosting issuance revenues for every N_i. Second, setting $\alpha_i = 1$ allows the intermediary to relax the AAA constraint, expanding debt issuance N_i.

Proposition 3.5. *Suppose that* $f(X) \geq f^\theta(X)$ *for* $X \leq N^\theta(1)/\underline{\epsilon}$ *and* $f_i^\theta(N^*(0)) > f^\theta(N^\theta(1))$. *Then, if* $\left[f\left(\dfrac{X}{\epsilon}\right) - f^\theta\left(\dfrac{X}{\epsilon}\right) \right]\dfrac{1}{\epsilon}$ *is concave in* ϵ *for* $X \leq N^\theta(1)/\underline{\epsilon}$, *cash flow pooling exacerbates overissuance due to neglected risk. Formally:*

$$N^\theta(1) - N^*(1) > N^\theta(0) - N^*(0).$$

Proof. The AAA constraint is binding across different pooling regimes and across rational expectations as well as neglect of downside risk. To begin, consider the function:

$$P(N) = \int_0^N \left[f(X) - f^\theta(X) \right] dX. \tag{A.3}$$

For N in the left tail, $P(N) > 0$, which causes debt issuance to be larger under neglected risk than under rationality. Because $f(X) \geq f^\theta(X)$ for all $X \leq N^\theta(1)$, which is assumed at the outset, function $P(N)$ is increasing: $P'(N) \geq 0$ for $X \leq N^\theta(1)$.

When risks are not pooled so that intermediaries are subject to idiosyncratic risk, the corresponding function is:

$$I(N) = \int_0^N \int_{\underline{\epsilon}}^{\bar{\epsilon}} \left[f\left(\dfrac{X}{\epsilon}\right) - f^\theta\left(\dfrac{X}{\epsilon}\right) \right]\dfrac{1}{\epsilon} g(\epsilon) d\epsilon\, dX. \tag{A.4}$$

Notice furthermore that:

$$P(N) \geq I(N)$$
$$\Leftrightarrow$$
$$\int_0^N \left[f(X) - f^\theta(X) \right] dX \geq \int_0^N \int_{\underline{\epsilon}}^{\bar{\epsilon}} \left[f\left(\dfrac{X}{\epsilon}\right) - f^\theta\left(\dfrac{X}{\epsilon}\right) \right]\dfrac{1}{\epsilon} g(\epsilon) d\epsilon\, dX,$$

which, by Jensen's inequality, is pinned down by the fact that

$$\left[f\!\left(\frac{X}{\epsilon}\right) - f^{\theta}\!\left(\frac{X}{\epsilon}\right) \right] \frac{1}{\epsilon}$$

is concave in ϵ, which we imposed at the outset. To see the implications for excess issuance, note that—after some algebra—one can find that under pooling and no pooling, respectively, the levels of issuance are pinned down by the equations:

$$\int_{N^{*}(1)}^{N^{\theta}(1)} f^{\theta}(X)dX = \int_{0}^{N^{*}(1)} \left[f(X) - f^{\theta}(X) \right] dX,$$

$$\int_{N^{*}(0)}^{N^{\theta}(0)} f_{i}^{\theta}(X)dX = \int_{0}^{N^{*}(0)} \left[f_{i}(X) - f_{i}^{\theta}(X) \right] dX.$$

Given that $N^{\theta}(0) < N^{\theta}(1)$, the right-hand side of the bottom condition is lower than the right-hand side of the top condition. As a result, a sufficient condition ensuring $N^{\theta}(1) - N^{*}(1) > N^{\theta}(0) - N^{*}(0)$ is that $f_{i}^{\theta}(N^{*}(0)) > f^{\theta}(N^{\theta}(1))$. (Again, remember that we are in the left tail, so densities are increasing.)

Pooling and Diversity

We now sketch the extension of the model in which it is possible to show that pooling of risks exacerbates fragility in secondary markets. The key to this extension is the idea that intermediaries issue debt and receive cash flows in two periods, and cash flow pooling in the first period exacerbates fragility when neglected risks resurface in the second period. The formal analysis of the two-period model is performed and explained in Gennaioli, Shleifer, and Vishny (GSV 2013). Here we illustrate the basic mechanism. Suppose that at $t=0$, intermediaries have legacy cash flows and debt. When at $t=0$ secondary market trading occurs, intermediaries receive cash flows from legacy projects and must pay off legacy debt. Denote by $\tilde{X}_{0,i}$ the idiosyncratic legacy cash flow of intermediary i realized at $t=0$ and by N_{-1} the amount of legacy debt (intermediaries are identical ex ante and hence they issue the same amount of debt). If $\tilde{X}_{0,i} < N_{-1}$, the intermediary does not have enough resources to repay its legacy debt and defaults.

Suppose, then, that at $t=0$ a bad aggregate state occurs, after the issuance of new debt N_0 that repays next period. The state is bad enough that the current realized cash flow $\tilde{X}_0 = \int \tilde{X}_{0,i}\, di$ does not suffice to pay off the totality of legacy debt: $\tilde{X}_0 < N_{-1}$. Suppose further that the bad aggregate state revealed by legacy cash flows renders market participants aware of the hidden risks in the new debt N_0 just issued and redeemable at $t=1$.

In this situation, besides default on some legacy debt, there are also fire sales on the newly issued debt N_0 given that neglected risk is revealed. However, legacy cash flows make some market liquidity available to support debt prices. Even if there is an aggregate shortfall of cash equal to $N_{-1} - \tilde{X}_0$, some intermediaries may have been lucky with their idiosyncratic bets and might have resources to buy the N_0 units of just issued new debt. The total resources available are equal to the aggregate legacy junior tranche earned by lucky intermediaries that did not default. If intermediaries pool a share α of projects, this corresponds to:

$$\int_{\frac{1}{1-\alpha}\left[1-\alpha+\frac{N_{-1}-\tilde{X}_0}{\tilde{X}_0}\right]}^{\bar{\epsilon}} \left[\tilde{X}_0 + (1-\alpha)\tilde{X}_0(\epsilon-1) - N_{-1}\right]g(\epsilon)d\epsilon.$$

The term $\tilde{X}_0 + (1-\alpha)\tilde{X}_0(\epsilon-1)$ in the integrand captures the cash flow obtained by a solvent intermediary. The term $-N_{-1}$ captures the repayment of legacy debt. Crucially, when pooling is complete, $\alpha=1$, the above integral is equal to zero. Intermediaries have no resources to support debt price during a fire sale. That is, the more intermediaries share idiosyncratic risk, the more they get exposed to systematic risk, and thus the more correlated their liquidity positions become. If, due to neglected risk, one intermediary unexpectedly defaults, they all default together, and no intermediary has spare profits to provide market liquidity.

Chapter 5

Proposition 5.1. *Suppose that* $\ln \tilde{X} \mid I_0 \sim N(\mu_0, \sigma_0^2)$ *and* $\ln \tilde{X} \mid I_{-1} \sim N(\mu_{-1}, \sigma_{-1}^2)$. *Then, provided* $(1+\theta)\sigma_{-1}^2 - \theta\sigma_0^2 > 0$, *the distorted density* $f^{\theta}(\tilde{X} \mid I_0)$ *is also lognormal with mean* $\mu_0(\theta)$ *and variance* $\sigma_0^2(\theta)$ *given by:*

$$\mu_0(\theta) = \mu_0 + \frac{\theta\sigma_0^2}{\sigma_{-1}^2 + \theta(\sigma_{-1}^2 - \sigma_0^2)}(\mu_0 - \mu_{-1}), \qquad (5.5)$$

$$\sigma_0^2(\theta) = \sigma_0^2 \frac{\sigma_{-1}^2}{\sigma_{-1}^2 + \theta(\sigma_{-1}^2 - \sigma_0^2)}. \qquad (5.6)$$

Proof. Consider the standard PDF of a lognormally distributed variable X:

$$\frac{1}{x\sigma\sqrt{2\pi}} e^{-\frac{(\ln x - \mu)^2}{2\sigma^2}}.$$

Recall the diagnostic density we want to compute is $f^{\theta}(X \mid I_0) = f(X \mid I_0)\left[\dfrac{f(X \mid I_0)}{f(X \mid I_{-1})}\right]^{\theta} Z$, where Z is a normalizing constant. Leaving the constant aside, the distorted density is given by:

$$\frac{1}{x\sigma_0\sqrt{2\pi}} e^{-\frac{(\ln x - \mu_0)^2}{2\sigma_0^2}} \left[\frac{\frac{1}{x\sigma_0\sqrt{2\pi}} e^{-\frac{(\ln x - \mu_0)^2}{2\sigma_0^2}}}{\frac{1}{x\sigma_{-1}\sqrt{2\pi}} e^{-\frac{(\ln x - \mu_{-1})^2}{2\sigma_{-1}^2}}}\right]^{\theta}.$$

Simplifying and rewriting the exponential functions together we obtain:

$$\frac{1}{x\,\dfrac{\sigma_0^{\theta+1}}{\sigma_{-1}^{\theta}}\sqrt{2\pi}}\,e^{\left[-\frac{(lnx-\mu_0)^2}{2\sigma_0^2}-\theta\frac{(lnx-\mu_0)^2}{2\sigma_0^2}+\theta\frac{(lnx-\mu_{-1})^2}{2\sigma_{-1}^2}\right]}.$$

The argument of the exponential function can be rewritten as:

$$\frac{1}{x\,\dfrac{\sigma_0^{\theta+1}}{\sigma_{-1}^{\theta}}\sqrt{2\pi}}\,e^{\left[-\frac{(\theta+1)\sigma_{-1}^2(lnx-\mu_0)^2-\theta\sigma_0^2(lnx-\mu_{-1})^2}{2\sigma_{-1}^2\sigma_0^2}\right]}.$$

Expanding the expression in the argument of the exponential function, we obtain:

$$\frac{1}{x\,\dfrac{\sigma_0^{\theta+1}}{\sigma_{-1}^{\theta}}\sqrt{2\pi}}\times$$

$$e^{\left\{-\frac{(\theta\sigma_{-1}^2+\sigma_{-1}^2-\theta\sigma_0^2)}{2\sigma_0^2\sigma_{-1}^2}\left[(lnx)^2-2lnx\frac{\theta\sigma_{-1}^2\mu_0+\sigma_{-1}^2\mu_0-\theta\sigma_0^2\mu_{-1}}{\theta\sigma_{-1}^2+\sigma_{-1}^2-\theta\sigma_0^2}+\frac{\theta\sigma_{-1}^2\mu_0^2+\sigma_{-1}^2\mu_0^2-\theta\sigma_0^2\mu_{-1}^2}{\theta\sigma_{-1}^2+\sigma_{-1}^2-\theta\sigma_0^2}\right]\right\}}.$$

Provided $\sigma_{-1}^2+\theta(\sigma_{-1}^2-\sigma_0^2)>0$, notice this last expression contains the kernel of a lognormal distribution where:

$$\sigma_0^2(\theta)=\frac{1}{\dfrac{(\theta\sigma_{-1}^2+\sigma_{-1}^2-\theta\sigma_0^2)}{\sigma_0^2\sigma_{-1}^2}}=\sigma_0^2\frac{\sigma_{-1}^2}{\sigma_{-1}^2+\theta(\sigma_{-1}^2-\sigma_0^2)}$$

$$\mu_0(\theta)=\frac{\theta\sigma_{-1}^2\mu_0+\sigma_{-1}^2\mu_0-\theta\sigma_0^2\mu_{-1}-\theta\sigma_0^2\mu_0+\theta\sigma_0^2\mu_0}{\theta\sigma_{-1}^2+\sigma_{-1}^2-\theta\sigma_0^2}$$

$$=\mu_0+\frac{\theta\sigma_0^2}{\sigma_{-1}^2+\theta(\sigma_{-1}^2-\sigma_0^2)}(\mu_0-\mu_{-1}).$$

To obtain the proper distribution, it suffices to multiply by a normalizing constant Z such that:

$$Z = e^{-\frac{(\theta\sigma_{-1}^2 + \sigma_{-1}^2 - \theta\sigma_0^2)}{2\sigma_0^2\sigma_{-1}^2}\left(\mu_0(\theta) - \frac{\theta\sigma_{-1}^2\mu_0^2 + \sigma_{-1}^2\mu_0^2 - \theta\sigma_0^2\mu_{-1}^2}{\theta\sigma_{-1}^2 + \sigma_{-1}^2 - \theta\sigma_0^2}\right)} \sigma_0^{\theta+1} \frac{1}{\sigma_{-1}^\theta} \frac{1}{\sigma_0^2(\theta)},$$

which proves the initial statement.

Proposition 5.2. *Agents neglect downside risk in the sense of definition 3.1 if and only if cash flow volatility has not increased relative to the past—namely, $\sigma_0^2 \leq \sigma_{-1}^2$. When this is the case, diagnostic beliefs neglect downside risk below the threshold $\underline{X}$ given by:*

$$\underline{X} = \mu_0 + \theta\varphi\left(\frac{\sigma_{-1}}{\sigma_0}\right)(\mu_0 - \mu_{-1}), \tag{5.7}$$

where $\varphi(\cdot)$ is a positive function that decreases in σ_{-1}/σ_0 such that

$$\lim_{\frac{\sigma_{-1}}{\sigma_0} \to 1} \varphi\left(\frac{\sigma_{-1}}{\sigma_0}\right) = +\infty.$$

Proof. Neglected downside risk $\underline{X}$, as per definition 3.1, implies that the diagnostic CDF must be below the rational CDF for all $X \leq \underline{X}$. In turn, this implies that this condition must hold at $X = 0$. In the lognormal case, this requires:

$$\lim_{x \to 0} \Phi\left(\frac{\ln x - \mu_0}{\sigma_0}\right) - \Phi\left(\frac{\ln x - \mu_0(\theta)}{\sigma_0(\theta)}\right) \geq 0.$$

Since the cdf is monotonically increasing and the argument is negative, the latter condition is satisfied whenever $\sigma_0 \geq \sigma_0(\theta)$, i.e.,

$$\sigma_0 \geq \sigma_0(\theta) \Leftrightarrow \sigma_0^2 \geq \sigma_0^2 \frac{\sigma_{-1}^2}{\sigma_{-1}^2 + \theta(\sigma_{-1}^2 - \sigma_0^2)} \Leftrightarrow \sigma_{-1}^2 - \sigma_0^2 \geq 0,$$

and thus a necessary condition for neglected downside risk is that $\sigma_0^2 \leq \sigma_{-1}^2$.

To compute the threshold $\underline{X}$, it is then sufficient to identify where the two cumulative distribution functions cross. In particular, let:

$$\Phi\left(\frac{\ln \underline{X} - \mu_0}{\sigma_0}\right) = \Phi\left(\frac{\ln \underline{X} - \mu_0(\theta)}{\sigma_0(\theta)}\right).$$

Because of strict monotonicity, we can write:

$$\frac{\ln \underline{X} - \mu_0}{\sigma_0} = \frac{\ln \underline{X} - \mu_0(\theta)}{\sigma_0(\theta)}.$$

Rearranging leads us to a threshold of the form:

$$\ln \underline{X} = \mu_0 + \frac{\theta \sigma_0 \, \sigma_0^2(\theta)/\sigma_{-1}^2}{\sigma_0 - \sigma_0(\theta)}(\mu_0 - \mu_{-1}),$$

which can be restated as:

$$\ln \underline{X} = \mu_0 + \varphi\left(\theta, \frac{\sigma_{-1}}{\sigma_0}\right)(\mu_0 - \mu_{-1}).$$

Note that for $\dfrac{\sigma_{-1}}{\sigma_0} = 1$ we have $\sigma_0^2(\theta) = \sigma_0^2$ and so $\varphi\left(\theta, \dfrac{\sigma_{-1}}{\sigma_0}\right) \to \infty$. Notice also that for $\dfrac{\sigma_{-1}}{\sigma_0} = \infty$ the numerator of the function goes to zero while the denominator remains positive, hence $\varphi\left(\theta, \dfrac{\sigma_{-1}}{\sigma_0}\right) = 0$.

To analyze the general behavior of the function as $\dfrac{\sigma_{-1}}{\sigma_0}$ varies, rewrite it as

$$\varphi\left(\theta, \frac{\sigma_{-1}}{\sigma_0}\right) = \frac{\theta \sigma_0^2(\theta)/\sigma_{-1}^2}{1 - \dfrac{\sigma_0(\theta)}{\sigma_0}}.$$

and notice $\dfrac{\partial \sigma_0^2(\theta)/\sigma_{-1}^2}{\partial \dfrac{\sigma_{-1}}{\sigma_0}} < 0$. Taking into account that the square

function is a monotone transformation on the positive orthant, we find

that $\dfrac{\partial \dfrac{\sigma_0(\theta)}{\sigma_0}}{\partial \dfrac{\sigma_{-1}}{\sigma_0}} < 0$ as well, so that we can state the general behavior of

the fraction characterizing the function: $\dfrac{\partial \varphi\left(\theta, \dfrac{\sigma_{-1}}{\sigma_0}\right)}{\partial \dfrac{\sigma_{-1}}{\sigma_0}} < 0.$

Proposition 5.3. *Denote by* $z^* < 0$ *the* δ^*-*percentile under a standard normal distribution. With diagnostic expectations, the AAA constraint takes the form:*

$$\ln N_0^\theta = \mu_0(\theta) + \sigma_0(\theta)z^*. \tag{5.8}$$

In equilibrium, safe debt issuance is excessive if $\mu_0 > \mu_{-1}$ *and* $\sigma_0^2 < \sigma_{-1}^2$.

Proof. Recall the AAA constraint is binding in equilibrium. Given that $\dfrac{\ln \tilde{X} - \mu}{\sigma}$ is standard normal, we can rewrite the AAA constraint as:

$$\Phi\left(\frac{\ln(N_0^\theta) - \mu_0(\theta)}{\sigma_0(\theta)}\right) = \delta^*.$$

Denote by $z^* < 0$ the δ^*-percentile in the standard normal, which is identified by $\Phi(z^*) = \delta^*$. Then, the AAA constraint implies:

$$\ln(N_0^\theta) = \mu_0(\theta) + \sigma_0(\theta)z^*.$$

Bond issuance is excessive, provided

$$\ln(N_0^\theta) = \mu_0(\theta) + \sigma_0(\theta)z^* > \ln(N^*) = \mu_0 + \sigma_0 z^*.$$

This condition holds, provided

$$[\mu_0(\theta) - \mu_0] + [\sigma_0(\theta) - \sigma_0]z^* > 0.$$

When $\mu_0 > \mu_{-1}$, the diagnostic mean is inflated and $\mu_0(\theta) > \mu_0$. When $\sigma_0 < \sigma_{-1}$, the diagnostic variance is deflated and $\sigma_0(\theta) < \sigma_0$. If both of those hold, the above condition holds and there is over-issuance, which proves the result.

Chapter 6

Proposition 6.1. *The believed distribution at t for $\hat{X}_{t+1}$ is normal, with variance σ^2 and expectation:*

$$\mathbb{E}_t^\theta(\hat{X}_{t+1}) = \rho \hat{X}_t + \rho\theta(\hat{X}_t - \rho\hat{X}_{t-1}). \tag{6.3}$$

Proof. First, notice that we can apply again the formula obtained in proposition 6.1 to compute the distorted expectation of the random variable of interest, as it holds both for a normal and lognormal distribution. Recall that we had derived:

$$\mu_0(\theta) = \mu_0 + \frac{\theta\sigma_0^2}{\sigma_{-1}^2 + \theta(\sigma_{-1}^2 - \sigma_0^2)}(\mu_0 - \mu_{-1}).$$

Consider the mean and variance of the target and comparison distributions here. The target distribution has the conditional mean $\mu_0 = \mathbb{E}_t(\hat{X}_{t+1}) = \rho\hat{X}_t$ and variance $\sigma_0^2 = \sigma^2$. The comparison distribution is the true distribution at t if in this period no news is received relative to $t - 1$. As a result, the comparison distribution has mean $\mu_{-1} = \mathbb{E}_{t-1}(\hat{X}_{t+1}) = \rho^2 \hat{X}_{t-1}$ and variance $\sigma_{-1}^2 = \sigma^2$.

By applying the above formula for the diagnostic mean, we can show:

$$\mathbb{E}_t^\theta(\hat{X}_{t+1}) = \rho\hat{X}_t + \rho\theta(\hat{X}_t - \rho\hat{X}_{t-1}). \tag{A.5}$$

We can also derive the diagnostic expectation under the alternative assumption whereby the comparison distribution is the true conditional distribution of $\hat{X}_{t+1}$ at $t-1$. This distribution has mean $\mu_{-1} = \mathbb{E}_{t-1}(\hat{X}_{t+1}) = \rho^2 \hat{X}_{t-1}$ and variance $\sigma_{-1}^2 = (1+\rho^2)\sigma^2$. By applying the formula above, we can show that the diagnostic expectation is given by:

$$\mathbb{E}_t^\theta(\hat{X}_{t+1}) = \rho \hat{X}_t + \frac{\theta}{1+(1+\theta)\rho^2} \rho(\hat{X}_t - \rho\hat{X}_{t-1}). \qquad (A.6)$$

Note the similarity between (A.5) and (A.6). Also, in the second case the distortion of expectations increases in θ. The only difference between (A.5) and (A.6) is that in the latter case the distortion depends on ρ.

Proposition 6.2. *Under diagnostic expectations $\theta > 0$, risky debt (and hence both total debt and the junk share) exhibits the following properties:*

i) It expands too much after good news, $cov(lnN_t^\theta, \epsilon_t) = \rho(1+\theta)\sigma^2$.

ii) It displays stronger reversals than fundamentals,
$$\frac{cov(lnN_t^\theta, lnN_{t-1}^\theta)}{var(lnN_{t-1}^\theta)} = \rho - \frac{\rho(1+\theta)\theta(1-\rho^2)}{[1+(1-\rho^2)\theta(2+\theta)]}.$$

iii) It is excessively volatile, $var(lnN_t^\theta) = \dfrac{\rho^2\sigma^2[1+(1-\rho^2)\theta(2+\theta)]}{1-\rho^2}.$

iv) Forecasts of future debt issuance are too optimistic after good news and too pessimistic after bad news, $\mathbb{E}_t[lnN_{t+1}^\theta - \mathbb{E}^\theta(lnN_{t+1}^\theta|t)] = -\rho^2\theta\epsilon_t.$

Proof. The dynamics of debt under diagnostic expectations are described by:

$$lnN_t^\theta = (1-\rho)\sigma z^* + \rho lnN_{t-1}^\theta + \rho(1+\theta)\epsilon_t - \rho^2\theta\epsilon_{t-1}.$$

Consider now how this expression implies all properties (*i*), (*ii*), (*iii*), and (*iv*).

Consider first property (*i*):

$$cov(lnN_t^\theta, \epsilon_t) = cov((1-\rho)\sigma z^* + \rho lnN_{t-1}^\theta + \rho(1+\theta)\epsilon_t - \rho^2\theta\epsilon_{t-1}, \epsilon_t)$$
$$= cov(\rho(1+\theta)\epsilon_t, \epsilon_t) = \rho(1+\theta)\sigma^2.$$

Consider next property (*ii*):

$$cov(lnN_t^\theta, lnN_{t-1}^\theta) = cov((1-\rho)\sigma z^* + \rho lnN_{t-1}^\theta + \rho(1+\theta)\epsilon_t - \rho^2\theta\epsilon_{t-1}, lnN_{t-1}^\theta)$$
$$= \rho var(lnN_{t-1}^\theta) - \rho^3\theta(1+\theta)\sigma^2$$
$$var(lnN_t^\theta) = cov[(1-\rho)\sigma z^* + \rho lnN_{t-1}^\theta + \rho(1+\theta)\epsilon_t - \rho^2\theta\epsilon_{t-1}, lnN_t^\theta]$$
$$= cov[\rho lnN_{t-1}^\theta + \rho(1+\theta)\epsilon_t - \rho^2\theta\epsilon_{t-1}, lnN_t^\theta]$$
$$= \rho^2 var(lnN_{t-1}^\theta) + \rho^2\sigma^2[1 + (1-\rho^2)\theta(2+\theta)],$$

which implies:

$$var(lnN_t^\theta) = \frac{\rho^2\sigma^2[1 + (1-\rho^2)\theta(2+\theta)]}{1-\rho^2},$$

so that:

$$\frac{cov(lnN_t^\theta, lnN_{t-1}^\theta)}{var(lnN_t^\theta)} = \rho - \frac{\rho(1+\theta)\theta(1-\rho^2)}{[1 + (1-\rho^2)\theta(2+\theta)]}.$$

Property (*iii*) has already been proved as we computed $var(lnN_t^\theta)$ in the previous point. Finally, let us turn to property (*iv*). The rational expectation of future debt issuance is:

$$\mathbb{E}_t lnN_{t+1}^\theta = (1-\rho)\sigma z^* + \rho lnN_t^\theta - \rho^2\theta\epsilon_t.$$

The past rational expectation of future debt issuance is:

$$\mathbb{E}_{t-1} lnN_{t+1}^\theta = (1-\rho)\sigma z^* + \rho\mathbb{E}_{t-1} lnN_t^\theta$$
$$= (1-\rho^2)\sigma z^* + \rho^2 lnN_{t-1}^\theta - \rho^3\theta\epsilon_{t-1}.$$

Exploiting the fact that $\mathbb{E}_t^\theta \ln N_{t+1}^\theta = \mathbb{E}_t \ln N_{t+1}^\theta + \theta(\mathbb{E}_t \ln N_{t+1}^\theta - \mathbb{E}_{t-1} \ln N_{t+1}^\theta)$, and substituting the expressions for $\mathbb{E}_t \ln N_{t+1}^\theta$, $\mathbb{E}_{t-1} \ln N_{t+1}^\theta$ and $\ln N_t^\theta$ we have that:

$$\mathbb{E}_t^\theta \ln N_{t+1}^\theta = (1-\rho)\sigma z^* + \rho \ln N_t^\theta,$$

which in turn implies:

$$\mathbb{E}_t \ln N_{t+1}^\theta - \mathbb{E}_t^\theta \ln N_{t+1}^\theta = -\theta\rho^2 \epsilon_t.$$

Proof of Proposition 6.3. By inspection.

Proposition 6.4. *The measure φ_t of the spread of risky debt issued at t satisfies the law of motion:*

$$\varphi_t = \rho\varphi_{t-1} + \rho^2\theta\epsilon_{t-1} - (\rho(1+\theta)-1)\epsilon_t. \tag{6.11}$$

Proof. Under log-utility and consumption proportional to aggregate risky endowment, we obtain that one unit of debt promising a payoff stream $R(\tilde{X}_{t+1})$ is valued at:

$$P_t^r = \beta\mathbb{E}_t^\theta\left[R(\tilde{X}_{t+1})\frac{\tilde{X}_t}{\tilde{X}_{t+1}}\right].$$

Substituting in the expression for the actual risky payoff $R(\tilde{X}_{t+1})$, this implies that:

$$P_t^r = \beta\mathbb{E}_t^\theta\left[\frac{\tilde{X}_t}{\tilde{X}_{t+1}}\right] - \beta\int_0^{N_t^\theta}\left(1-\frac{\tilde{X}_{t+1}}{N_t^\theta}\right)\frac{\tilde{X}_t}{\tilde{X}_{t+1}}\left[e^{-\frac{(\ln\tilde{X}_{t+1} - \mathbb{E}_t^\theta(\ln\tilde{X}_{t+1}))^2}{2\sigma^2}}\frac{1}{\tilde{X}_{t+1}\sigma\sqrt{2\pi}}\right]d\tilde{X}_{t+1},$$

$$\tag{A.7}$$

where the second term on the right-hand side of (A.7) can be rewritten as:

$$\beta\left[\int_0^{N_t^\theta} \frac{\tilde{X}_t}{\tilde{X}_{t+1}}\left[\frac{e^{-\frac{(ln\tilde{X}_{t+1} - \mathbb{E}_t^\theta(ln\tilde{X}_{t+1}))^2}{2\sigma^2}}}{\tilde{X}_{t+1}\sigma\sqrt{2\pi}}\right]d\tilde{X}_{t+1} - \delta * e^{ln\tilde{X}_t - lnN_t^\theta}\right].$$

On the other hand, the first term in square brackets above can be developed as follows:

$$\int_0^{N_t^\theta} \frac{\tilde{X}_t}{\tilde{X}_{t+1}}\left[\frac{e^{-\frac{(ln\tilde{X}_{t+1} - \mathbb{E}_t^\theta(ln\tilde{X}_{t+1}))^2}{2\sigma^2}}}{\tilde{X}_{t+1}\sigma\sqrt{2\pi}}\right]d\tilde{X}_{t+1} = \tilde{X}_t \int_{-\infty}^{lnN_t^\theta} \frac{e^{-u - \frac{(u - \mathbb{E}_t^\theta(ln\tilde{X}_{t+1}))^2}{2\sigma^2}}}{\sigma\sqrt{2\pi}}du.$$

After some algebra, one can see that the exponent of the integrand is equal to:

$$-\frac{u^2 - 2u[\mathbb{E}_t^\theta(ln\tilde{X}_{t+1}) - \sigma^2] + \mathbb{E}_t^\theta(ln\tilde{X}_{t+1})^2}{2\sigma^2},$$

so the integrand multiplied by $e^{\left[\mathbb{E}_t^\theta(ln\tilde{X}_{t+1}) - \frac{\sigma^2}{2}\right]}$ is a normal density with mean $[\mathbb{E}_t^\theta(ln\tilde{X}_{t+1}) - \sigma^2]$ and variance σ^2. As a result, one can write:

$$\int_{-\infty}^{lnN_t^\theta} \frac{e^{-u - \frac{(u - \mathbb{E}_t^\theta(ln\tilde{X}_{t+1}))^2}{2\sigma^2}}}{\sigma\sqrt{2\pi}}du = e^{\frac{\sigma^2}{2} - \mathbb{E}_t^\theta(ln\tilde{X}_{t+1})}Pr(u < lnN_t^\theta),$$

where the probability is computed using a normal with mean $\mathbb{E}_t^\theta(ln\tilde{X}_{t+1}) - \sigma^2$. Overall, then, we have that the second term on the right-hand side of (A.7) is given by:

$$\beta\left[e^{ln\tilde{X}_t + \frac{\sigma^2}{2} - \mathbb{E}_t^\theta(ln\tilde{X}_{t+1})}Pr(u < lnN_t^\theta) - \delta * e^{ln\tilde{X}_t - lnN_t^\theta}\right].$$

To obtain P_t^r we now need to compute the first term on the right of equation (A.7):

$$\mathbb{E}_t^\theta\left[\frac{\tilde{X}_t}{\tilde{X}_{t+1}}\right]=\int_0^{+\infty}\frac{\tilde{X}_t}{\tilde{X}_{t+1}}\left[\frac{e^{-\frac{(ln\tilde{X}_{t+1}-\mathbb{E}_t^\theta(ln\tilde{X}_{t+1}))^2}{2\sigma^2}}}{\tilde{X}_{t+1}\sigma\sqrt{2\pi}}\right]d\tilde{X}_{t+1}$$

$$=\tilde{X}_t\int_{-\infty}^{+\infty}e^{-u}\left[\frac{e^{-\frac{(u-\mathbb{E}_t^\theta(ln\tilde{X}_{t+1}))^2}{2\sigma^2}}}{\sigma\sqrt{2\pi}}\right]du$$

$$=\tilde{X}_t\,e^{\frac{\sigma^2}{2}-\mathbb{E}_t^\theta(ln\tilde{X}_{t+1})}=e^{ln\tilde{X}_t+\frac{\sigma^2}{2}-\mathbb{E}_t^\theta(ln\tilde{X}_{t+1})}. \tag{A.8}$$

After some algebra, the price of risky debt can then be written as:

$$P_t^r=\beta e^{ln\tilde{X}_t+\frac{\sigma^2}{2}-\mathbb{E}_t^\theta(ln\tilde{X}_{t+1})}-\beta e^{ln\tilde{X}_t+\frac{\sigma^2}{2}-\mathbb{E}_t^\theta(ln\tilde{X}_{t+1})}Pr(u<\mathbb{E}_t^\theta(ln\tilde{X}_{t+1})+\sigma z^*)$$
$$+\beta\delta*e^{ln\tilde{X}_t-\mathbb{E}_t^\theta(ln\tilde{X}_{t+1})+\sigma z^*}.$$

The price of safe debt is given by (A.8) times β. As a result, the difference between the price of safe and risky debt is given by:

$$P_t^s-P_t^r=\beta e^{ln\tilde{X}_t+\frac{\sigma^2}{2}-\mathbb{E}_t^\theta(ln\tilde{X}_{t+1})}Pr(u<\mathbb{E}_t^\theta(ln\tilde{X}_{t+1})+\sigma z^*)$$
$$-\beta\delta*e^{ln\tilde{X}_t-\mathbb{E}_t^\theta(ln\tilde{X}_{t+1})+\sigma z^*}$$
$$=\beta e^{ln\tilde{X}_t-\mathbb{E}_t^\theta(ln\tilde{X}_{t+1})}\left[e^{\frac{\sigma^2}{2}}Pr(u<\mathbb{E}_t^\theta(ln\tilde{X}_{t+1})+\sigma z^*)-\delta*e^{\sigma z^*}\right].$$

As a first step, note that the expression in square brackets is positive. The term $Pr(u<\mathbb{E}_t^\theta(ln\tilde{X}_{t+1})+\sigma z^*)$ in fact does not depend on $\mathbb{E}_t^\theta(ln\tilde{X}_{t+1})$, and furthermore can be expressed as:

$$Pr(u<\sigma+z^*)=\int_{-\infty}^{z^*+\sigma}\frac{e^{-\frac{u^2}{2}}}{\sqrt{2\pi}}du=\gamma>\delta*.$$

Denote therefore by $k>0$ the term in square brackets so we can write:

$$P_t^s - P_t^r = \beta k e^{\frac{\sigma^2}{2} + \ln\tilde{X}_t - \mathbb{E}_t^\theta(\ln\tilde{X}_{t+1})}.$$

Due to the properties of diagnostic expectations, we can write this expression as:

$$P_t^s - P_t^r = \beta k e^{\frac{\sigma^2}{2} + \rho[\ln\tilde{X}_{t-1} - \mathbb{E}_{t-1}^\theta(\ln\tilde{X}_t)] + \rho^2\theta\epsilon_{t-1} - [\rho(1+\theta)-1]\epsilon_t},$$

which in turn implies:

$$P_t^s - P_t^r = \beta k e^{\frac{\sigma^2}{2} + \rho\ln(P_{t-1}^s - P_{t-1}^r) - \rho\left(\ln\beta k + \frac{\sigma^2}{2}\right) + \rho^2\theta\epsilon_{t-1} - [\rho(1+\theta)-1]\epsilon_t}.$$

Taking as a measure of the spread the logarithm of the price difference $\hat{\varphi}_t = \ln(P_t^s - P_t^r)$, the above formula implies that:

$$\hat{\varphi}_t = (1-\rho)\left(\ln\beta k + \frac{\sigma^2}{2}\right) + \rho\hat{\varphi}_{t-1} + \rho^2\theta\epsilon_{t-1} - [\rho(1+\theta)-1]\epsilon_t.$$

Defining, with abuse of notation, the spread as $\varphi_t = \left(\hat{\varphi}_t - \ln\beta k - \frac{\sigma^2}{2}\right)$, we find:

$$\varphi_t = \rho\varphi_{t-1} + \rho^2\theta\epsilon_{t-1} - [\rho(1+\theta)-1]\epsilon_t,$$

which proves the proposition.

This result can be also used to evaluate errors in forecasting future spreads. The diagnostic expectation of the spread in the next period is in fact equal to:

$$\mathbb{E}_t^\theta(\varphi_{t+1}) = \mathbb{E}_t(\varphi_{t+1}) + \theta[\mathbb{E}_t(\varphi_{t+1}) - \mathbb{E}_{t-1}(\varphi_{t+1})]$$

$$\mathbb{E}_t^\theta(\varphi_{t+1}) = \rho\varphi_t + \rho^2\theta\epsilon_t + \theta[\rho^2\varphi_{t-1} + \rho^3\theta\epsilon_{t-1} - \rho[\rho(1+\theta)-1]\epsilon_t$$
$$+ \rho^2\theta\epsilon_t - \rho^2\varphi_{t-1} - \rho^3\theta\epsilon_{t-1}]$$

$$\mathbb{E}_t^\theta(\varphi_{t+1}) = \rho\varphi_t + \theta\rho\epsilon_t.$$

The average forecast error is then given by:

APPENDIX

$$\mathbb{E}_t[\varphi_{t+1} - \mathbb{E}_t^\theta(\varphi_{t+1})] = -\rho(1-\rho)\theta\epsilon_t.$$

There is excess optimism after good news $\epsilon_t > 0$ and excess pessimism after bad news $\epsilon_t < 0$.

Proposition 6.5. *Within each of the two regimes described above, a linear approximation of investment around the steady state expected productivity $\mathbb{E}_t^\theta(\ln A_{t+1}) = 0$ yields the following law of motion:*

$$I_t \approx a_0(1-\rho) + \rho I_{t-1} - a_1\rho^2\theta\epsilon_{t-1} + a_1\rho(1+\theta)\epsilon_t, \qquad (6.12)$$

where a_0, a_1 are positive constants.

Proof. Suppose that the borrowing constraint is binding. Given that $\beta_h, \beta_l \to 1$, the amount of risky investment I_t is given by:

$$I_t = q(I_t)\int_0^{\frac{N_{t+1}^\theta}{q(I_t)}} A h_t^\theta(A)dA + N_{t+1}^\theta(1-\delta^*).$$

The right-hand side is the payment received by investors on average. The ratio $\dfrac{N_{t+1}^\theta}{q(I_t)}$ is determined by the risk constraint $\int_0^{\frac{N_{t+1}^\theta}{q(I_t)}} h_t^\theta(A)dA = \delta^*$ —namely, $\ln\dfrac{N_{t+1}^\theta}{q(I_t)} = \mathbb{E}_t^\theta(\ln A_{t+1}) + \sigma z^*$. As a result:

$$\frac{I_t}{q(I_t)} = \int_0^{e^{\mathbb{E}_t^\theta(\ln A_{t+1})+\sigma z^*}} A h_t^\theta(A)dA + e^{\mathbb{E}_t^\theta(\ln A_{t+1})+\sigma z^*}(1-\delta^*).$$

The ratio of investment to output increases in expected productivity $\mathbb{E}_t^\theta(\ln A_{t+1})$. Assuming a production function $q(I_t) = I_t^\alpha$, and by linearizing investment around $\mathbb{E}_t^\theta(\ln A_{t+1}) = 0$, we find:

$$I_t = a_0 + a_1\mathbb{E}_t^\theta(\ln A_{t+1}),$$

where coefficients a_0 and a_1 are positive because i) investment at long run productivity is positive, and ii) investment depends positively on future expected productivity. This is true both at an interior optimum and along the risk constraint. By exploiting the expression for diagnostic expectations, this can be written as:

$$I_t = a_0 + a_1 [\rho \ln A_t + \rho \hat{\theta} \epsilon_t]$$
$$I_t = a_0 (1 - \rho) + \rho I_{t-1} - a_1 \rho^2 \hat{\theta} \epsilon_{t-1} + a_1 \rho (1 + \hat{\theta}) \epsilon_t.$$

Hence, investment also follows an ARMA(1,1) process.

REFERENCES

Acharya, Viral V., Philipp Schnabl, and Gustavo Suarez. 2013. "Securitization without Risk Transfer." *Journal of Financial Economics* 107 (3): 515–36.

Adam, Klaus, Albert Marcet, and Johannes Beutel. 2017. "Stock Price Booms and Expected Capital Gains." *American Economic Review* 107 (8): 2352–408.

Adrian, Tobias, and Hyun Song Shin. 2010. "Liquidity and Leverage." *Journal of Financial Intermediation* 19 (3): 418–37.

Amromin, Gene, and Steven A. Sharpe. 2014. "From the Horse's Mouth: Economic Conditions and Investor Expectations of Risk and Return." *Management Science* 60 (4): 845–66.

Armona, Luis, Andreas Fuster, and Basit Zafar. 2016. "Home Price Expectations and Behavior: Evidence from a Randomized Information Experiment." Federal Reserve Bank of New York Staff Report 798.

Bacchetta, Philippe, Elmar Mertens, and Eric van Wincoop. 2009. "Predictability in Financial Markets: What Do Survey Expectations Tell Us?" *Journal of International Money and Finance* 28 (3): 406–26.

Ball, Laurence M. 2018. *The Fed and Lehman Brothers: Setting the Record Straight on a Financial Disaster*. Cambridge: Cambridge University Press.

Barberis, Nicholas C. 2013. "The Psychology of Tail Events: Progress and Challenges." *American Economic Review: Papers and Proceedings* 103 (3): 611–16.

Barberis, Nicholas C., Robin Greenwood, Lawrence Jin, and Andrei Shleifer. 2015. "X-CAPM: An Extrapolative Capital Asset Pricing Model." *Journal of Financial Economics* 115 (1): 1–24.

———. 2018. "Extrapolation and Bubbles." *Journal of Financial Economics*, forthcoming.

Barberis, Nicholas C., and Ming Huang. 2008. "Stocks as Lotteries: The Implications of Probability Weighting for Security Prices." *American Economic Review* 98 (5): 2066–100.

Barberis, Nicholas C., Andrei Shleifer, and Robert W. Vishny. 1998. "A Model of Investor Sentiment." *Journal of Financial Economics* 49 (3): 307–43.

Baron, Matthew, and Wei Xiong. 2017. "Credit Expansion and Neglected Crash Risk." *Quarterly Journal of Economics* 132 (2): 713–64.

Ben-David, Itzhak, John R. Graham, and Campbell R. Harvey. 2013. "Managerial Miscalibration." *Quarterly Journal of Economics* 128 (4): 1547–84.

Benmelech, Efraim, Ralf Meisenzahl, and Rodney Ramcharan. 2017. "The Real Effects of Liquidity during the Financial Crisis: Evidence from Automobiles." *Quarterly Journal of Economics* 132 (1): 317–65.

Bernanke, Ben S. 1983. "Non-monetary Effects of the Financial Crisis in the Propagation of the Great Depression." *American Economic Review* 73 (3): 257–76.

———. 2008. "Reducing Systemic Risk." Speech delivered at the Federal Reserve Bank of Kansas City's Annual Economic Symposium, Jackson Hole, WY, August 22.

———. 2015. *The Courage to Act: A Memoir of a Crisis and Its Aftermath*. New York: W. W. Norton.

Bernanke, Ben S., Carol Bertaut, Laurie Pounder DeMarco, and Steven Kamin. 2011. "International Capital Flows and the Returns to Safe Assets in the United States, 2003–2007." International Finance Discussion Paper 1014, Federal Reserve Board, Washington, DC, February. https://www.federalreserve.gov/pubs/ifdp/2011/1014/ifdp1014.pdf.

Bernanke, Ben S., Mark Gertler, and Simon Gilchrist. 1999. "The Financial Accelerator in a Quantitative Business Cycle Framework." Chap. 21 in vol. 1 of *Handbook of Macroeconomics*, edited by John B. Taylor and Michael Woodford, 1341–93. Amsterdam: North-Holland Elsevier.

Board of Governors of the Federal Reserve System. 2008. "Current Economic and Financial Conditions: Summary and Outlook." Pt. 1 of Greenbook prepared for the August 5, 2008, Federal Open Market Committee (FOMC) meeting.

———. 2017. "Debt Outstanding, Domestic Nonfinancial Sectors, Households— LA154104005.Q: 1945–2017." December. https://www.federalreserve.gov /releases/z1/default.htm.

Bordalo, Pedro, Katherine B. Coffman, Nicola Gennaioli, and Andrei Shleifer. 2016a. "Stereotypes." *Quarterly Journal of Economics* 131 (4): 1753–94.

———. 2016b. "Beliefs about Gender." NBER Working Paper 22972, National Bureau of Economic Research, Cambridge, MA, December. http://www.nber .org/papers/w22972.

Bordalo, Pedro, Nicola Gennaioli, Rafael La Porta, and Andrei Shleifer. 2017. "Diagnostic Expectations and Stock Returns." NBER Working Paper 23863, National Bureau of Economic Research, Cambridge, MA, September. http:// www.nber.org/papers/w23863.

Bordalo, Pedro, Nicola Gennaioli, Yueran Ma, and Andrei Shleifer. 2018. "Over-reaction in Macroeconomic Expectations." Working paper. Oxford Said Business School, Università Bocconi, and Harvard University, March.

Bordalo, Pedro, Nicola Gennaioli, and Andrei Shleifer. 2018. "Diagnostic Expectations and Credit Cycles." *Journal of Finance* 73 (1): 199–227.

Brunnermeier, Markus, and Lasse H. Pedersen. 2009. "Market Liquidity and Funding Liquidity." *Review of Financial Studies* 22 (6): 2201–38.

Brunnermeier, Markus K. 2009. "Deciphering the Liquidity and Credit Crunch 2007–2008." *Journal of Economic Perspectives* 23 (1): 77–100.

Brunnermeier, Markus K., and Jonathan A. Parker. 2005. "Optimal Expectations." *American Economic Review* 95 (4): 1092–118.

Bubb, Ryan, and Alex Kaufman. 2014. "Securitization and Moral Hazard: Evidence from Credit Score Cutoff Rules." *Journal of Monetary Economics* 63 (C): 1–18.

Caballero, Ricardo J., and Alp Simsek. 2013. "Fire Sales in a Model of Complexity." *Journal of Finance* 68 (6): 2549–87.

Campbell, John Y., and John H. Cochrane. 1999. "By Force of Habit: A Consumption-Based Explanation of Aggregate Stock Market Behavior." *Journal of Political Economy* 107 (2): 205–51.

Campbell, John Y., and Robert J. Shiller. 1987. "Cointegration and Tests of Present Value Models." *Journal of Political Economy* 95 (5): 1062–88.

———. 1988. "Stock Prices, Earnings, and Expected Dividends." *Journal of Finance* 43 (3): 661–76.

Case, Karl E., Robert J. Shiller, and Anne K. Thompson. 2012. "What Have They Been Thinking? Homebuyer Behavior in Hot and Cold Markets." *Brookings Papers on Economic Activity* (Fall 2012): 265–315.

Casscells, Ward, Arno Schoenberger, and Thomas B. Graboys. 1978. "Interpretation by Physicians of Clinical Laboratory Results." *New England Journal of Medicine* 299 (18): 999–1001.

Chen, Daniel L., Tobias J. Moskowitz, and Kelly Shue. 2016. "Decision Making under the Gambler's Fallacy: Evidence from Asylum Judges, Loan Officers, and Baseball Umpires." *Quarterly Journal of Economics* 131 (3): 1181–242.

Cheng, Ing-Haw, Sahil Raina, and Wei Xiong. 2014. "Wall Street and the Housing Bubble." *American Economic Review* 104 (9): 2797–829.

Chodorow-Reich, Gabriel. 2014. "The Employment Effects of Credit Market Disruptions: Firm-level Evidence from the 2008–09 Financial Crisis." *Quarterly Journal of Economics* 129 (1): 1–59.

Coibion, Olivier, and Yuriy Gorodnichenko. 2015. "Information Rigidity and the Expectations Formation Process: A Simple Framework and New Facts." *American Economic Review* 105 (8): 2644–78.

Collin-Dufresne, Pierre, Robert S. Goldstein, and J. Spencer Martin. 2001. "The Determinants of Credit Spread Changes." *Journal of Finance* 56 (6): 2177–207.

Coval, Joshua, Kevin Pan, and Erik Stafford. 2014. "Capital Market Blind Spots." Working paper, Harvard University, Cambridge, MA, October.

Coval, Joshua D., Jakub W. Jurek, and Erik Stafford. 2009a. "Economic Catastrophe Bonds." *American Economic Review* 99 (3): 628–66.

———. 2009b. "The Economics of Structured Finance." *Journal of Economic Perspectives* 23 (1): 3–25.

Cutler, David M., James M. Poterba, and Lawrence H. Summers. 1990. "Speculative Dynamics and the Role of Feedback Traders." *American Economic Review Papers and Proceedings* 80 (2): 62–68.

Daniel, Kent, David Hirshleifer, and Avanidhar Subramanyam. 1998. "Investor Psychology and Security Market Under- and Overreactions." *Journal of Finance* 53 (6): 1839–85.

De Bondt, Werner F. M., and Richard H. Thaler. 1985. "Does the Stock Market Overreact?" *Journal of Finance* 40 (3): 793–805.

DeFusco, Anthony A., Charles G. Nathanson, and Eric Zwick. 2017. "Speculative Dynamics of Prices and Volume." NBER Working Paper 23449, National Bureau of Economic Research, Cambridge, MA, May. http://www.nber.org /papers/w23449.

DeLong, J. Bradford, Andrei Shleifer, Lawrence H. Summers, and Robert J. Waldmann. 1990. "Noise Trader Risk in Financial Markets." *Journal of Political Economy* 98 (4): 703–38.

Diamond, Douglas W., and Philip H. Dybvig. 1983. "Bank Runs, Deposit Insurance, and Liquidity." *Journal of Political Economy* 91 (3): 401–19.

Dominguez, Kathryn. 1986. "Are Foreign Exchange Forecasts Rational? New Evidence from Survey Data." *Economics Letters* 21 (3): 277–81.

Eggertsson, Gauti B., and Paul Krugman. 2012. "Debt, Deleveraging, and the Liquidity Trap: A Fisher-Minsky-Koo Approach." *Quarterly Journal of Economics* 127 (3): 1469–513.

Erel, Isil, Taylor Nadauld, and René M. Stulz. 2014. "Why Did Holdings of Highly Rated Securitization Tranches Differ So Much across Banks?" *Review of Financial Studies* 27 (2): 404–53.

Fahlenbrach, Rüdiger, Robert Prilmeier, and René M. Stulz. 2017. "Why Does Fast Loan Growth Predict Poor Performance for Banks?" *Review of Financial Studies* 31 (3): 1014–63.

Federal Open Market Committee (FOMC). 2008. Transcript of "Meeting of the Federal Open Market Committee on August 5, 2008."

Federal Reserve Bank of Philadelphia. 2017a. "Survey of Professional Forecasters: 1968–2017." https://www.philadelphiafed.org/research-and-data/real-time -center/survey-of-professional-forecasters.

———. 2017b. "Greenbook Data Set: 1966–2012." Board of Governors of the Federal Reserve System. https://www.philadelphiafed.org/research-and-data /real-time-center/greenbook-data.

Federal Reserve Bank of St. Louis. 2017a. "Homeownership Rate for the United States—RHORUSQ156N: 1965–2017." U.S. Bureau of the Census. https://fred.stlouisfed.org/series/RHORUSQ156N.

———. 2017b. "Disposable Personal Income—DPI: 1947–2017." U.S. Bureau of Economic Analysis. https://fred.stlouisfed.org/series/DPI.

———. 2017c. "Asset-backed Commercial Paper Outstanding—DTBSPCKAM: 2001–2017." Board of Governors of the Federal Reserve System. https://fred.stlouisfed.org/series/DTBSPCKAM.

———. 2017d. "CBOE Volatility Index: VIX—VIXCLS: 1990–2017." Chicago Board Options Exchange. https://fred.stlouisfed.org/series/VIXCLS.

Financial Crisis Inquiry Commission, 2011. *The Financial Crisis Inquiry Report: Final Report of the National Commission on the Causes of the Financial and Economic Crisis in the United States.* Washington, DC: U.S. Government Printing Office.

Fitch Ratings. 2007. "Inside the Ratings: What Credit Ratings Mean: August 2007." Research report. http://pages.stern.nyu.edu/~igiddy/articles/what_ratings_mean.pdf.

Foote, Christopher L., Kristopher S. Gerardi, and Paul S. Willen. 2012. "Why Did So Many People Make So Many Ex Post Bad Decisions? The Causes of the Foreclosure Crisis." In *Rethinking the Financial Crisis*, edited by Alan S. Blinder, Andrew W. Lo, and Robert M. Solow, 136–86. New York: Russell Sage Foundation.

Frankel, Jeffrey A., and Kenneth A. Froot. 1987. "Using Survey Data to Test Standard Propositions regarding Exchange Rate Expectations." *American Economic Review* 77 (1): 133–53.

French, Kenneth R., Martin N. Baily, John Y. Campbell, et al. 2010. *The Squam Lake Report: Fixing the Financial System.* Princeton, NJ: Princeton University Press.

Fuster, Andreas, David Laibson, and Brock Mendel. 2010. "Natural Expectations and Macroeconomic Fluctuations." *Journal of Economic Perspectives* 24 (4): 67–84.

Geanakoplos, John. 1997. "Promises, Promises." In *The Economy as an Evolving Complex System, II*, edited by W. Brian Arthur, Steven N. Durlauf, and David A. Lane, 285–320. Reading, MA: Addison-Wesley.

———. 2010. "The Leverage Cycle." *NBER Macroeconomics Annual* 24: 1–65.

Gennaioli, Nicola, Yueran Ma, and Andrei Shleifer. 2015. "Expectations and Investment." *NBER Macroeconomics Annual* 30 (1): 379–431.

Gennaioli, Nicola, and Andrei Shleifer. 2010. "What Comes to Mind." *Quarterly Journal of Economics* 125 (4): 1399–433.

Gennaioli, Nicola, Andrei Shleifer, and Robert W. Vishny. 2012. "Neglected Risks, Financial Innovation, and Financial Fragility." *Journal of Financial Economics* 104 (3): 452–68.

———. 2013. "A Model of Shadow Banking." *Journal of Finance* 68 (4): 1331–63.

Gerardi, Kristopher, Andreas Lehnert, Shane M. Sherlund, and Paul Willen. 2008. "Making Sense of the Subprime Crisis." *Brookings Papers on Economic Activity* (Fall 2008): 69–159.

Gigerenzer, Gerd. 1996. "On Narrow Norms and Vague Heuristics: A Reply to Kahneman and Tversky." *Psychological Review* 103 (3): 592–96.

Gilboa, Itzhak, and David Schmeidler. 1989. "Maxmin Expected Utility with Non-Unique Prior." *Journal of Mathematical Economics* 18 (2): 141–53.

Giroud, Xavier, and Holger M. Mueller. 2017. "Firm Leverage, Consumer Demand, and Employment Losses during the Great Recession." *Quarterly Journal of Economics* 132 (1): 271–316.

Glaeser, Edward L. 2013. "A Nation of Gamblers: Real Estate Speculation and American History." *American Economic Review Papers and Proceedings* 103 (3): 1–42.

Glaeser, Edward L., and Charles G. Nathanson. 2017. "An Extrapolative Model of House Price Dynamics." *Journal of Financial Economics* 126 (1): 147–70.

Goldstein, Itay, and Ady Pauzner. 2005. "Demand–Deposit Contracts and the Probability of Bank Runs." *Journal of Finance* 60 (3): 1293–327.

Gorton, Gary B., and Andrew Metrick. 2010a. "Haircuts." *Federal Reserve Bank of St. Louis Review* 92 (6): 507–19.

———. 2010b. "Regulating the Shadow Banking System." *Brookings Papers on Economic Activity* (Fall 2010): 261–97.

———. 2012. "Securitized Banking and the Run on Repo." *Journal of Financial Economics* 104 (3): 425–51.

Gourio, François, Anil K. Kashyap, and Jae Sim. 2017. "The Tradeoffs in Leaning against the Wind." NBER Working Paper 23658, National Bureau of

Economics Research, Cambridge, MA, August. http://www.nber.org/papers /w23658.

Graham, Jesse, Brian Nosek, and Jonathan Haidt. 2012. "The Moral Stereotypes of Liberals and Conservatives: Exaggeration of Differences across the Political Spectrum." *PLoS One* 7 (12): 1–13.

Greenlaw, David, Jan Hatzius, Anil K. Kashyap, and Hyun Song Shin. 2008. "Leveraged Losses: Lessons from the Mortgage Market Meltdown." U.S. Monetary Policy Forum Report No. 2. Rosenberg Institute, Brandeis International Business School and Initiative on Global Markets, University of Chicago Graduate School of Business.

Greenspan, Alan. 1998. "Private-sector Refinancing of the Large Hedge Fund, Long-Term Capital Management." Testimony of Chairman Alan Greenspan before the Committee on Banking and Financial Services, U.S. House of Representatives, October 1.

Greenwood, Robin, and Samuel G. Hanson. 2013. "Issuer Quality and Corporate Bond Returns." *Review of Financial Studies* 26 (6): 1483–525.

———. 2015. "Waves in Ship Prices and Investment." *Quarterly Journal of Economics* 130 (1): 55–109.

Greenwood, Robin, and Andrei Shleifer. 2014. "Expectations of Returns and Expected Returns." *Review of Financial Studies* 27 (3): 714–46.

Greenwood, Robin, Andrei Shleifer, and Yang You. 2018. "Bubbles for Fama." *Journal of Financial Economics*, forthcoming.

Hansen, Lars Peter, and Thomas J. Sargent. 2001. "Robust Control and Model Uncertainty." *American Economic Review* 91 (2): 60–66.

Hart, Oliver D., and John H. Moore. 1995. "Debt and Seniority: An Analysis of the Role of Hard Claims in Constraining Management." *American Economic Review* 85 (3): 567–85.

Hilton, James, and William Von Hippel. 1996. "Stereotypes." *Annual Review of Psychology* 47: 237–71.

Hirshleifer, David, Jun Li, and Jianfeng Yu. 2015. "Asset Pricing in Production Economies with Extrapolative Expectations." *Journal of Monetary Economics* 76 (2015): 87–106.

Hong, Harrison, and Jeremy C. Stein. 1999. "A Unified Theory of Underreaction, Momentum Trading, and Overreaction in Asset Markets." *Journal of Finance* 54 (6): 2143–84.

Initiative on Global Markets (IGM) Economic Experts Panel. 2017. "Factors Contributing to the 2008 Global Financial Crisis," October 17. http://www.igmchicago.org/surveys-special/factors-contributing-to-the-2008-global-financial-crisis.

International Monetary Fund (IMF). 2007a. *Global Financial Stability Report, April 2007: Market Developments and Issues.* Washington, DC: IMF.

———. 2007b. *Global Financial Stability Report, October 2007—Financial Market Turbulence: Causes, Consequences, and Policies.* Washington, DC: IMF.

———. 2008a. *Global Financial Stability Report, April 2008—Containing Systemic Risks and Restoring Financial Soundness.* Washington, DC: IMF.

———. 2008b. *Global Financial Stability Report, October 2008—Financial Stress and Deleveraging: Macro-Financial Implications and Policy.* Washington, DC: IMF.

———. 2009a. *Global Financial Stability Report, April 2009: Responding to the Financial Crisis and Measuring Systemic Risks.* Washington, DC: IMF.

———. 2009b. *Global Financial Stability Report, October 2009: Navigating the Financial Challenges Ahead.* Washington, DC: IMF.

Investment Company Institute. 2008–2012. "Weekly Money Market Fund Assets." www.ici.org/research/stats.

Jarrow, Robert A., Li Li, Mark Mesler, and Donald R. van Deventer. 2008. "CDO Valuation: Fact and Fiction." In *The Definitive Guide to CDOs: Market, Application, Valuation and Hedging*, edited by Gunter Meissner, 429–56. London: Risk Books.

Jordà, Òscar, Moritz Schularick, and Alan M. Taylor. 2015. "Betting the House." *Journal of International Economics* 96 (S1): S2–S18.

Kahana, Michael. 2012. *Foundation of Human Memory.* Oxford: Oxford University Press.

Kahneman, Daniel, and Amos Tversky. 1974. "Judgment under Uncertainty: Heuristics and Biases." *Science* 185 (4157): 1124–31.

———. 1979. "Prospect Theory: An Analysis of Decision under Risk." *Econometrica* 47 (2): 263–92.

————. 1983. "Extensional versus Intuitive Reasoning: The Conjunction Fallacy in Probability Judgment." *Psychological Review* 90 (4): 293–315.

Kashyap, Anil K., and Jeremy C. Stein. 2012. "The Optimal Conduct of Monetary Policy with Interest on Reserves." *American Economic Journal: Macroeconomics* 4 (4): 266–82.

Keys, Benjamin J., Tanmoy Mukherjee, Amit Seru, and Vikrant Vig. 2010. "Did Securitization Lead to Lax Screening? Evidence from Subprime Loans." *Quarterly Journal of Economics* 125 (1): 307–62.

Kindleberger, Charles P. 1978. *Manias, Panics, and Crashes: A History of Financial Crises*, 1st ed. New York: Basic Books.

Kirti, Divya. 2018. "Lending Standards and Output Growth." IMF Working Paper WP/18/23, International Monetary Fund, Washington, DC, January. https://www.imf.org/en/Publications/WP/Issues/2018/01/26/Lending -Standards-and-Output-Growth-45595.

Kiyotaki, Nobuhiro, and John Moore. 1997. "Credit Cycles." *Journal of Political Economy* 105 (2): 211–48.

Krishnamurthy, Arvind, Stefan Nagel, and Dmitry Orlov. 2014. "Sizing Up Repo." *Journal of Finance* 69 (6): 2381–417.

Kuchler, Theresa, and Basit Zafar. 2017. "Personal Experiences and Expectations about Aggregate Outcomes." Working paper. New York University Stern School of Business and Arizona State University, November.

La Porta, Rafael. 1996. "Expectations and the Cross-Section of Stock Returns." *Journal of Finance* 51 (5): 1715–42.

Lakonishok, Josef, Andrei Shleifer, and Robert W. Vishny. 1994. "Contrarian Investment, Extrapolation, and Risk." *Journal of Finance* 49 (5): 1541–78.

Landier, Augustin, Yueran Ma, and David Thesmar. 2017. "New Experimental Evidence on Expectations Formation." Working paper. HEC Paris, Harvard University, MIT Sloan School of Management, and the Center for Economic and Policy Research, November.

Lettau, Martin, and Sydney Ludvigson. 2001. "Consumption, Aggregate Wealth, and Expected Stock Returns." *Journal of Finance* 56 (3): 815–49.

López-Salido, David, Jeremy C. Stein, and Egon Zakrajšek. 2017. "Credit-Market Sentiment and the Business Cycle." *Quarterly Journal of Economics* 132 (3): 1373–426.

Lucas, Robert E., Jr. 1976. "Econometric Policy Evaluation: A Critique." In vol. 1 of *The Phillips Curve and Labor Markets: Carnegie-Rochester Conference Series on Public Policy*, edited by Karl Brunner and Allan H. Meltzer, 19–46. New York: American Elsevier.

Mago, Akhil, and Sihan Shu. 2005. "HEL Bond Profile across HPA Scenarios." *U.S. ABS Weekly Outlook*, Lehman Brothers Fixed-Income Research, August 15.

Malmendier, Ulrike, and Stefan Nagel. 2011. "Depression Babies: Do Macroeconomic Experiences Affect Risk-Taking?" *Quarterly Journal of Economics* 126 (1): 373–416.

Manski, Charles F. 2004. "Measuring Expectations." *Econometrica* 72 (5): 1329–76.

Markit. 2017. "ABX Home Equity Index (ABX.HE): 2006–2017." Accessed August 15, 2017. https://ihsmarkit.com/products/markit-abx.html.

Merrill, Craig B., Taylor Nadauld, Rene M. Stulz, and Shane M. Sherlund. 2014. "Were There Fire Sales in the RMBS Market?" Working paper, Ohio State University, Fisher College of Business, Columbus, Ohio, May. https://econ papers.repec.org/paper/eclohidic/2014-09.htm.

Mian, Atif, and Amir Sufi. 2009. "The Consequences of Mortgage Credit Expansion: Evidence from the U.S. Mortgage Default Crisis." *Quarterly Journal of Economics* 124 (4): 1449–96.

———. 2011. "House Prices, Home Equity-Based Borrowing, and the U.S. Household Leverage Crisis." *American Economic Review* 101 (5): 2132–56.

———. 2014a. "What Explains the 2007–2009 Drop in Employment?" *Econometrica* 82 (6): 2197–223.

———. 2014b. *House of Debt: How They (and You) Caused the Great Recession, and How We Can Prevent It from Happening Again*. Chicago: University of Chicago Press.

———. 2017. "Household Debt and Defaults from 2000 to 2010: The Credit Supply View." In *Evidence and Innovation in Housing Law and Policy*, edited by Lee Anne Fennell and Benjamin J. Keys, 257–88. Cambridge: Cambridge University Press.

Mian, Atif, Amir Sufi, and Emil Verner. 2017. "Household Debt and Business Cycles Worldwide." *Quarterly Journal of Economics* 132 (4): 1755–817.

Minsky, Hyman P. 1977. "The Financial Instability Hypothesis: An Interpretation of Keynes and an Alternative to 'Standard' Theory." *Nebraska Journal of Economics and Business* 16 (1): 5–16.

Muth, John F. 1961. "Rational Expectations and the Theory of Price Movements." *Econometrica* 29 (3): 315–35.

Myers, Stewart C. 1977. "Determinants of Corporate Borrowing." *Journal of Financial Economics* 5 (2): 147–75.

Niu, Geng, and Arthur van Soest. 2014. "House Price Expectations." IZA Discussion Paper 8536, Institute for the Study of Labor, Bonn, Germany, October. http://ftp.iza.org/dp8536.pdf.

Palmer, Christopher J. 2015. "Why Did So Many Subprime Borrowers Default during the Crisis: Loose Credit or Plummeting Prices?" Working paper, University of California–Berkeley, Berkeley, CA, September. http://faculty.haas.berkeley.edu/palmer/papers/cpalmer-subprime.pdf.

Piskorski, Tomasz, Amit Seru, and James Witkin. 2015. "Asset Quality Misrepresentation by Financial Intermediaries: Evidence from the RMBS Market." *Journal of Finance* 70 (6): 2635–78.

Prescott, Edward C. 1977. "Should Control Theory Be Used for Economic Stabilization?" *Carnegie-Rochester Conference Series on Public Policy* 7: 13–38.

Rabin, Matthew. 2013. "An Approach to Incorporating Psychology into Economics." *American Economic Review* 103 (3): 617–22.

Rabin, Matthew, and Dimitri Vayanos. 2010. "The Gambler's and Hot-Hand Fallacies: Theory and Applications." *Review of Economic Studies* 77: 730–78.

Rajan, Raghuram G. 2006. "Has Finance Made the World Riskier?" *European Financial Management* 12 (4): 499–533.

Reinhart, Carmen M., and Kenneth S. Rogoff. 2009. *This Time Is Different: Eight Centuries of Financial Folly*. Princeton, NJ: Princeton University Press.

Rognlie, Matthew, Andrei Shleifer, and Alp Simsek. 2018. "Investment Hangover and the Great Recession." *American Economic Journal: Macroeconomics* 10 (2): 113–53.

Saiz, Albert. 2010. "The Geographic Determinants of Housing Supply." *Quarterly Journal of Economics* 125 (3): 1253–96.

Schularick, Moritz, and Alan M. Taylor. 2012. "Credit Booms Gone Bust: Monetary Policy, Leverage Cycles, and Financial Crises, 1870–2008." *American Economic Review* 102 (2): 1029–61.

Shiller, Robert J. 1981. "Do Stock Prices Move Too Much to Be Justified by Subsequent Changes in Dividends?" *American Economic Review* 71 (3): 421–36.

———. 2016. *Irrational Exuberance: Revised and Expanded Third Edition*. Princeton, NJ: Princeton University Press.

Shleifer, Andrei, and Robert W. Vishny. 1992. "Liquidation Values and Debt Capacity: A Market Equilibrium Approach." *Journal of Finance* 47 (4): 1343–66.

———. 1997. "The Limits of Arbitrage." *Journal of Finance* 52 (1): 35–55.

Sims, Christopher. 2003. "Implications of Rational Inattention." *Journal of Monetary Economics* 50 (3): 665–90.

Sorkin, Andrew R. 2009. *Too Big to Fail: The Inside Story of How Wall Street and Washington Fought to Save the Financial System—and Themselves.* New York: Viking.

Stein, Jeremy C. 2012. "Monetary Policy as Financial-Stability Regulation." *Quarterly Journal of Economics* 127 (1): 57–95.

———. 2013. "Lean, Clean, and In-Between." Speech delivered at the National Bureau of Economic Research Conference: Lessons from the Financial Crisis for Monetary Policy, Boston, MA, October 18.

———. 2014. "Incorporating Financial Stability Considerations into a Monetary Policy Framework." Speech delivered at the International Research Forum on Monetary Policy, Federal Reserve Board of Governors, Washington, DC, March 21.

Taleb, Nassim Nicholas. 2007. *The Black Swan: The Impact of the Highly Improbable.* New York: Random House.

Tenenbaum, Joshua B., and Thomas Griffiths. 2001. "The Rational Basis of Representativeness." *Proceedings of the Annual Meeting of the Cognitive Science Society* 23: 1036–41.

U.S. Bureau of Labor Statistics. 2012. "The Recession of 2007–2009." *BLS Spotlight on Statistics*, February.

U.S. Treasury Department. 2008. "'Break the Glass' Bank Recapitalization Plan," April 15. https://www.scribd.com/document/21266810/Too-Big-To-Fail -Confidential-Break-the-Glass-Plan-from-Treasury.

———. 2009. "Public–Private Investment Program." Press release, March 23. https://www.treasury.gov/press-center/press-releases/Documents/ppip _whitepaper_032309.pdf.

Vissing-Jorgensen, Annette. 2004. "Perspectives on Behavioral Finance: Does 'Irrationality' Disappear with Wealth? Evidence from Expectations and Actions." *NBER Macroeconomics Annual* 18: 139–94.

Woodford, Michael. 2003. "Imperfect Common Knowledge and the Effects of Monetary Policy." In *Knowledge, Information, and Expectations in Modern Macroeconomics: In Honor of Edmund S. Phelps*, edited by Philippe Aghion, Roman Frydman, Joseph Stiglitz, and Michael Woodford, 25–58. Princeton, NJ: Princeton University Press.

INDEX

Page numbers in *italics* refer to figures and tables.

245